Delivering Family Justice in Late Modern Society in the wake of Legal Aid Reform

Legal aid for family cases in private law, mainly divorce and separation, where the state is not directly involved as it is in public law cases where there are issues of domestic violence or neglect or abuse of children, came to an abrupt end together with help for welfare and immigration cases on April 1st 2013 when the Legal Aid Sentencing and Punishment of Offenders Act (LASPO) came into effect. This book presents an account of the wide ranging problems which the researchers and practitioners expected to ensue. Sadly, their fears have been realised in many areas of legal help and advice. The National Audit Office was to take the view in 2014 that although the Ministry of Justice had succeeded in making considerable savings in the cause of austerity that they had failed to investigate or understand the impact of these cuts on the individuals concerned and society as a whole.

This book was previously published as a special issue of the *Journal of Social Welfare & Family Law*.

Mavis Maclean has carried out empirical research in family justice for many years, and founded the Oxford Centre for Family Law and Policy with John Eekelaar in Oxford in 2001. She has worked as an academic adviser to the Ministry of Justice, and edits the *Journal of Social Welfare & Family Law* with Helen Stalford.

Delivering Family Justice in Late Modern Society in the wake of Legal Aid Reform

Edited by
Mavis Maclean

Routledge
Taylor & Francis Group
LONDON AND NEW YORK

First published 2017
by Routledge
2 Park Square, Milton Park, Abingdon, Oxon, OX14 4RN, UK

and by Routledge
711 Third Avenue, New York, NY 10017, USA

Routledge is an imprint of the Taylor & Francis Group, an informa business

British Library Cataloguing in Publication Data
A catalogue record for this book is available from the British Library

ISBN 13: 978-1-138-21427-9

Typeset in Times New Roman
by RefineCatch Limited, Bungay, Suffolk

Publisher's Note
The publisher accepts responsibility for any inconsistencies that may have arisen during the conversion of this book from journal articles to book chapters, namely the possible inclusion of journal terminology.

Contents

Citation Information

The chapters in this book were originally published in the *Journal of Social Welfare & Family Law*, volume 35, issue 1 (March 2013). When citing this material, please use the original page numbering for each article, as follows:

Editorial

Late modern justice for the family
Mavis Maclean and Helen Stalford
Journal of Social Welfare & Family Law, volume 35, issue 1 (March 2013), pp. 1–2

Chapter 1

Legal aid reform: its impact on family law
Stephen Cobb
Journal of Social Welfare & Family Law, volume 35, issue 1 (March 2013), pp. 3–19

Chapter 2

Analysing the economic justification for the reforms to social welfare and family law legal aid
Graham Cookson
Journal of Social Welfare & Family Law, volume 35, issue 1 (March 2013), pp. 21–41

Chapter 3

Self-represented litigants: the overlooked and unintended consequence of legal aid reform
Chris Bevan
Journal of Social Welfare & Family Law, volume 35, issue 1 (March 2013), pp. 43–54

Chapter 4

Changing the immigration rules and withdrawing the 'currency' of legal aid: the impact of LASPO 2012 on migrants and their families
F. Meyler and S. Woodhouse
Journal of Social Welfare & Family Law, volume 35, issue 1 (March 2013), pp. 55–78

Chapter 5

The impact of cuts in legal aid funding on charities
Debra Morris and Warren Barr
Journal of Social Welfare & Family Law, volume 35, issue 1 (March 2013), pp. 79–94

Chapter 6

Back for the future: a client centred analysis of social welfare and family law provision

Alexy Buck and Marisol Smith

Journal of Social Welfare & Family Law, volume 35, issue 1 (March 2013), pp. 95–113

Chapter 7

Arbitration in financial dispute resolution: the final step to reconstructing the default(s) and exception(s)?

Lucinda Ferguson

Journal of Social Welfare & Family Law, volume 35, issue 1 (March 2013), pp. 115–138

Chapter 8

When legal rights are not a reality: do individuals know their rights and how can we tell?

Catrina Denvir, Nigel J. Balmer and Pascoe Pleasence

Journal of Social Welfare & Family Law, volume 35, issue 1 (March 2013), pp. 139–160

Notes on Contributors

Nigel J. Balmer is Reader in Law and Social Statistics in the Faculty of Laws, University College London, UK.

Warren Barr is Professor of Law in the Charity Law & Policy Unit, School of Law and Social Justice, University of Liverpool, UK.

Chris Bevan is Assistant Professor in Property Law in the Faculty of Social Sciences, University of Nottingham, UK.

Alexy Buck works for the Ministry of Justice in the UK. She was previously Head of the Legal Services Research Centre (LSRC), London, UK.

Stephen Cobb is a British High Court judge on the Family Division bench. He served as Chairman of the Family Law Bar Association from 2010–2011.

Graham Cookson is Professor of Economic and Public Policy in the Department of Health Care Management and Policy, University of Surrey, UK.

Catrina Denvir is Lecturer in the Sydney Law School, University of Sydney, Australia.

Lucinda Ferguson is Associate Professor of Family Law, and Director of Studies (Law), at Regent's Park College, Oxford University, UK.

Mavis Maclean has carried out empirical research in family justice for many years, and founded the Oxford Centre for Family Law and Policy with John Eekelaar in Oxford in 2001.

F. Meyler is an Honorary Fellow in the School of Law and Social Justice, University of Liverpool, Liverpool, UK.

Debra Morris is Professor of Law in the Charity Law & Policy Unit, School of Law and Social Justice, University of Liverpool, UK.

Pascoe Pleasence is Professor of Empirical Legal Studies and co-director of the Centre for Empirical Legal Studies in the UCL Faculty of Laws, University College London, UK.

Marisol Smith is an Independent Social Researcher. She previously worked for the Legal Services Research Centre, Legal Services Commission, London, UK.

Helen Stalford is Professor of Law in the Liverpool Law School, University of Liverpool, UK.

S. Woodhouse is Lecturer in the School of Law and Social Justice, University of Liverpool, Liverpool, UK.

Introduction: Late modern justice for the family

Mavis Maclean and Helen Stalford

Just over a year ago the *Journal of Social Welfare and Family Law* published a special issue on Family Law in Hard Times (2011, 33(4)). This was devoted to identifying the problems associated with the government's plans to remove large areas of family law from the scope of legal aid. The policy paper announcing the changes[1] adopted a rather surprising approach to family disputes, describing them as 'not of the highest importance' where they are thought to arise from the personal decisions of those concerned. While there is widespread support for the view that family disputes may be more comfortably and appropriately managed and resolved managed outside the legal system, and for the addition of the various forms of Alternative Dispute Resolution (ADR) to the repertoire of helping services, nevertheless there is, and will be for the foreseeable future, a small group of people who are so troubled, vulnerable and/or conflicted that they need the help of the court to sort out and manage their dispute and offer some assurance that a fair arrangement will be enforced.

This issue takes up the debate at the point where the Legal Aid, Sentencing and Punishment of Offenders Act (LASPO) comes into force on 1 April 2013. This is happening at the same time as a number of welfare reforms come into force, which are likely to add to the pressures on family life by further reducing the public and private resources available to deal with them.

The first part of this special issue looks in detail at the effects of LASPO on family and social welfare-related advice and support. We are grateful to Stephen Cobb (formerly Chairman of the Family Law Bar Association) for setting out the nature of many of the changes affecting family law with clarity and authority.

We then turn to the question of how effective the changes will be achieving the Government's aim of reducing public expenditure, set out by Graham Cookson. This contribution, from the perspective and experience of an economist, will, we hope, focus more attention on the use which can be made of existing data while highlighting the acknowledged need for more. Chris Bevan's article develops a number of points raised by Stephen Cobb, by offering a practitioner's view of the potential impact of an increase in the number of self-represented parties on the work of the family courts. A further insightful practitioners' perspective is presented in Frances Meyler and Sarah Woodhouse's contribution, which highlights the 'double-jeopardy' experienced by families in the context of immigration proceedings. The effect of the cuts in this regard will be particularly profound for immigration advice providers and service users alike, insofar as they will tighten the noose around an already highly regulated, poorly funded and politically contentious area of social justice. These contributions are, in turn, complemented by Debra Morris and Warren Barr's reflections on the significant (and, as yet, under-acknowledged) impact of the legal aid cuts on charities, particularly those who fulfil a vital advice and advocacy role for the socially and economically marginalised.

The second part of this issue explores other ways of delivering and receiving family and social welfare law advice in late modern society and how these might serve to limit some of the damage caused by LASPO. Alexy Buck and Marisol Smith describe an earlier attempt at taking a more holistic approach to delivering social welfare and family law-related advice. Their client-centred analysis highlights both the benefits and challenges of an integrated service model. These benefits should not be forgotten as policy develops in the future. In the same vein, Lucinda Ferguson raises questions about the potential role of arbitration in family matters.

Finally, we turn to the issue of public knowledge and awareness of the law. As alternative dispute resolution is welcomed by government, it is assumed that such services function in the shadow of the law, in that those coming to the courts are expected to understand what it is they are asking for. And as web-based information and advice hubs and services develop, these too presume some public understanding of the law. Catrina Denvir, Nigel Balmer and Pascoe Pleasence give a critical account of attempts to measure public legal knowledge. The late modern move away from professional care and support, towards asking more of the individuals involved in family disputes, demands a great deal of the parties in terms of awareness of their legal position and what might be done to secure the best possible outcomes. The complex analysis in this last paper and, indeed, in other contributions, of the methodological issues and findings which can be obtained if we try to understand the state of public knowledge and awareness, send a clear message: don't assume too much.

Taken together, this collection of papers provides an insightful and timely commentary of the likely impacts of the legal aid reforms on the quality and accessibility of advice in relation to family and social welfare provision. These are difficult times, but the contributions suggest a number of potential routes to addressing the social injustice caused by such reforms. The human rights arguments offer a particularly persuasive legal route, at least in theory, but the contributions indicate that it is more the shared resilience and commitment to social justice, of service providers and users alike, that will yield an inspiring level of ingenuity and resourcefulness. This will not come without some radical adjustments, however, not to mention a significant amount of personal sacrifice. In the longer term, it is to be hoped that austerity may act as a trigger to stimulate the development of much more responsive, evidence-based, cost-effective policies rather than the wielding of blunt instruments. We hope this special issue makes an important contribution to that process.

Note

1. White Paper and Draft Legal Aid, Sentencing and Punishment of Offenders Bill, Ministry of Justice 2011 Annex B paras 2 and 3.

Legal aid reform: its impact on family law

Stephen Cobb

Chairman of the Family Law Bar Association 2010–2011

This paper seeks to give an overview of the Legal Aid reform leading to the enactment of the Legal Aid, Sentencing and Punishment of Offenders Act 2012 ("LASPO"). It provides a context for the reforms heralded by consultation in 2010, and discusses the interplay with the simultaneous Family Justice Review. The paper goes on to look at the structural and constitutional changes brought about by the LASPO Act 2012, the impact on the Courts, and the removal of many cases from the 'scope' of public funding leading to the increase in the numbers of Litigants in Person. The paper discusses the 'exceptional' cases, the cases in which children are joined as parties, and mediation. The article looks briefly at the impact on the legal profession brought about by the legal aid reforms together with the reduction in fees under the Family Advocacy Scheme (also introduced in 2011).

Introduction

The modern legal aid system was established by the Legal Aid and Advice Act 1949, and has, since the passing of that legislation, been regarded as central in providing access to justice to many; it ensures equality before the law, and promotes and enhances the right to a fair trial. Over the 60 or so years since its inception, the administration[1] of legal aid as well its scope and structure has been modified and adapted to meet the needs of the public and the law; inevitably, given the greater complexity of the law, and the heightened awareness of Human Rights, legal aid has been made available in a wider range of areas. The Government perceives that expenditure has grown but in fact the legal aid budget has been contained since about 2003 (and has in fact dropped in real terms by about 11%). One of the biggest issues facing successive governments has been to contain the expenditure of legal assistance.

Unsurprisingly, at a time of significant economic crisis nationally (and globally), the legal aid budget was bound to be vulnerable to public spending review. Cuts were first identified in the Government's Consultation document (Proposals for the Reform of Legal Aid) launched on 15 November 2010 and were forecast to be the most wide-ranging and deeply administered in the history of legal aid. Notwithstanding significant opposition to many of the proposed reforms, the Legal Aid, Sentencing and Punishment of Offenders Act 2012 (hereafter 'the 2012 Act') received Royal Assent in largely the same form (on family law funding) as had been foreshadowed by the consultation.

There is no doubt that the 2012 Act reflects the most radical revision of legal aid since the inception of the modern scheme. The legal aid cuts are likely seriously to affect the operation of the courts. There is a risk that cuts will impede access to justice for many of the most vulnerable people in society.

The Government introduced the legal aid reform programme some months after the fundamental review of the family justice system had been launched (this had been initiated by the previous government administration in January 2010, having been commissioned by the Ministry of Justice, the Department for Education, and the Welsh Government). This review – conducted by a panel chaired by David Norgrove – had been charged to look at all aspects of the family justice system. Specifically (see Annex A to the Interim Report for its complete terms of reference) it was expected to consider and advise on the promotion of informed settlement and agreement, and management of the family justice system. Inevitably effective management of the family justice system requires proper funding; this led, on one view, to tensions between the two reform programmes.

The implications of the legal aid reform on the administration of family justice, and on the Family Justice Modernisation programme (being overseen by Ryder J), are potentially extremely significant. In this piece, I highlight only some of the likely effects of the 2012 Act on family justice.

Legal aid reform in context

The proposals for the Reform of Legal Aid in November 2010 were said to be needed in order (in part) to manage the wider economic crisis which the Coalition Government had inherited earlier that year; the proposals were further said to be in part to achieve a 'fundamental review' of the legal aid scheme. It was reasonably clear from the Government's Consultation that the primary objective was to demonstrate how the Ministry of Justice could save £350m p.a. by the year 2014–2015. The essential thrust of the proposals was essentially cost-saving, and the proposals did little to explore positive ways to achieve the delivery of publicly funded justice for the benefit of the public.

That all said, there was some uncertainty in the material produced about whether (a) £350m was ever indeed the true target figure, and (b) how that saving was actually to be achieved. The Cumulative Impact Assessment of the Consultation contained proposals which would have saved an estimated £395m to £478m once the full savings had been realised. Not only were the Impact Assessment(s) on which the consultation was based deficient in relation to financial data, the evaluation of the effects of the Government's proposals on that (substantial) part of the legal profession which conducts criminal and civil legal aid work had been only superficially studied and (insofar as they had been appraised at all) had been seriously underestimated.

There could be little doubt that £200m could not be removed from the legal aid budget in family law (just under a third of the current legal aid budget in family cases) without creating an adverse impact on the supports upon which many victims of family breakdown rely. This was likely to create a domino effect of problems as citizens who have problems do not tend to have one problem; they tend to experience clusters of problems. One problem leads to another: family breakdown often casts one party onto welfare benefits, and creates housing issues, which in turn leads to mental health difficulties. Not only does the 2012 Act remove large numbers of those experiencing family breakdown from the scope of Legal aid to assist them in receiving *family law* advice, the Act also removes from scope many cases relating to *welfare benefits*[2], the vast majority of *debt cases*[3], and almost all cases in the field of *immigration* will be excluded.[4] As we know – because the Government recognises this – the Act will have a disproportionate impact upon women, on ethnic minorities and on people with disabilities[5]; 97% of legally aided parties now are in the bottom two income quintiles.

During the Legal Aid Reform consultation, and at all stages as the Bill progressed through Parliament, the Family Law Bar Association (FLBA) (of which I was Chairman at the time), warned of the irreversible loss to the public of the current range of publicly funded areas of law, how the courts will become gridlocked with litigants in person, and how that damage can be avoided. These warnings were regrettably in large measure unheeded. It was the view of the Family Law Bar Association that the Legal Aid Reform programme runs the risk of placing the family justice system (already stretched to breaking point) under yet more strain, aggravating the considerable difficulties facing those who currently seek effective access to family justice, and those who work in the field of family justice. Litigants, and potential litigants, need not only access to justice, but effective access to justice; as Article 47 of the European Charter of Fundamental Rights 2000 makes clear: 'Legal aid shall be made available to those who lack sufficient resources in so far as such aid is necessary to ensure effective access to justice.'

In many instances those entering the family and civil courts are socially, intellectually, emotionally and/or economically very vulnerable. If there are difficulties and obstacles in seeking the advice they clearly require, in many cases the only alternative will be to abandon justice – compromising the very rights and freedoms which underpin our society and, more worryingly, imperilling the lives of vulnerable.

Legal aid reform and the Family Justice Review

The Government – in launching the legal aid reform programme – rightly acknowledged the valuable work of the Family Justice Review (FJR); it recognised that the FJR was actively considering options for a quicker, simpler, more cost-effective and fairer system, whilst continuing to protect children and vulnerable adults from risk of harm.[6]

The Government maintained that the proposals for the reform of legal aid 'complement the aims'[7] of the FJR. While acknowledging that both reform programmes examined conscientiously the benefits of out-of-court settlement and mediation, in significant respects the reform programmes were arguably operating in opposite directions. In the first instance, the FJR itself proposed[8] a radical re-organisation of legal aid – namely that it be part of the overall budget of the Family Justice Service:

> Family legal aid is a major part of the government spend on family justice. Were it managed as part of the overall family justice budget there would be opportunities to shift money between activities, from court work to mediation for example. The Family Justice Service should manage relationships with mediators, legal providers and experts. In time, with responsibility for the legal aid budget, it could procure their services.

Yet the Government forged ahead with its legal aid reform plans while this fundamental review of the family justice system was being undertaken. In this respect, the Government made clear that the legal aid reform proposals were 'stand-alone proposals and ... not dependent on the implementation of those wider reforms', including the FJR reforms.[9] Yet the two reform programmes were in my view inextricably bound together; the work of the FJR was undoubtedly more profound and far-reaching.

By way of example (as discussed more fully below), the removal of large numbers of people from the scope of legal aid will inevitably bring many more litigants in person into the family courts (discussed further by Barton, this issue); this will have the inevitable and serious consequence that the courts will become more densely populated with unrepresented parties. The FJR focused in particular on addressing (and removing) the weaknesses from the system, and building on its strengths; in this respect, the FJR (in its interim report) observed:

> Proposed changes to legal aid, should they go ahead, will mean more people choosing to represent themselves as litigants in person. This complexity will, as a result, become an *increasingly important weakness.*[10]

The FJR was concerned about the 'overlap between public and private law'[11], yet the legal aid proposals – while preserving the grant of legal aid in the public law sphere – removed it from private law. Furthermore, the FJR expressed its profound concern about the "significant" number of private law cases in which there was an identifiable risk of abuse, reporting that:

> Serious child protection concerns are raised, or come to light, in *a significant proportion of private law cases*. Where there are concerns for the child's safety or for a vulnerable adult swift and decisive action must be taken to protect them.[12] (emphasis added)

The Government's proposals for the Reform of Legal Aid meant that large numbers of these cases would fall outside the scope of public funding.

The scale and nature of the problem surrounding private law cases on the edge of public law was illustrated by the publication by the NSPCC during the period of the Bill's passage through Parliament of its report 'All babies count.' This report revealed that: just under 20,000 babies (under a year old) are living with a parent who has used Class A drugs in the last year; nearly 100,000 babies (under a year old) live with a parent who is a problem drinker; and nearly 150,000 babies (under a year old) live with a parent who has a common mental health problem.[13]

When noting that one in every two cohabiting couples will have separated by the time their children are five years old, this gives some idea of the number and potential complexity of private law cases which contain a factor which poses a potential if not an actual safeguarding concern.[14] And it is often these cases of family breakdown which occur in, or indeed spawn, other multiple problems including housing, welfare, immigration, or crime (see above). In short, it is clear that when these 'broken families' break, they shatter into many pieces.

The FJR contemplated that, notwithstanding the emphasis on out-of-court/mediated arrangements, a number of cases will still require court intervention (and that 'the judiciary remain central to the successful management of cases'[15]) namely: 'those with significant complexity, a point of law or pivotal point of fact to be considered, or where there are serious welfare concerns' – this covers a wider range of cases than those contemplated by the Legal Aid Bill and Response to consultation.[16] The cases will not be captured by the modest revisions to the legal aid proposals.

Structural change

The 2012 Act adopts a significantly different structure from its predecessor legislation in the manner in which legal aid provision is to be granted. The predecessor, the Access to Justice Act 1999, had specified the categories of case which were *excluded* from legal aid (the default being that, unless excepted, legal aid was available). The 2012 Act (by contrast) specifies what is *included* in legal aid, on the basis that unless specifically *in*cluded, it is not within the scope of legal aid.

Constitutional change

The 2012 Act further imported a significant constitutional change in defining the Lord Chancellor's responsibilities. Section 1 of the 2012 Act was drafted to read:

> The Lord Chancellor must secure that legal aid is made available in accordance with this Part.

It was notable that the Government rejected pleas to re-draft the provision to read:

> The Lord Chancellor must secure that legal aid is made available **in order to ensure practical and effective access to justice**.

The actual effect of the legislation is to substitute a narrower 'access to justice' provision in the 2012 Act than previously existed. Under Section 4 of the 1999 Act (now repealed), the LSC was established in order to develop the Community Legal Service:

> *for the purpose of promoting the availability to individuals of services of the descriptions specified in subsection (2) and, in particular,* ***for securing (within the resources made available, and priorities set, in accordance with this Part) that individuals have access to services that effectively meet their needs.*** (emphasis added)

The scope of legal aid

The most significant impact of the legal aid reform is the removal of large areas of family law dispute (and consequently large numbers of people) from the scope of legal aid. By the 2012 Act, save in limited circumstances, legal aid will now no longer be available for the majority of private law disputes.

The consultation elicited strong opposition to the proposal to remove large numbers of cases from scope. Of those who responded to the proposals, there was an almost unanimous view expressed against the proposal. A paltry 3%[17] of the respondents to the consultation supported the Government's proposal to remove large numbers of cases from scope. This response was disappointingly not reflected in the ultimate decision on legal aid, the Government declaring itself satisfied that:

> Although a significant majority of responses disagreed with the proposals, the Government remains convinced that reform is necessary to avoid unnecessary litigation, reduce the cost of legal aid and deliver better overall value for money.[18]

The Government's response[19] on this vital issue contained some general comments (intended to be re-assuring) about three 'factors' which (it was said) 'will help to mitigate' the impact of removing legal aid from private family proceedings; it is and was the view of the Family Law Bar Association view that these factors will in fact apply to relatively few of the cases. The aspired-for success of mediation was the single prominent factor which the Government relied on to mitigate the impact of legal aid; the facility of the court to award interim lump sums in financial claims was another. In our view, successful mediation and interim lump sums will relieve the stress of unfunded support in a small minority of cases. The third factor – namely the unspecified 'other avenues of support and advice to the extent they remain available' – would be unlikely to have much, if any, impact (whatever they are).

Most worrying is the fact that many families in private law disputes reflect a very similar profile to those who are subject to statutory interventions in public law cases, struggling on the lowest rung of the ladder until an incident or combination of factors coupled with a breakdown of co-operation and trust between the parents and professionals results in statutory intervention.[20] The parties to this litigation (private or public family law) often have combinations of ill health and socio economic difficulties (coupled with personal vulnerability factors) which demand that they have representation in the courts, where the issues arising in the context of their family crisis demand it.

This result may reduce the immediate costs to the Ministry of Justice but there is a real concern that it will add immeasurably to the costs to society. The court system does not operate in a vacuum: removing an area of legal redress from scope does not resolve the original problem; it merely pushes the problem onto a different service. Without looking at the potential incremental costs that will be incurred in the police service, education services, welfare services, homeless organisations, the NHS and community mental health organisations, the Legal Aid reform programme appears to be taking a significant risk with public money.

There can be no doubt that the proposals to remove large numbers of cases from scope will place a significant burden on the functioning of the civil and family courts. This will have considerable cost implications for Her Majesty's Court and Tribunal Service (HMCTS). It is a matter of significant concern that Government has proceeded with its proposals for reform on the basis that the proposed reforms only ***might*** lead to an increase in the volume of cases where people choose to represent themselves in court or at a tribunal without using legal representation (litigants in person). The Government has wrongly assumed that any such effect should not have a significant impact on ongoing court or tribunal operating costs.[21] Vital research in this area was surprisingly never undertaken.

Alongside the legal aid reforms, the Government reversed the abolition of the increased application fee for public law proceedings (notwithstanding the clear views expressed by Francis Plowden in his report 'Review of court fees in child care proceedings' dated 16 September 2009). This may mean that many Local Authorities 'think twice' about issuing public law proceedings in some of the borderline neglect/abuse cases.

It is appropriate to note Mr Plowden's comments (ref. Summary @ §1.16 and 1.18):

> I have been told of a number of cases where it appears that local authorities may have deferred taking proceedings for budgetary reasons. In addition, there is a widespread concern on the part of the judiciary about some family placements with which, while private law cases, the local authority may be involved. There is some corroborating evidence from national data which shows an increasing number of s37 directions. These allow the family courts to direct a local authority to investigate with a view to considering s31 proceedings where the Court is concerned that a child within the family may be at risk of significant harm

At the margins, there is a risk that resource issues can play a part in determining when and if care proceedings are initiated or that alternative courses of action are preferred – at least for the time being. In drawing this conclusion, it is unlikely that children have been left at avoidable risk, certainly not knowingly, on the part of the local authority. More plausibly, a child may be left in voluntary accommodation for longer than desirable or a sub-optimal placement with a family member attempted which, in due course, may prove unworkable.

Cuts which are taking place across local government are already having an impact on the delivery of children's services. It seems highly likely that there will be an increase in the incidence of those borderline child protection cases which are diverted by local authorities into private law proceedings by the Local Authority recommending that one or other parent seeks residence. This results in them dropping off the Local Authority radar, and they cease to be the subject of a child protection plan because they are in the hands of the court. Parents in these cases ought to be publicly funded, were it not for private proceedings there would be child protection activity and / or care proceedings – both of which are more costly.

The points above reinforce the importance of the Revised Private Law Programme (RPLP). Note, for instance, what is said in para.1.3 of the RPLP about the importance of the safety of the child:.

> ...the acceptance that Court orders, even those made by consent, must be scrutinised to ensure that they are safe and take account of any risk factors.

These cases (on the edge of public law) are now going to fall (or are going to continue to fall) in the private law sphere – where Judges will be dealing with parents unrepresented.

Litigants in Person

The proposals to exclude large numbers of the public from the scope of legal aid in family cases are likely to have a range of consequences. Most serious is the high probability that those who seek access to the courts will do so themselves, without representation.

Representation brings the following benefits (which are elaborated upon by Barton, this Issue):

- parties with legal advice may in fact be deterred or discouraged from initiating court process altogether;
- parties receive advice as litigation proceeds; at intermediate stages, litigation can be settled or concluded;
- the preparation of cases by lawyers is focused, with concentration on the issues; the court documentation is prepared in a form which encourages efficient court hearings;
- advocates concentrate on the key issues; court hearings take less time;
- legal advice post-hearings will avert unmeritorious appeals;
- There will be a lower likelihood of a miscarriage of justice; where unrepresented parties appear before the court there is a risk that Judges will not have relevant information and evidence placed before it. This is particularly regrettable at a time of heightened public anxiety regarding child protection;
- Representation assures equality of arms as between privately funded and legally aided parties.

In relation to public law (care) proceedings, Julia Brophy in her *Review of child care proceedings under the Children Act 1989* (University of Oxford) (May 2006) looked at research undertaken, including that relating to the profile of parents, in care proceedings. She found the following:

> As the profile of children and parents indicate, combinations of ill health and socio economic difficulties coupled with personal vulnerability factors indicate that the vast majority of families subject to statutory interventions are struggling on the lowest rung of the ladder – until an incident or combination of factors – coupled with a breakdown of co-operation and trust between the parents and professionals results in statutory intervention. (p. 17)

Many members of the public who fall into this profile appear in the family courts in private law disputes – just on the edge of formal statutory court intervention, but very possibly with Local Authority social services involvement in their lives. These people are the most likely to be adversely affected by the growing advice deserts around the country.

While some litigants in person will be intelligent, and marshal their cases well, many will be emotional and obsessional about what has happened to them; many are very nervous, often upset, sometimes very angry, and it is invariably a real challenge for the Judge to be able to get the best out of people who are in that state.

The Lord Chancellor's own experience summarised the position accurately:

> I personally accept that every court dreads suddenly discovering that there is a difficult case where one of the litigants insists on appearing in person (Lord Chancellor evidence to the Justice Select Committee: 15.12.10).

It follows that an influx of litigants in person into the family courts will have a serious impact on the delays likely to be caused to the family court lists.

One of the most difficult classes of hearings for judges to manage is those where a serious allegation (for example, one of domestic violence or sexual abuse) is made against a litigant in person. For with no professional representation, the court must be scrupulous to ensure that the Respondent not only has the opportunity to refute the allegations, but also that he (or she) understands the full potential consequences of any adverse findings. There is little scope for negotiation or compromise in such cases. At the same time the judge must be astute to ensure that the complainant is properly protected from further potential distress or abuse whilst giving evidence, as the alleged perpetrator will be in a position to ask questions of each witness directly. This class of case will become far more frequent an occurrence before the court, with consequent inevitable delays to the listing of other cases.

It should be remembered too that in cases such as those mentioned in the paragraph above, as in every species of case, there are those where language barriers may play a significant part – in some courts particularly in urban areas this happens very frequently. In such cases, in the absence of representation, interpreters are unlikely to have been arranged before a hearing. The prospect of a party who does not speak English as a first language being able to grasp legal concepts or procedures adequately in court are slim however much additional time or effort the court may be able to invest where such a situation arises.

The Government's own literature review[22] (commissioned alongside its response) revealed that, as a result of the legal aid reform, the public will face: poorer case outcomes; longer delays in resolution of cases; lower prospects of settlement; and vulnerable people forced to present their own cases.

The Government's literature review on the impact of Litigants in Person ('LiP') on family cases confirms the representations of the many respondents to the legal aid reform consultation, who spoke of the harmful effect on the court system of the inevitable increase in the number of LiPs in the family courts. Notably, reference to the LiP review in the Response is rather patchy. While reference is made to delay, the finding of "poorer outcomes" is not mentioned in several locations where the LiP issue is addressed.

The research was, sadly, of limited value, but nevertheless does little if anything to support the Government's proposals and goes some way to corroborate the fears expressed by the consultees to the Government's response about the impact of the reform proposals. It was, as the authors of the research admit 'not a fully systematic review'. The research revealed (it is acknowledged) 'limited' good quality evidence on which the Government could base its proposals. It is conceded that there was little 'robust' evidence for the research questions (*comment:* while ostensibly ignoring the clear evidence from the judiciary in their response to the consultation, for example – see below). The relevance of international comparative studies was shown (as we predicted) to be 'problematic' given the different eligibility criteria, cultural differences, and legal context. In the final analysis, it shows that there are 'gaps' in the Government's 'understanding' of the impact of litigants in person in the courts (described as 'limited').

Nevertheless, the research told us the following information about LiPs:

Profile of LiPs

> LiPs tended to be younger, with lower income, and educational levels than those who obtained representation;
>
> In family cases, the one study to examine the issue revealed that a significant minority of unrepresented litigants (20% of injunction cases, and 15% of children cases) had a 'specific indication of vulnerability (such as being victims of violence, having depression, a problem with alcohol/drug use, having a mental illness or being extremely young parents)', raising serious questions about their ability effectively to access the courts / justice.

Effect on the cases and on the courts

> Family cases where one or both parties were unrepresented tended not to settle, increasing case duration (and, therefore, cost);

'The weight of the evidence indicated that lack of representation generally had a negative effect on case outcomes';

LiPs tended to experience 'a number of problems' in presenting their cases '... which, in turn, impact on the court' – LiPs were (according to a number of sources) '... overwhelmed by the procedural and oral demands of the courtroom';

A number of sources noted the extra burden that unrepresented litigants create for court staff and judges.

Where active unrepresented litigants were involved, cases were seen to take longer. This was particularly so for family cases, where the absence of a representative was linked to longer case duration as they were less likely to settle than cases involving a representative (Dewar *et al.* 2000, Hunter,, 2003, Moorhead and Sefton, 2005, Rosenbloom, 2003: see Literature Review for details of this research.),

Failure to pursue claims as a result of lack of advice / representation

The Government conceded that there was a gap in the research, in that it did not examine the potential impact of changes to access to legal funding on whether people with problems amenable to resolution in the justice system would be reluctant or unwilling to participate in the justice system if they did not have legal advice; what they do instead, and the effectiveness of the alternatives they may turn to.

In contrast with this literature review, it is appropriate to note what the Judge's Council[23] said in its response to the Consultation Paper on Legal Aid. There is a highly relevant, detailed, discussion of the impact of LiPs on the management and outcome of cases, from an informed and experienced perspective. In summary, the Council reports (§6):

One of the major concerns running through our comments is that the proposals would lead to a huge increase in the incidence of unrepresented litigants, with serious implications for the quality of justice and for the administration of the justice system in terms of additional costs and delays – at a time when courts are having to cope in any event with closures, budgetary cut-backs and reductions in staff numbers. The consultation paper shows an awareness of the issue but fails to recognise the depth of the problem. Even if one focuses on cost alone, there is a real question whether the cost savings arising from the proposed cutbacks in the scope of civil and family legal aid would be offset by the additional costs imposed on the system by dealing with the increase in litigants in person.

And alongside the Judge's Council, it is further revealing to note what the Interim Report of the Family Justice Review said (§5.55–5.57) on this topic:

Should the proposals go ahead as set out in the Green Paper, the reduction in the scope of legal aid may result in greater numbers of people representing themselves, or litigants in person. Such people often have limited legal expertise and need greater support from the court during their proceedings, which may lead to longer cases. Litigants in person may also be disadvantaged by not knowing their entitlements.

There should be much more readily-available information for litigants in person. People should not have to fork out huge legal fees, go on benefits or be disadvantaged by a lack of information on appearing as a litigant-in-person - just so that they can put forward their case regarding the most important things in their lives i.e. their children. [Parent, call for evidence submission.]

We share these concerns, both as to the ability of litigants in person to conduct their case effectively and as to the inevitable increased burden in terms of time and resources this will place on the court. We are also concerned that some parents will simply not pursue their dispute leading to some children losing contact with a parent.

We await the government's conclusions, following the consultation and their response to these concerns."

The Government's summary of the research[24] reads as follows:

> In the consultation paper we undertook to review the research available on litigants-in-person, and their impact on the conduct and outcome of proceedings. The Government has completed its review, which it has published separately today. Overall the review found that the evidence available on litigants-in-person tends to suggest a mixed impact in length of proceedings. This was affected by case type and how active the litigants were. It was suggested that cases took longer when the unrepresented litigant was active but could take less time when the litigant was inactive.[25]

The 'mixed impact' should not be misunderstood: this includes cases where the litigant was 'inactive' – that is to say, took no part in the proceedings at all.

Finally, it is noted that the 'Government will examine the system to support litigants-in-person as part of the post-implementation review and will report the findings to Parliament'.[26] There has been little indication of what the post-implementation review may look like.

Domestic Abuse and the Court process

Where relationship breakdown has been accompanied by the trauma of domestic abuse, the victim is inevitably in a state of considerable distress. This distress is undoubtedly exacerbated if the victim has to relive the experience of abuse by giving evidence about it in court. The stress facing the victim will be significantly heightened by being confronted – directly in court – by the unrepresented abuser. The legal process contemplated by these legal aid proposals, will place the victim not just in court with the unrepresented abuser, but being faced by direct questioning by the abuser. Far from protecting the abuser from the abuse, this will only serve to perpetuate (and increase) the experience of abuse.

The Family Law Bar Association was concerned about the situation which will routinely arise in a family court in which the victim will be cross-examined by the perpetrator as to the allegations in an unrestricted way; this situation is avoided to a considerable extent in the criminal courts by virtue of Section 41, Youth Justice and Criminal Evidence Act 1999, and Criminal Procedure Rules 2010 Part 36.

There is a risk that these provisions may deter vulnerable victims from pursuing court protection if they know that they will have to face direct cross-examination from the person who has abused them.

One further issue is where one party is represented, and the other is not. This situation was described by Lord Justice Munby in a recent appeal (*Re K* [2010] EWCA Civ 1546) in which he said:

> Any dispassionate observer sitting in this court might be forgiven for thinking that there is unfairness in that state of affairs and something very far from the equality of arms which is supposed, consistently with Article 6 of the European Convention, to underlie proceedings of this sort as indeed all proceedings. Justice, as was memorably observed so many years ago, must not merely be done but must be seen to be done. Although I am confident that, despite the mother's forensic disabilities, justice has been done, I am much less confident that any dispassionate observer having watched these proceedings today would think that justice has been seen to be done, given the disparity in the resources which the State has made available to the one litigant and not to the other.

Rule 16.2/Rule 16.6 cases (Family Procedure Rules 2010)

There was surely a powerful argument that legal aid should be available for all parties in which an order under Rule 16.2 is made, where the child is to participate in proceedings without a guardian, or where the child is to be the applicant or respondent to the application. These cases are by definition extremely complex and sensitive (in accordance with the *Airey* criteria); they include cases.[27]

- Where there are serious allegations of physical, sexual or other abuse in relation to the child;
- Where there are complex medical or mental health issues to be determined or there are other unusually complex issues;
- Where there is an intractable dispute over residence or contact, including where all contact has ceased, or where there is irrational but implacable hostility to contact or where the child may be suffering harm associated with the contact dispute (see above);
- Where there are international complications outside child abduction, in particular where it may be necessary for there to be discussions with overseas authorities or a foreign court;
- Where there is a contested issue about blood testing.

These cases are invariably not suitable for mediation. The Courts will therefore have unrepresented litigants before them:

- Being required to marshal the relevant evidence in a case concerning physical or sexual abuse of a child, where there may be, for example, concurrent police involvement / investigations;
- Having to deal with (and cross-examine on) expert evidence relevant to serious allegations of physical or sexual harm of a child,
- Having to consider and deal with expert evidence relevant to the court practice of a foreign jurisdiction;
- With "mental health issues", who will be expected to represent themselves even though the "significant difficulty" envisaged in the case is precisely the fact that the parent has such a condition.

Regrettably, only the child will benefit from a public funding certificate in such cases.

Exceptional cases[28]

The exclusion of important cases from the scope of legal aid is not remedied by the incorporation into the 2012 Act of section 10. At consultation stage, the FLBA contended that – having regard to the decision of *Airey* v. *Ireland* 32 Eur Ct HR Ser A (1979): [1979] 2 EHRR 305 – the lack of legal aid in the majority of private law family cases raised serious ECHR issues (a matter taken up further by Meyler and Woodhouse in the context of immigration proceedings in their contribution to this issue).

In *Airey*, the Court held that a right of access to a court for the determination of the applicant's civil rights (recognised by *Golder* v. *UK* [1975] 1EHRR 524) could be violated by lack of legal aid for legal representation in those proceedings. The fact that the litigant was free to act as a LIP is not conclusive of the matter, as ECHR guarantees practical and effective, not theoretical and illusory rights [24]. In some cases, acting as a LIP would not breach Article 6 rights, but 'much must depend on the particular circumstances' [26].

So in *Airey* the question was whether Mrs Airey's theoretical ability to represent herself would be effective, i.e. whether she would be able to present her case properly and satisfactorily [24].

It was noted that the fact that her husband would be represented by a lawyer would put her at a disadvantage. But even putting that aside, Mrs Airey could not effectively conduct her own case *in litigation of this nature,* despite the assistance that judge would afford to her as a LIP because: of the complex procedure of High Court (how would it compare by reference to the Family Procedure Rules?); of the complex points of law; there would be requirement to prove grounds for judicial separation, possibly with expert evidence and other witnesses; and 'What is more, marital disputes often entail an emotional involvement that is scarcely compatible with the degree of objectivity required by advocacy in court.'

When the issue was looked at again in *McVicar* v. *UK* (Application no. 46311/99; (2002) 35 EHRR 21, a case concerning the lack of legal aid in defamation actions) it was held that one of the important features of the decision in *Airey* was that there was an inevitable emotional involvement – this was a particular feature of family cases which 'regulate the legal relationship between two individuals and may have serious consequences for any children of the family' [61].

It is appropriate also to look at *R* v. *Legal Services Commission ex parte Jarrett* ([2001] EWHC Admin 389). The current exceptional funding criteria were amended following the domestic decision in *Jarrett* where it was held that the then criteria (overwhelming importance to client or significant public interest) failed to capture all issues pertinent to Article 6. This led to the addition of the clause that reads:

> there is convincing evidence that there are exceptional circumstances such that without public funding for representation it would be practically impossible for the client to bring or defend proceedings, or the lack of public funding would lead to obvious unfairness in the proceedings.

An oddity immediately arises from the *prima facie* exclusion of private family law from legal aid, given the apparent Strasbourg view that at least some non-domestic violence private family cases (note: there was some history of domestic violence in *Airey*, but that played no part in the Court's decision that legal aid was required for Mrs Airey's judicial separation petition) can be sufficiently important to require legal aid given the importance of the issues to the lives of the parties, especially the children.

So we contended that the exclusion of private family cases had been drawn too tightly, such that the blanket rule may well be unlawful in terms of Article 6. There was clearly room for challenge on this point, given the Government's complete inattention to the ample evidence of lawyers' role in settling cases, and the available evidence about the experience of litigants in person in family cases.

If the blanket rule was not itself a breach, that conclusion would have to be in part on the basis that the exceptional funding provision would be applied in such a way to ensure Article 6 compliance. What proportion of cases might be expected to require legal aid? It is interesting to note the Government view that mediation is all that is needed in these cases (with supporting legal work) and the expectation that, domestic violence and child abuse-related cases remaining in scope, only a further 5% of private family cases will find their way back into legal aid via exceptional funding [impact assessment Annex A, Table 3].

It is also relevant to consider *P, C and S* v. *UK* ((ECHR) 56547/00), in which it was said that while there is no automatic right under the Convention for legal aid or legal representation to be available for an applicant who is involved in proceedings which determine his or her civil rights, nonetheless, Article 6 may be engaged under two interrelated aspects. First, assistance is indispensable for effective access to court, either because legal representation is rendered *compulsory* as is the case in certain Contracting States for various types of litigation, or by reason of the *complexity* of the procedure or the type of case (see *Airey* v. *Ireland*, judgment of 9 October 1979, Series A no. 32, pp. 14–16, §§ 26–28, where the applicant was unable to obtain the assistance of a lawyer in judicial separation proceedings). Factors identified as relevant in *Airey* in determining whether the applicant would have been able to present her case properly and satisfactorily without the assistance of a lawyer included the complexity of the procedure, the necessity to address complicated points of law or to establish facts, involving expert evidence and the examination of witnesses, and the fact that the subject matter of the marital dispute entailed an emotional involvement that was scarcely compatible with the degree of objectivity required by advocacy in court. In such circumstances, the Court found it unrealistic to suppose that the applicant could effectively conduct her own case, despite the assistance afforded by the judge to parties acting in person.

Second, the key principle governing the application of Article 6 is *fairness*. In cases where an applicant appears in court notwithstanding lack of assistance by a lawyer and manages to conduct his or her case in the teeth of all the difficulties, the question may nonetheless arise as to whether this procedure was fair (see, for example, *McVicar* v. *the United Kingdom*, Application no. 46311/99, §§ 50–51, ECHR 2002-III). There is the importance of ensuring the appearance of the fair administration of justice and a party in civil proceedings must be able to participate effectively, *inter alia*, by being able to put forward the matters in support of his or her claims. Here, as in other aspects of Article 6, the seriousness of what is at stake for the applicant will be of relevance to assessing the adequacy and fairness of the procedures

In short, it was our view that the legal aid reform programme in this respect raised legitimate Article 6 issues in light of *Airey*; we suggested that it was wrong to apply an additional hurdle of 'exceptionality' in order to satisfy Article 6 rights. We suggested that section 10 (as it became) did not go far enough to ensure that there was provision for funding in appropriate cases. The proposed scheme for funding exceptional (excluded) cases where it was shown to be necessary in order for the United Kingdom to meet its legal obligations was unduly narrow and would not be sufficient to counter the adverse effects of litigants being forced to pursue litigation in person, in areas of civil and family law where legal representation is important for the proper conduct of the case (see on this issue §9 of the response of the Judge's Council to the Consultation Paper).

It is not easy to ascertain, without more information, how the Director will exercise discretion in the individual case; this may become clearer when the Guidance is published. However, it seems extremely unlikely that this discretion will be invoked in the many cases in which we consider the vulnerable will encounter difficulties in accessing justice.

Minor changes to the Bill

As the Bill made its passage through Parliament, small changes to the proposed legislation were made. Most notably, perhaps, was the concession wrung out of the Government late in the day when it relented in adopting the ACPO definition of domestic abuse within schedule 1.[29] Initially it had been proposed that domestic abuse would be satisfied by proof that 'the victim is at risk of physical harm' (§4.64), and 'an ongoing risk of physical harm' §4.67. For most of the consultation period, and Parliamentary review of the Bill, domestic abuse was limited to that falling within the definition of physical harm.

The concession achieved was important given the incidence of, and the profile of, those who suffer domestic abuse.

Further success was scored in relation to domestic child abduction, following amendments tabled by Baroness Elizabeth Butler-Sloss (designed to ensure legal aid for those who seek to *prevent* child abduction or to take steps to ensure the *return* of the child further to such a removal).

Mediation and dispute resolution

Mediation and Dispute Resolution Services are given a prominent billing in the FJR report, as indeed they were in the Government's Legal Aid Reform Programme. To some extent this is right; mediation has an important part to play in dispute resolution. But some of the most dysfunctional or disadvantaged in society will not be readily amenable to mediation. For many, mediation will simply be inappropriate. As Lord Neuberger said, 'Citizens are bearers of rights, they are not simply or merely consumers of services'.[30] He further spoke of a perceived:

> ... tendency, which has found increasing favour in some circles particularly those in which saving money is the main aim, that mediation is a sort of universal panacea, which, properly developed, should obviate the need for an effective civil courts system in England and Wales.

He made clear that such a tendency would be 'not merely wrong' but 'misconceived, and actually risk undermining the very argument that their supporters wish to maintain'.

Lord Neuberger further spoke of the 'proper role' for mediation being 'one which focuses on its proper function as an adjunct to justice, as a complement to the justice system and not as a substitute for effective access to justice. If it is conceived of as a substitute for securing effective access to justice, the risk is run that we will institutionalise the denial of effective access to justice for some citizens.'

He added:

> If we expand mediation beyond its proper limits as a complement to justice we run the risk of depriving particular persons or classes of person of their right to equal and impartial justice under the law. Citizens are bearers of rights, they are not simply or merely consumers of services.

There is a large number of people for whom mediation will not be suitable. Quite apart from those who have experienced domestic violence, we include here parties who have learning disabilities, parties with mental illnesses, parties whose lives have been so affected by drink or drugs that they need support or assistance to function or reason independently. There are also those where the relationship is a significant power imbalance between the parties, and for whom mediation becomes not only unworkable but potentially abusive.

Indeed the power imbalance which affects parties' abilities to participate in this service is not addressed. Enforced mediation will thus have a disproportionately negative effect on women, particularly those from ethnic minority groups when cultural pressures have a part to play in the parties' abilities to negotiate on issues of money and children post separation. Where English is not the first language of either of the parties or the mediator, is it intended that interpreters are used? If so, are they to be neutral court appointed interpreters? It would not be appropriate for family members to do the translating. Has the Government considered who is to pay for the official translator if one is needed?

So while out-of-court solutions may be appropriate for some (we suggest fewer than contemplated by the Government or perhaps by the Review Panel) self-help in court will become the 'norm' for many. As mentioned earlier, this is surely going to increase the 'scandalous' delays in the family courts as DIY litigants absorb increasing amounts of court time as they endeavour – overwhelmed by the processes – to seek solutions or remedies.[31] Increased delays in the courts will cause or at best aggravate injustice. Delay is said to be the deadliest form of denial: delay and you will prevent justice being done at all.

Impact on the legal profession

Shortly after the consultation period closed on the Legal Aid reform proposals, on 9 May 2011, the Government introduced a new fee scheme for practitioners in the family courts – the Family Advocacy Scheme (FAS – this was introduced by the Community Legal Service (Funding) (Amendment) Order 2011 (No. 1027) and is also to be found in section 7 of the 2012 Standard Civil Contract (Family and Housing) (the Family Specification)).

The FAS is a Graduated Fee Scheme providing a separate payment regime for advocacy for all advocates regardless of their professional status during the life of family proceedings. It operates alongside the arrangements for payment of non-advocacy work in these proceedings including payments under the Care Proceedings Graduated Fee Scheme (CPGFS) and the Private Family Law Representation Scheme (PFLRS). The FAS was designed to achieve not only the harmonising of rates of pay for advocates in the family courts (whether they be barristers or solicitors) but also cost control. One of the important purposes of the scheme is to 'guarantee the sustainable provision of family legal aid services by controlling the increasing cost of family legal aid and reducing the amount spent on work outside of legal advice and representation'. The FAS replaced the FGFS for barristers – a scheme introduced in 2001, and to which there has been no real increase in the rates since its inception, not even to take account of any increase in the cost of living.

There was no review of the impact of this new (FAS) scheme on the delivery and supply of family justice before the Government imposed further 10% cuts in family fees on family lawyers under the Legal Aid reform proposals.

There is a risk that the depth and breadth of the legal aid cuts, coupled with the absence of any proposals for considering other sources of funding, may well threaten the viability of the publicly funded legal profession practising in family law as a whole, praised by Lord Carter in his review of legal aid (and others, see Lord Justice Moses[32]) for their industry. Regrettably, the Legal Aid reform programme has had the effect of undermining professional confidence in the Government's commitment to retaining quality advocacy in the publicly-funded justice system.

There is a further risk that the 10% cuts in fees for the legal profession (part of the associated legal aid reform – though not specifically contained in the 2012 Act), far from 'protecting and promoting the interests of consumers', will undermine these interests. Given the acknowledged discriminatory impact of the proposals the legal profession will not emerge 'independent, strong, diverse and effective'; countless women and black and minority ethnic practitioners – whose practices rely more extensively on public funds than their other professional colleagues – will be forced away from the work.

The proposed cuts in fees (running alongside the proposed removal of cases from scope) is likely to place a strain on many solicitors firms, as publicly funded work becomes wholly uneconomic; advice deserts may well emerge; access to justice for the public will become harder. It is no wonder that 88%[33] of the respondents to the consultation opposed the cuts to legal fees. That 88% figure is not likely, we suggest, to represent simply those whose livelihoods depend on public funding.

At the Bar, women and BME practitioners will be the hardest hit by these fee proposals.[34] Overall, the legal profession (and in due course the judiciary) will become less representative of the public it serves.

This is not, as has been said already, mere self-interested lawyers complaining about the cuts to its fees; this is the view of the senior Judiciary (§10: Judge's Council response):

> There is a real concern, especially in relation to family and criminal work, that the pool of skilled advocates willing to undertake the work will diminish, to the disadvantage of litigants and to the detriment of the efficient running of cases. Moreover, there are likely to be longer term adverse consequences for the recruitment of able advocates into these fields of work and, at the other end of the spectrum, for the existence of a sufficiently large and diverse pool of able advocates suitable for appointment as judges in such cases.

Conclusion

The FLBA has been concerned about the 'Jenga'[35] effect of the Legal Aid Reform programme. There is a risk that by removing cases from scope, the edifice of the Family Justice System will rock on its foundations; decimate the fees paid to the dedicated lawyers who prop up the system, and they leave; the edifice rocks further.

In particular, there remains a risk that the most vulnerable in society will go without proper legal advice and representation at a crucial – and often traumatic – time in their lives and that vulnerable adults and children will remain trapped in situations where they are exposed to (potentially increasing) risk of harm. There will inevitably be an increase in unrepresented parties in the courts which, in turn, will increase the length of cases and the costs (usually publicly funded) of the other parties. There may well be an upsurge in the number of appeals, given the high risk that the first instance courts will not have relevant information and evidence placed before it. This is particularly regrettable at a time of heightened public anxiety regarding child protection. It will increase the burden on other areas of public spending as more people become dependent on social and mental health services. There are likely to be many cases in which there is a proper cause for concern about an inequality of arms, where one side is privately funded, and the other is (absent legal aid) required to litigate in person (see *Re K* [2010] EWCA Civ 1546). It is, of course, to be hoped that that the legal aid reforms introduced by LASPO Act 2012 do not adversely impact upon the energetic programme of family justice modernisation, and damage the confidence of the public in the family court system. Only time will tell.

Notes

1. Initially vested with the Law Society, then with the Legal Aid Board (1988), and then (post-1999) the Legal Services Commission.
2. £25m: This will remove advice in this category for 113,000 clients per annum.
3. 75,000 clients (i.e. unless there is an immediate risk to the home, significant amount of housing – a cut of a little under 40%).
4. This includes family reunion cases engaging Art. 8 and other visa cases. In Immigration it is in general all cases (other than asylum and detention). See further Meyler and Woodhouse, this issue.
5. Impact Assessment: Equality impacts: November 2010: our initial analysis of the impacts of the proposed changes on clients is that there is a potential disproportionate impact on women and BAME clients, in that the proportion of clients affected adversely by the proposed changes that fall within these groups is likely to be high relative to the proportion of people in those groups in the population.
6. Page 20, §46: The Government Response: CM8072.
7. Page 116, para. 21 (Annex B) The Government's Response.
8. Family Justice Review Interim Report §3.88.
9. §2.13 of the Government's Consultation Paper 'Proposals for the Reform of Legal Aid'.
10. Family Justice Review Interim Report, §2.47.
11. Family Justice Review Interim Report, §5.61.

12. §106 Interim Report of the Family Justice Review (p. 20).
13. All Babies Count [November 2011].
14. FJR report/NSPCC report/marriage statistics.
15. Family Justice Review Interim Report §74 (p. 15).
16. Family Justice Review Interim Report §5.125.
17. Annexe B, para. 2: The Government Response: CM 8072.
18. Annex B, para. 3: The Government Response: CM 8072.
19. The Government Response: CM 8702, §45 p. 20.
20. See Julia Brophy's research for her 'Review of child care proceedings under the Children Act 1989' (University of Oxford) (May 2006).
21. See IAMoJ28, para. 39.
22. http://www.justice.gov.uk/downloads/publications/research-and-analysis/moj-research/litigants-in-person-literature-review.pdf
23. http://www.judiciary.gov.uk/Resources/JCO/Documents/Consultations/response-judges-council-legal-aid-reform-consultation.pdf
24. The Government Response §138, p. 40.
25. Note that the 'poorer outcomes' finding was NOT mentioned in this section of the Response paper.
26. The Government Response Chapter 4, §16, p. 115.
27. See President's Practice Direction: Representation of Children in Family Proceedings (2004) reported at [2004] 1 FLR 1188.
28. With particular thanks to Jo Miles, University Lecturer, Director of Studies and Fellow in Law, Trinity College, Cambridge, for her assistance with the narrative in this part of the article.
29. The ACPO definition above (or something very close to it), had been adopted by many official and governmental bodies, including the Association of Chief Police Officers: Guidance on Investigating Domestic Abuse (2008); the Crown Prosecution Service Policy for Prosecuting Cases of Domestic Violence (2010); the Ministry of Justice, in Domestic Violence: A Guide to Civil Remedies and Criminal Sanctions (February 2003, updated March 2007); and the UK Border Agency, in Victims of Domestic Violence: Requirements for Settlement Applications.
30. Lord Slynn Memorial Lecture: November 2010.
31. See the Response of the Judges Council to the Legal Aid Reform consultation.
32. *Law Society* v. *LSC & Others* [2010] EWHC 2550 (Admin).
33. Annex H of the Government's response to the Consultation §4, p. 227.
34. King's College Survey: 2008: This is a quantitative study of the work of the family bar in 2008, and the current functioning of the legal aid graduated fee system for barristers in family law cases. The study was commissioned in June 2008 by the Family Law Bar Association (FLBA), and was undertaken by researchers in the King's Institute for the Study of Public Policy (KISPP) at King's College London, from July 2008 to December 2008. Data were gathered through surveys of (i) chambers where any family work is undertaken, (ii) barristers who undertook any family work (whether publicly funded or privately paid) in the year to 30 August 2008 and (iii) all family work completed by barristers in England and Wales in a random week, known as the 'Week-At-A-Glance'.
35. Jenga is the game where wooden blocks are stacked and removed one at a time until the tower collapses.

Analysing the economic justification for the reforms to social welfare and family law legal aid

Graham Cookson

Department of Management, King's College London, London, UK

The Ministry of Justice plans on saving £450 million per annum from the legal aid budget through reforms contained in the Legal Aid, Sentencing and Punishment of Offenders Act 2012.Over 60% of these savings will be found by removing whole areas of law and types of problem from the scope of legal aid support. One of the principal justifications for these reforms is the economic imperative; reducing legal aid expenditure is necessary to meet the Government's fiscal targets. This article examined whether these reforms will generate the substantial savings identified in the Government's impact assessment, or whether these costs will be passed on to other areas of government. Data from the Civil and Social Justice Survey were used to model the behavioural responses of people no longer eligible for legal aid under the scope changes. Economic costs were estimated for these responses where they will be incurred by the state, although many of these costs are likely to be underestimates. Many costs could not be estimated including, inter alia, the cost of increased criminality where people seek redress outside of the justice system. The analysis focused on family and social welfare law, which together represent 82% of the proposed savings from the scope reforms. Based upon this analysis, the Government is unlikely to save more than 40% of its prediction. At the same time, these minimal savings could generate inequality of access to justice and overburden an already struggling alternative advice sector. A significant uptake in funded mediation within family law is predicted.

Introduction

The economic justification for reforming legal aid

Since its inception in 1949, the legal aid system in England and Wales has enabled equality of access to justice for those people unable to afford legal advice or representation. Access to justice is considered a hallmark of a civil society (Ministry of Justice 2010b) and therefore many people were surprised by the extent of the cuts contained in the the *Legal Aid, Sentencing and Punishment of Offenders* (LASPO) Act 2012, which received Royal Assent in May 2012. LASPO will save £450 million[1] per annum according to government projections (Ministry of Justice 2011d). While £160 million will come from fee reform and £10 million will come from changes to the eligibility criteria, the majority (£270 million) of the savings will come from changes to the scope of legal aid, i.e. what areas of law and types of cases are covered (Ministry of Justice 2011d). The Act removes entire areas of law from the scope of legal aid reforms. Social welfare and family law are particularly exposed to the scope cuts with 84% of this £270 million saving coming from these areas of law.[2] For example, all private family law cases will no longer be eligible unless there is evidence of domestic violence, child abuse or cases which fall under the Government's obligations under the European Convention on Human Rights. Even fewer exceptions are made for social welfare law (*c.f.* Ministry of Justice 2010b, Annex F). There are various measures of legal aid expenditure and volume reported by the Government and the Legal Services Commission, but the trends are similar (Cookson 2011).

The cuts to the legal aid budget were predicated on two main arguments. First, that current legal aid expenditure is too great (Ministry of Justice 2010b). People are too willing to litigate rather than negotiate, as is indicated by England and Wales spending almost four times as much per capita on legal aid than New Zealand with a similar, common law, system (Bowles and Perry 2009). Second, that legal aid is not immune from the public spending cuts aimed at reducing the UK fiscal deficit. The UK, along with much of the world, is amidst one of the worst economic crises ever witnessed. In response, the current government pledged to reduce public expenditure by £81 billion by 2015 (HM Treasury 2010). As part of this commitment, the Ministry of Justice is required to make savings of £2 billion per annum by 2015 (Ministry of Justice 2011d), which represents 23% of its annual budget. Legal aid expenditure was £2.1 billion in 2009–2010, of which £941 million was spent on family and civil law cases (Ministry of Justice 2010b). Therefore there is a public finance imperative or wider economic justification for the legal aid reforms.

There has been extensive research on both the legal and humanitarian implications of the legal aid reforms, but very little attention has been paid to the economic or financial aspects. Perhaps this is because researchers, policymakers and society are uncomfortable placing a price on access to justice. However, for these reforms to contribute to tackling the fiscal deficit – the main justification for such extensive cuts – they must not generate substantial 'knock-on' costs in other areas of government expenditure. As the Justice Select Committee stated: 'Reducing spending on legal aid may have financial implications – and indeed may inflate costs – in other parts of the legal system' (Justice Select Committee 2011). Yet the Government's impact assessment suggested that the scope changes proposed in LASPO could generate additional knock-on costs including reduced social cohesion, increased criminality, reduced business and economic efficiency, increased resource costs to other departments, and increased transfer payments from other departments (Ministry of Justice 2011a). For instance, in the area of family law, if a parent is unable to secure access to their child because they do not have the benefit of legal aid funded legal advice or representation, then they may seek justice outside of the legal system for example, in extremis, taking the child abroad.

Very little is known about the potential consequential costs of cutting access to legal aid funded services. A recent public commission in Canada found cutting legal aid expenditure to be a false economy because it merely shifted the costs of unresolved problems onto other departments in government (Doust 2011). As noted by the Justice Select Committee (Justice Select Committee 2011) and acknowledged by the Ministry of Justice (Ministry of Justice 2011b), the magnitude of these knock-on costs has not been estimated. It is therefore not possible to determine whether the reduction in legal aid expenditure within the Ministry of Justice will generate a net saving to the public purse. This article will address this question.

Data and methods

Estimating the counterfactuals

The basic method for determining the net impact of the reform is straightforward: estimate the knock-on costs and subtract these from the Government's predicted savings. To do this it is necessary to determine the likely actions or behavioural responses of people who no longer receive legal aid – what the Government called the 'counterfactuals' in the impact assessment (Ministry of Justice 2011a). Once the volume of people taking each action has been determined, the cost to the public purse of these actions must be estimated.

The ideal situation for determining the counterfactuals would be to conduct a (randomised control) trial where some people continued to receive legal aid support (control) and others did not (treatment), and people were randomised into the treatment and control groups. The next best option would be to observe a selection of people before and after the policy change and using statistical controls remove confounding effects to determine the overall effect of the policy. None of these options are available as the policy is yet to be implemented. Instead, responses to the Civil and Social Justice Survey (CSJS) are used to predict behaviour after LASPO is implemented. The method is explained in detail below. Once the possible responses and the numbers of people choosing these responses has been determined using data from the CSJS, the cost to the public purse of these decisions must be estimated. Again, the method to estimate these costs is explained in detail below. In the next section, the counterfactuals and their associated costs are populated with data on the current family and social welfare law system to predict the impact of the legal aid reforms on the public purse.

The Civil and Social Justice Survey

The English and Welsh Civil and Social Justice Survey (CSJS) studies people's experiences of civil justice problems and the strategies adopted to deal with them (Pleasence *et al.* 2010). The latest version of the CSJS reported in 2009 using data from 2006–2009. It contained responses from 10,537 adults from 6234 randomly selected households, and was 'broadly representative of the residential household population of England and Wales' (ibid). Of the respondents, 36% (3752) experienced one or more 'difficult to solve civil justice problems' (ibid), a total of 5815 justice problems. Housing problems account for the largest proportion (26%) of problems, followed by consumer (23%), family (11%) and debt (11%) problems. There is good coverage of the types of people and cases that will be affected by the LASPO reforms. The CSJS survey provides useful information on the responses to civil justice problems by respondents, some with legal aid funding and some without access to legal aid funding. Further, it asks questions that help identify counterfactuals such as what the respondent would have done if their first choice advisor did not exist, and how much they would have been prepared to pay to solve the problem.

Seeking alternative advice

As the impact assessment acknowledges, the key to estimating the knock-on costs of the reforms is to determine the likely responses to the removal of legal aid advice. What alternative courses of actions, so-called 'counterfactuals' will people adopt. The CSJS helpfully asks: 'Which of the following would you have done if [adviser] hadn't existed?' Analysing the responses of those who used a solicitor for their first choice of advisor and experienced a family or social welfare problem, 11% (of 209 respondents) would not seek alternative advice (margin of error: ±4.8%[3]) and 13% 'didn't know'. Grouping the other responses together, between 75 and 89% would seek alternative advice depending upon where the 'don't know' responses are included. Among the subset of respondents who reported having free or partially free legal advice, 10% (margin of error: ±6.7%) said that they would not seek alternative advice. And finally, among the subset who reported having this legal advice paid for by legal aid, the percentage of respondents who would not seek alternative advice was 11% (margin of error: ± 10%)[4]. Including all areas of law, 20% (margin of error: ± 2.6%) of clients would not seek any advice and 16% 'don't know', of 890 responses to this question.

Therefore the best estimate of the proportion of people not seeking alternative advice when legal aid is no longer available will be 11% (confidence interval: 6–15%). If all of the don't knows did not seek advice then this proportion could increase to 24% (confidence interval 18–30%). Determining whether this alternative advice is self-funded private legal advice or one of the plethora of free-at-source advice services is critical to calculating the knock-on costs. The CSJS also asks respondents who received free or partially free advice whether and how much they would have been prepared to pay for the advice that they received. Only 19% of those receiving free advice from a solicitor (in the areas of law under study) would be willing to pay more than £100 for the advice they received. Only 7% were willing to pay £500 or more. There was no significant variation by the source of funding (e.g. legal aid versus conditional fee arrangements). Pooling those respondents who were willing to pay more than £100 for the advice generates a median of £300 (interquartile range: £200–£1,000) and pooling all respondents who were willing to pay any positive amount, the median fell to £200 (interquartile range: £100–£625).

Although the average legal aid claim for advice in 2009–2010 for many areas of law was less than £300 including family, housing, debt and welfare law for instance (Legal Services Commission 2010b), this is advice provided at controlled rates. Private sector legal advice is significantly more expensive. For example, the Master of Rolls outlined guideline hourly costs for solicitors in 2010 between £111 and £409 per hour depending upon location and the number of years of post-qualification experience (Master of Rolls 2010). Further, a 2006 survey on behalf of the Norwich Union found the average cost of legal advice during a divorce was £1818 per person (Norwich Union 2006). Given that 80% of legal aid recipients are in the bottom income quartile this result is expected (Association of Lawyers for Children 2011). Very few people who received free legal advice are willing to pay reasonable sums for legal advice. While around 19% were willing to pay more than £100, only 7% were willing to pay £500 or more. A recent enquiry into the cost of advice for an undefended divorce petition where both parties were in agreement, found that private costs were approximately £500 (in Southampton) and over £1000 (in London) (Miller personal communication by email 2011).

Giving up or going it alone

Analysis of the CSJS has determined that approximately 11% of people denied legal aid will not seek alternative advice. Following this choice, people will either give up on their social justice problem or attempt to tackle it on their own. The proportion of people who, at present, 'give up' and 'tackle their problem alone' after failing to obtain advice can be used as an estimate of the same strategies for those who are denied legal aid and do not seek alternative advice. This proportion varies by area of law with 65% of people who failed to obtain family law advice tackling their problem alone compared to 83% in social welfare law. This difference may reflect the greater complexity of family law and the higher proportion of cases which end up in court.

Legal representation versus self-representation

So far the analysis has focused on the responses to legal aid being removed for legal advice. Some cases will end up in court and this propensity varies by area of law. For example, almost 40% of family law cases involving respondents to the CSJS ended up in court. For those who do not receive legal representation paid for by legal aid there are few options available. The principal options will be to self-represent or to pay for private legal counsel. Only nine respondents in the entire survey received free advice from a barrister. Of these only 22% (margin of error: ±33%) were willing to pay for that advice had it not been free. Given the very small sample, this is consistent with the proportion that was willing to pay for legal advice from a solicitor (19%). Therefore, approximately 80% of people would self-represent. Again, given the small sample sizes extreme caution must be used. While in some areas of the law, there may be alternatives including an increased use of conditional fee arrangements in clinical negligence cases, this is unlikely in family and social welfare law especially given the implementation of the Jackson proposals on litigation reform.

Unintended costs – estimating the costs

The previous sub-section explained how data from the CSJS were used to determine the likely behavioural responses of people who will be denied legal aid following the implementation of LASPO. The analysis predicted the choices and their likely popularity. To understand the impact on public expenditure it is necessary to determine the costs of each of these actions including, *inter alia*, simply giving up, seeking alternative advice, self-representing or using government funded mediation services. Each area of cost is considered in turn.

Cost of screening applicants

The Government has proposed a telephone 'gateway' for incoming legal aid enquiries. The service will act as a triage service directing qualifying clients (and/or cases) to appropriate legal aid providers. Those not qualifying for legal aid will be directed to alternative advice or support services, including mediation in private family law cases, and not-for-profit alternative advice services. Initially the mandatory single gateway will only apply to four areas of law (debt where it remains in scope, special educational needs, discrimination and community care). Whether or not this telephone gateway is adopted more widely, ineligible clients will still need to be screened out of the new system at a cost to Government that has not been identified in the impact assessment for the scope changes. It is likely that the proposed telephone gateway would do this at lowest cost and therefore any alternative system adopted is likely to increase estimates of the knock-on cost. Further, it is possible that people may call the telephone gateway regarding areas of law that are outside its scope simply because they have failed to locate alternative advice themselves.

The Ministry of Justice estimates the average cost of a 'triage' call to the telephone gateway would cost £8 per call (Ministry of Justice 2010b p. 11, para. 45) which will be adopted in this analysis. Additionally there are one-off costs involved in establishing the telephone system: procurement to cover expansion in case volume and areas of law is estimated to cost around £1 million, and marketing of the new service is assumed to cost £1 million (Ministry of Justice p. 10, para. 42–43). There is a further risk that these estimates for the implementation of a single telephone gateway may understate, or fail to anticipate, additional costs and consequences of creating such a complex information service as occurred with the Legal Services Commission's online supplier management system (National Audit Office 2011).

Cost of giving up

A simple measure of the cost of giving up is the difference between the benefit obtained from receiving advice and that obtained when somebody gives up. Presuming that there is no benefit from giving up then only a measure of benefit for those obtaining advice is required. While this is not readily available there are data on the adverse consequences suffered when people experience justiciable problems and the improvements in these adverse conditions following advice.

Earlier versions of the CSJS survey have been used in previous research on the impact of justiciable problems on people, and in particular to measure the adverse consequences of these problems. A significant proportion of legal problems generated one or more adverse consequence for respondents. In family and social welfare law, stress (34%) was the most commonly reported impact, followed by physical ill health (27%), loss of confidence (17%), and loss of income (14%). An LSRC paper, *Mounting problems* (Pleasence *et al.* 2007) used data from the 2004 survey to estimate the economic cost of these adverse consequences to the public purse. For example, 66% of survey respondents reported visiting their GP regarding a physical health problem resulting from their legal problem, which the LSRC estimated incurred an average cost of £113 per visit (Pleasence *et al.* 2007). The type and extent of these adverse consequences varies by area of law and during the analysis appropriate adjustments will be made.

The average cost per person of these adverse consequences are reported in Table 1 and are calculated using cost data reported in Pleasence *et al.* (2007). These are estimates based upon responses to the CSJS questions relating to the impact of the adverse consequences on respondents and their use of public services as a result of these impacts. It is not possible to calculate the adverse consequences or impact of 'giving up' on a justiciable problem compared to obtaining advice or tackling the problem alone as clients are not observed under both situations. Instead only the reported improvement in the adverse consequence following advice is reported in the CSJS. For example, almost half (44%) of people suffering from stress reported an improvement, almost a third (30%) reported improvements in their physical health problems and approximately a quarter (22%) improvements in their housing situation.

During the analysis, the prevalence of the adverse consequences for each area of law will be combined with the improvement in these adverse consequences following advice and the cost of the adverse consequences to produce a crude measure of the cost to the public purse of 'giving up' on a justiciable problem as detailed in Table 1.

Cost of alternative advice

One of the reasons stated for removing areas of law from scope is the availability of so-called 'alternative sources of advice'. The availability of this alternative advice is key to mitigating the impact of the reforms. While alternative advice is usually free at the point of use, it is rarely free of cost to the providing organisations, which are often funded or subsidised via the state. For instance, in 2010, Citizens Advice received almost 80% of its income from Government sources (Citizens Advice Bureau 2010a). Therefore, while an increase in the use of alternative advice may not directly cost the Ministry of Justice through increased legal aid expenditure it may lead to an increase in funding from other Government sources, offsetting any saving made to the legal aid budget. For example, the Government announced in early 2011 that the Financial Inclusion Fund will continue to be funded for another year at an additional cost of £27 million. The scheme funds approximately 500 specialist debt advisors and helps 100,000 people each year.

Table 1. Economic costs of adverse consequences.

Adverse consequence	Average cost	% improvement[1]	Value of improvement[2]
Physical ill health	£440[3]	30	£132
Stress-related illness	£100[4]	44	£44
Personal violence	£255[5]	12	£31
Property damage	£126[1]	N/A	£0
Costs of moving home	£5,640[6]	22	£1,236
Loss of jobs	£1,057[7]	7	£70
Loss of employment	£8,140[8]	7	£536

Source: Pleasence *et al.* (2007) updated with CSJS 2009 data[9]
[1] Using the data from CSJS 2009 on the proportion of respondents who reported an improvement in their adverse consequence after receiving advise.
[2] Multiplying the second and third columns of the table generates a crude measure of the value of improvement which will be used as a measure of the 'cost' of 'giving up' on the assumption that clients who give up on their problem do not realise this benefit or improvement.
[3] Of respondents who reported physical ill health resulting from their justiciable problem 66% visited a GP (£113), 43% visited a hospital as an out-patient (£528), 13% visited another healthcare worker (£319) and 11% were treated at a hospital as an in-patient (£883). The figures in parentheses are the average costs of this treatment based upon 2004 NHS Reference Costs and using responses from the CSJS to estimate the number of 'visits' and the length of these visits. All of these costs exclude respondents who reported a personal injury or clinical negligence problem. For patients who reported one of these legal problems the in-patient hospital cost was £1,938 and the out-patient cost £1,842. The average cost of ill health in these cases was therefore £1,103 and the value of improvement £331. A full explanation of the costing methodology is in Pleasence *et al.* (2007)
[4] Of respondents who reported stress resulting from their justiciable problem 22% visited a GP (£113), 4% visited a counsellor (£258), 2% a Community Psychiatric Nurse (£2224) and 2% another healthcare worker (£319). The figures in parentheses are the average costs of this treatment using Pleasence *et al.* (2007)
[5] Pleasence *et al.* (2007) estimated the cost of physical assault and property damage as £255 and £126 per case respectively based upon data from Duoborg and Hamed (2005).
[6] Of respondents who reported a loss of home as an adverse consequence, 46% of them were unable to move into a new home immediately and had to spend time in temporary accommodation. Pleasence *et al.* (2007) estimate the cost of rent provided by the local authority as £150 per week or a total of £5640 per instance.
[7] Loss of employment often results in a claim for state benefits and this is more likely for clients eligible for legal aid as they are less likely to have savings or alternative income sources. For respondents claiming unemployment benefit resulting from losing a job as a result of a social justice problem, the average claim length was 19 weeks at an average cost of £1,057.
[8] Unemployed people also represent an opportunity cost to society in terms of the economic output they have not produced. Pleasance et al use annual GDP per capita data from ONS and multiply by 19/52 to generate the economic cost of the average unemployed spell as £8140.
[9] The costs reported here are based upon those reported in Pleasence *et al.* (2007) and use 2003 or 2004 price data combined with responses to 2004 CSJS on the impact of social justice problems. The responses to 2004 survey are indistinguishable from those to 2009 survey in this respect.

It is difficult to ascertain the true cost of alternative advice because most advice agencies do more than simply offer advice (e.g. campaigning or offering grants themselves), and because they receive huge levels of volunteer labour which is difficult to account for correctly. For example, CAB calculates that is receives £86 million of 'volunteer hours' each year (Citizens Advice Bureau 2010a). However, various estimates are available. CAB estimates the cost of giving advice (specifically debt advice) at between £67 and £454 with an average cost of £85 per client across all areas of advice (Citizens Advice Bureau 2010b). Similarly, using expenditure on 'housing services' and client numbers from Shelter produces a crude average cost of £130 per client (Shelter 2011),[5] The National Audit Office when evaluating the Financial Inclusion Fund stated that the average cost of providing face-to-face debt advice to 270,000 people was £311 (range £201 to £377[6]) over the two phases of the scheme and an average of £265 in the second phase. (National Audit Office 2010). Given that the clients under analysis would have previously required specialist legal advice for their social welfare problems, it is a reasonable assumption that their particular problems are towards the complex end of the spectrum. Further, given the robustness of the data the NAO figure of £265 per client is the baseline figure adopted for the cost of providing alternative 'face-to-face' advice.

However, the Government would not be liable for this full cost. The Government provides support for charitable advice organisations in a number of ways. First, through core grant-aid to organisations such as Citizens Advice. Second, through specific funding for advice projects and partnerships such as the Financial Inclusion Fund. And third, through Gift Aid[7] for charitable donations.[8] Taken together a conservative estimate is that alternative advice will cost the Government 55% of this rate, or £146 per client. Government funding of advice charities is complex and changing from year to year. Shelter (2010) reported 21% income coming from Government grants, while Citizens Advice (2010) received approximately 80% of its income for the parent organisation from the Government (which falls to roughly 30% of the entire network's income). These are some of the largest providers in the sector and therefore a 25% contribution from Government has been assumed. In addition, for every £1 donated through gift aid the Government remits 25 pence in taxation back to the charity. The final 5% is an estimate of the number of corporate or higher taxpayers who claim back tax themselves on donations made.

Cost of mediation

A key aim of the reforms in relation to family law is to incentivise mediation over litigation in divorce and relationship breakdown, especially where children are involved (Ministry of Justice 2010b). The rationale being that mediation is less combative, reducing emotional distress. Publicly funded mediation has been proposed as a cost-effective and less damaging alternative to litigation, with a maximum cost of £1700 per case. The figure of £1700 per mediation case is generated by summing (i) the legal fees promised in the consultation paper of £150 per person, (ii) the additional £200 of legal fees to draft an order as promised in the response to the consultation exercise,[9] and (iii) the £1200 mediation cost reported in the Impact Assessment.[10] As a comparison, £16.2 million was spent in 2009–2010 funding 14,500 full mediation cases, and 55,000 willingness tests which is broadly comparable (Quartermain 2011).

While the average cost is easily established as £1700 the per person cost is less easy to establish. At present, the Government funds mediation where either (or both) party is eligible for legal aid support. Thus if every legal aid client was mediating with somebody who is not eligible then the per person cost to the legal aid budget would be £1550,[11] and where both parties were legal aid eligible it would be £850. A further complication is that the £200 of funding available for drawing up an order based upon a settlement is only payable if the mediation is successful. In reality 58% of publicly funded mediation cases involve two legal aid funded clients (*ibid*). This results in an average mediation cost of £909 per legal aid funded client plus an average of £126 per legal aid funded client if the mediation is successful.

The Government predicts that its outlay on mediation services will not exceed an additional £10 million (net) on an extra 6000–10,000 cases per annum. If legal aid reforms provide unexpected incentives to send a case to mediation (rather than, say, through private legal advice) the predicted costs of mediation could be much higher than Government predictions. Fee caps and legal aid funding cuts will likely reduce incomes for many small legal firms of solicitors and independent advisors. With funding provided for private family law mediation such firms will have incentives to encourage potential clients to mediate, even where they may otherwise seek private advice or representation, because mediation costs will be met by the Government. As such, uptake of Government-funded mediation could be much higher than predicted. The Justice Select Committee (2011) and The Law Society (2011) have cast doubt on the Government's forecasts for mediation utilisation post-reforms, and evidence from the recent Family Justice Review (2011) on the introduction of a pre-application protocol in the family courts highlights potentially strong demand for mediation services. The Family Justice Review (p. 154) reports a 22% increase in mediation information and assessment meetings in the period April–June 2011 (compared to the same period in 2010) following the introduction of compulsory attendance at a mediation information meeting before applicants are allowed to take their case to court.

Cost of self-representation

Self-representation, or more formally a litigant in person is a situation where an individual (litigant) has no formal legal representation in court or tribunal. A 2003 study established a positive relationship between the unavailability of legal aid and self-representation (Hunter 2003). According to respondents to the LASPO consultation and the Government's own impact assessment, self-representing is likely to be a greater feature of our courts and tribunal services following the reforms (Ministry of Justice 2011d). Two factors will lead to an increase in self-representation. First, removing funding for legal advice may increase the number of people who will issue proceedings rather than being deterred by legal advice of the merits of their cases. Second, even where good private or alternative advice has been sought, removing legal representation for many cases will increase the likelihood that motivated litigants with meritorious cases, but without the funds for private representation, will pursue their cases to court or tribunal themselves.

In certain key respects a rise in litigants in person will have noticeable, material unintended consequences to Government: poorer outcomes for litigants, greater burden on HMCTS, greater legal costs for legal aid – represented litigants and for government-run organisations such as the NHS (Moorhead 2010, Moorhead *et al.* 2005). Research on self-representation indicates that they may be a lower burden on the court system *where they are inactive or passive* participants in the court process, for example, in non-contentious divorce proceedings. However, active litigants in person place a significant burden on courts (Williams 2011, Moorhead 2010, Moorhead *et al.* 2005, Bowcott 2011). The emotive nature of issues in family law is liable to make for more active and engaged litigants in person with over 60% of adoption and divorce cases already involving active unrepresented litigants (Williams 2011). Evidence suggests that almost 80% of cases which will fall out of scope under the reforms will relate to people in the bottom income quintile, and whom are unversed in court procedure (Williams 2011). A rise in unrepresented litigants therefore risks '[...] cases taking longer, particularly where the applicant or both parties were unrepresented' (Williams 2011). Cases with active litigants in person are also less likely to be settled (Hunter 2003, Moorhead 2010, Rosenbloom 2002, Dewar *et al.* 2000) and are more likely to be thrown out of court (Advice Services Alliance 2011). In cases involving children where both parents are self-representing there is likely to be an increase in the number of r16.4 appointments[12] of guardians which will increase costs to Cafcass both in terms of their officers' time and their own legal costs.

A final impact of litigants in person is on other court users. If their cases take longer this could generate longer waiting lists for hearing dates and a higher prospect of hearings being adjourned due to over-running cases. Where these users are legal aid funded clients or Government parties it will generate a knock-on cost for the state. Further in some cases, and particularly in family cases, this delay may lead to a change in circumstances requiring further evidence (e.g. Cafcass reports) including refreshed expert evidence. To the extent that organisations such as Cafcass are state funded this could generate a knock-on cost.

While it is clear that litigants in person generate knock-on costs the magnitude of this impact is uncertain. The consultation response from the Council of Her Majesty's Circuit Court Judges estimated that the increase in court time, and therefore court cost of litigants in person, was 30–50% depending upon the type of hearing (Martin 2011). In Canada (Matthews 2011) and Australia (PriceWaterhouseCoopers 2009) a 'conservative estimate' of 20% has been used although there seems to be little empirical basis for this. The upper estimate of a 50% increase in costs for cases involving litigants in person will be adopted for the following reasons: (i) while an increased hearing length will increase court costs it will also delay other court users who could themselves be funded by the state (or be the state) therefore generating a further 'spillover' effect not captured by simply measuring the increased case length, (ii) the crude average case cost[13] measure adopted will significantly underestimate the cost of 'contentious' cases as it was not possible to differentiate between contested and uncontested cases, where the later significantly outweigh the former, and (iii) in a number of cases involving children there will also be a knock-on cost to Cafcass but this will not be a linear relationship with the length of time the case costs and will not be true for all cases. Using this estimate, each litigant in person is expected to generate a knock- on cost of £273.50[14] per person.

Additionally, HMCTS may suffer a reduction in fee income if litigants in person are granted fee remissions, as these fees would have been paid under the legal aid scheme previously. The Government estimated the total impact of fee remission on HMCTS at £8 million (Ministry of Justice 2011a). No detail is provided on how this figure was generated, nor is it possible to calculate the impact for each area of law based upon the current fee tariff. A crude estimate weighted by area of law is therefore created using the proportion of the total legal representation expenditure is being saved in each area of law. For family law this is 80%[15] and for social welfare law this is 2%.[16]

Analysis and results

In this section, the likelihood of the various responses to the removal of legal aid funding are combined with the estimates of the costs of these responses which were detailed in the previous section. Together with historical data on case volumes for each area of law, the flow through the civil justice system following LASPO can be projected and the total knock-on costs to Government estimated.

Family law

Family law is one of the most significant areas of law to be affected by LASPO, generating 60% of the total saving. Based upon 2009–10 data, the Ministry of Justice anticipates saving £170 million (gross) from excluding all private family law cases from scope unless they involve domestic violence, child abuse or child parties (Ministry of Justice 2011a). The impact assessment identifies costs of £6–10 million resulting from an increased use of publicly funded mediation services, generating a net saving of £160 million per annum (Ministry of Justice 2011a). An estimated 210,000 people will be affected by these changes (Ministry of Justice 2011a), reducing the volume of legal help cases by 74% and the volume of legal representation cases by 40%. Overall, the family law budget will only be reduced by 28% because public family law will remain in scope.[17]

Trends in family law

Expenditure on family law legal aid has been relatively stable over the past decade, but with an increase of approximately 8% in real terms over the past six years. Family law represents a considerable portion of all civil legal aid expenditure, some £597 million in 2009–10 or 63% of total civil expenditure. It is therefore not surprising that it faces the largest absolute cuts under LASPO. Evidence presented to the Justice Select Committee (2011) suggests that the increase in family law expenditure was driven by a dramatic increase in the number and cost of public law cases following the publicity surrounding the 'Baby Peter' case. Data from the Legal Services Commission demonstrates falling volumes and expenditure for private family law over the past five years compared with rising public law volumes and expenditures.

Costs to the public purse

There is likely to be a significant knock-on cost to the public purse as a result of excluding most private family law cases from scope. While the net effect of the proposals should be positive (i.e. a saving) this is likely to be substantially less than the Government's initial estimates. Figure 1 maps the flow of the clients who no longer receive legal aid support through the private family justice system. The flows (as percentages) are based upon the responses to the CSJS reported in the data section above and validated by data from the Legal Services Commission on outcomes for legal aid cases in 2008–9. The cost of these responses to the public purse was discussed in the methods section. Knock-on costs are indicated in green lettering and the vertical dashed line separates those who do not seek advice from those that continue to seek advice.

As stated in the impact assessment, 266,000 clients will require screening at a minimum cost of £8 per client using the telephone gateway at a total cost of £2.1 million. Of the 210,000 people who are denied legal aid under the reforms, 89% are expected to seek advice from another provider yet only 19% of these respondents were willing or able to pay for it. The remainder will access alternative advice services, and a knock-on cost of £22.1 million is calculated based upon an average cost of £146. The remaining 11% of people who do not seek advice either give up (33%) at a cost of £2 million, or they tackle the problem alone (66%). Giving up may generate or prolong adverse consequences including mental and physical health problems as discussed earlier. For family law cases, this is estimated at an average cost of £263 per person.

The Ministry of Justice argues that approximately half of the people losing eligibility under the reforms would find mediation inappropriate either because of the nature of the problem (e.g. a name change) or because they are no longer proceeding with their problem (e.g. due to reconciliation). This has been included in Figure 1 by reconciling the data from CSJS on how problems are solved with data from the Legal Services Commission on client outcomes as recorded by solicitors. These outcomes are thought to apply equally to clients using private (legal) advice or alternative advice and are reported under the horizontal green brace in Figure 1. From LSC data, approximately 14% of family law clients either reconcile with their partner or required advice only. This matches well with the 15% of respondents in the CSJS who reported that their problem had 'sorted itself out' after receiving advice. From the CSJS, 17% of respondents give up after receiving advice, and

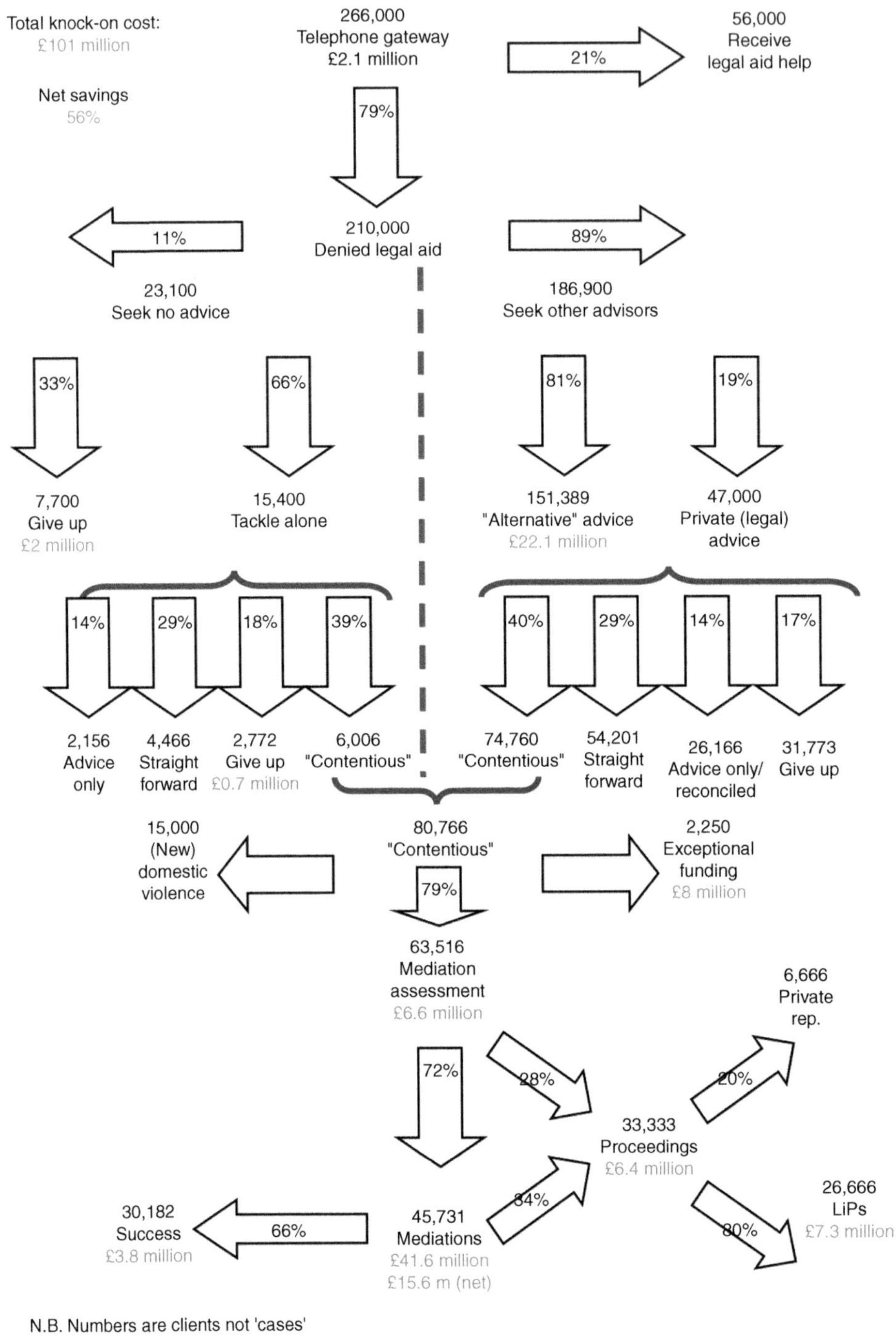

Figure 1. Flows through the family law system (2009–10 Baseline & CSJS data).

from the LSC 17% of clients 'cease providing instructions'. The Ministry of Justice believes that for some types of problems mediation is inappropriate, including family wills, name changes and straightforward divorces or nullities (Ministry of Justice 2011b). The proportion of these 'straightforward' cases was estimated by using their proportion in the 2008–9 LSC dataset, of 29%. These cases will frequently end up in court (e.g. for a divorce) but they are usually non-contentious and should not create further knock-on costs to the courts. However, without proper legal advice the outcomes of these cases may be unfair or they may generate additional work for court staff and the judiciary if they are unable to complete the required paperwork correctly. The remaining 40% of cases are labelled 'contentious' and may include serious disputes (e.g. Children Act cases or divorces involving ancillary relief).

The approach was repeated for clients who tackle their problems alone. Obviously the LSC does not have data for people who tackled their problem alone but the CSJS does have this information. For instance, 14% of respondents reported their problem had 'sorted itself out' after tackling it alone. From LSC data, approximately 14% of clients required advice only. Again, 18% of people in the CSJS gave up after tackling their problem alone. This compares to 17% in the LSC dataset. The CSJS does not record information on the exact nature of the problem and so the LSC data must be relied upon to provide a proportion of clients who experience 'straightforward' problems. The remaining 39% are assumed to have more contentious problems that may be suitable for mediation.

Together 40% of people who obtained advice and 39% of people who tackled their problem alone experience problems that may require court proceedings. It is assumed that 2250 exit the flow here as part of the exceptional funding scheme to avoid double counting. The Ministry of Justice estimates that 5% of 45,000 legal representation cases no longer falling in scope will be readmitted under the exceptional funding scheme. At an average cost of £278 for a family legal help claim and £3282 for the average family legal representation claim, this cost is estimated at £8 million per annum, based upon averages presented in LSC (2010c). Given the uncertainty in the final wording of the scheme this is likely to rise substantially by the time the reforms are enacted. It is further assumed that this is where the additional cases involving domestic violence will exit the system and attract legal aid representation. The Government's impact assessment estimates this figure to be approximately a quarter of the cases which do not automatically remain in scope (domestic violence and public family law cases). A figure of 15,000 cases is used here.

Of the remaining 'contentious' cases they are all assumed to be potentially suitable for mediation. A key assumption here is that all of these (63,516) people attend mediation assessment to determine whether mediation is appropriate. In 2010–11, there were 60,000 willingness tests, and there were targets to get 40-50% of these to proceed to mediation assessment, and for 50–60% of these mediation assessments to proceed to substantive mediation (Legal Services Commission 2010a). This is therefore a strong assumption but seems reasonable given the evidence from the pre-application protocol introduced into the family court, the few alternatives available for people no longer receiving legal aid funding for advice or representation, the legal aid advice which comes attached to the mediation pathway, and finally the success rate of mediation. Mediation information and assessment sessions come at a cost of £104.40 per person or a total of £6.6 million.[18] A key assumption regards the proportion of clients assumed to progress from mediation assessment to substantive mediation. The current rate is approximately 60% (Legal Services Commission 2010a) but the Government accepts that this rate will rise (Ministry of Justice 2011c). Recent evidence based on in-court mediation suggests a conversion rate of 72% (Baksi 2010). Using this rate, an estimated 45,731 people would progress to around

29,000 mediations at an estimated cost of £41.6 million per annum.[19] Of these 66% are expected to be fully settled through mediation and will therefore attract a further £3.8 million in legal aid solicitor fees.

Finally, not all cases will be successfully resolved by mediation. An estimated 34% are not settled. In addition, a suggested 28% of people will not proceed with mediation following the assessment meeting. Together these (33,333) people are expected to begin court proceedings. Based upon the responses to the CSJS survey, 80% of people are likely to self-represent rather than pay for private representation. Given the knock-on costs of litigants in person, the total knock-on cost to the courts is estimated to be £7.3 million per annum.[20] Finally the proceedings may not attract court fees if the clients are eligible for fee remissions. This cost to HMCTS is estimated at £6.4 million.

Table 2 summarises the knock-on costs shown in Figure 1. The total knock-on cost is almost £101 million per annum but removing the mediation cost already accounted for by the Government, leaves a net knock-on cost of £74 million. This generates a net saving of approximately 56% of the predicted saving of £170 million per annum.

Social welfare law

Social welfare law is made up of housing, debt and welfare benefit problems. Taken together, social welfare law represents 13% of the total civil legal aid budget. However, the Ministry of Justice estimates that changes to the scope of social welfare law will generate 21% of the total scope savings. Over 400,000 people received legal aid support for their social welfare problems in 2009–10 at a total cost of £121 million. According to the LASPO impact assessment, almost 300,000 people will no longer receive legal aid funding for their social welfare problems generating an estimated £58 million saving per annum. This saving will be achieved by removing all welfare benefits law cases from scope without exception, all debt cases unless there is an immediate risk of homelessness and all housing cases unless there is an immediate risk of homelessness, or disrepair cases where there is a serious risk to health or life. In addition homelessness assistance and County Court anti-social behaviour cases remain in scope.

Trends in social welfare law

Many people experience social welfare problems. In 2009–10, the Citizens Advice Bureaux (CAB) helped 583,000 people with debt problems, 278,000 people with housing

Table 2. Summary of knock-on costs for family law.

Description	Total cost	'Unit' cost	Number of clients
Give Up	£12,518,800	£263	10,472
Telephone Gateway	£2,128,000	£8	266,000
Alternative Advice	£17,666,000	£146	151,389
Mediation Assessment	£8,124,480	£104	63,516
Mediation	£44,040,618	£783	45,731
Mediation Orders	£2,834,748	£126	30,182
Litigant in Person	£9,708,703	£273.50	26,666
Fee Remission	£6,400,000	N/A.	N/A.
Exceptional Funding	£8,010,000	£3560	2250
Sub Total	£100,691,562		
Net Total	**£74,691,562**		

problems and 690,000 people with benefits and tax credit problems (Citizens Advice Bureau 2009). Demand for social welfare advice is large and growing (Citizens Advice Bureau 2009). Spending patterns across all three areas of social welfare law have been very similar, which is to be expected as various sources claim that these problems cluster together (Pleasence *et al.* 2007). For example, 19% of people with a welfare benefit problem also reported a housing problem (including 6% of homelessness) in the 2009 CSJS (Pleasence *et al.* 2010). Sixteen percent of respondents with welfare benefits problems also reported experiencing debt problems. The connections are clear; for example, financial problems that may be caused or exacerbated by difficulty accessing welfare benefits, may in turn cause wider debt problems.

Real expenditure in this area has increased by over 60% since 2004–05 to £121 million in 2009–10. Expenditure on housing problems has been relatively flat (increasing by 13% in real terms over the entire period), while real expenditure on debt advice has more than trebled, and on welfare benefits advice has more than doubled. This rising expenditure has been driven by rapidly increasing case volume. The number of housing and welfare benefit cases has almost doubled over the 2004–05 to 2009–10 period while the number of debt cases has increased by 150%. This increase in social law case volume (and therefore total expenditure) has likely been driven by an increase in the number of underlying social justice problems, combined by Labour's willingness to divert resources to meeting previously unmet demand.

Costs to the public purse

Due to the high case volume in social welfare law, there is likely to be a large knock-on cost to the state, although this is unlikely to be met by the Ministry of Justice directly. These costs are summarised in Table 3 while Figure 2, which follows the same template as the family law flow diagram (Figure 1), demonstrates the flow through the civil justice system. Taken together, there were 407,000 social law clients who were supported by legal aid in 2009–10. If a telephone triage service is used to filter out those cases that no longer fall under the legal aid scheme this could cost the Ministry of Justice over £3 million per annum. According to the Ministry of Justice's projections 292,000 clients will no longer receive legal aid funded advice under the reforms of which an estimated 210,000 people will seek alternative advice at an approximate cost of £30.7 million, based upon an average cost of £146.

A sign that the Government accepts that their proposals will generate such a knock-on cost, and that they will have to contribute to alternative advice provision, is the agreement to continue the Financial Inclusion Fund for another year, plus the agreement to consider the impact of the proposals on the advice sector more broadly. Moreover, £20 million has

Table 3. Summary of knock-on costs for social welfare law.

Description	Total Cost	'Unit' Cost	Number of clients
Give up	£238,050	£45	5,290
Telephone Gateway	£3,256,000	£8	407,000
Alternative Advice	£30,733,438	£146	210,503
Fee remission	£160,000	N/A.	N/A.
Exceptional proceedings	£828,000	£2,762	300
Total cost	**£35,216,088**		

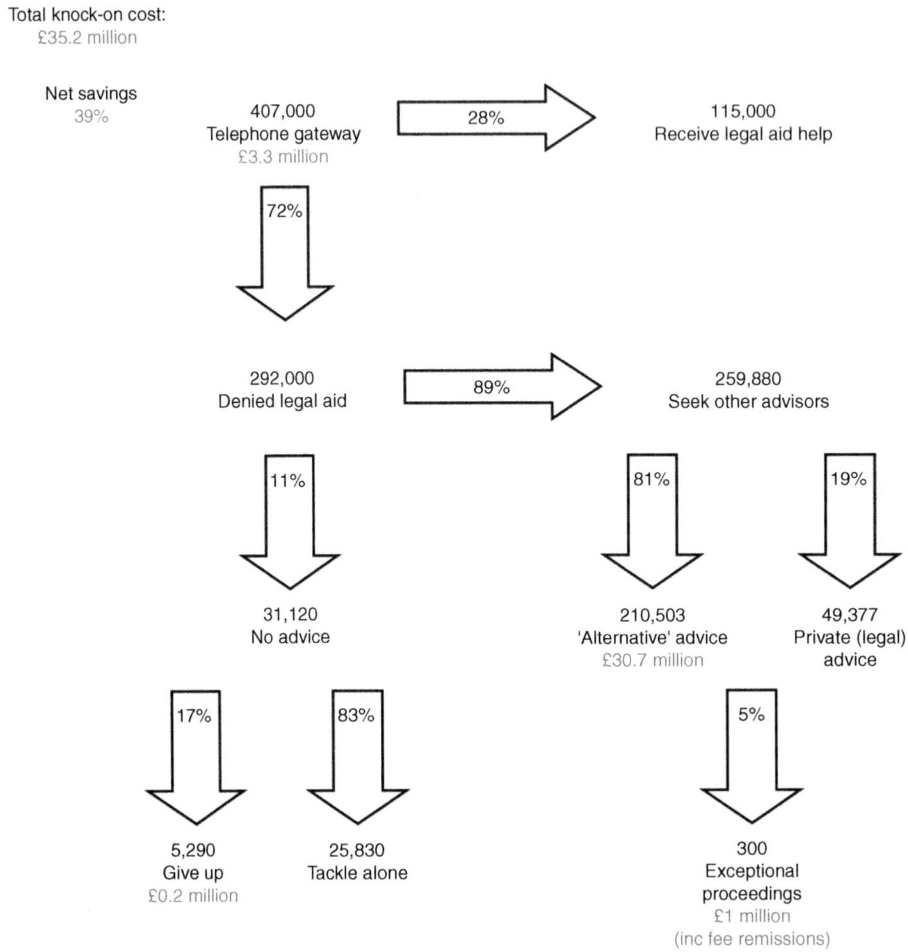

Figure 2. Flows through the social welfare law system (2009/10 baseline & CSJS data).

been earmarked for helping the sector improve the efficiency of providing advice. Based on the estimates here, funding of this magnitude may be needed in future years to fund advice agencies to fill the void left by the reforms.

A predicted 49,000 people will seek private advice, although given the nature of many of the problems (indebtedness or access to welfare benefits) the proportion able to afford private legal advice is likely to be less than this figure. There is a risk therefore, that the knock-on cost for alternative advice could increase by a further £7.2 million, although this has not been included in this analysis.

The majority (83%) of the predicted 11% of people (31,120) who decide not to obtain advice following the removal of legal aid funding will tackle their problem alone. A small proportion of them (17%) will simply 'give up' – an estimated 5290 people. Using the methodology outlined earlier, the estimated knock-on cost to the state of 'giving up' is over £200,000 per annum.[21] This is likely to be a significant underestimate. For example, Pleasence *et al.* (2007) estimate each debt problem costs the state £1000. No evidence exists which helps to identify whether this cost is reduced following the receipt of legal aid (or other) advice, or on the differential outcomes by advisor on the costs to the state. This is not a net effect because the Government may be a net beneficiary of people giving up. For example, the state will save money if clients can no longer challenge (incorrect) decisions not to grant benefits. This is impossible to determine at this stage.

The knock-on cost of unfair outcomes which may occur when clients are unable to access professional legal advice is impossible to estimate. For example, clients who cannot access specialist legal advice may have worse outcomes than they would have had. Similarly, those who tackle their problem alone may do worse. The Government estimates that up to 25% of housing legal representation cases may be re-admitted under the exceptional funding scheme (Ministry of Justice 2011a). At a current average cost of £2542 for legal representation and £220 for legal help, this could generate a knock-on cost of £0.8 million per annum (Legal Services Commission 2010b). Additionally, HMCTS fee remissions for housing cases no longer funded by legal aid are estimated at £160,000 per annum.

As reported in Table 3, the total knock-on cost of these proposals within social welfare law is over £35 million per annum, generating a net saving of 39% of that predicted by the Government.

Discussion and conclusion

The remit of this article was to focus on the claim that the reforms would generate a large saving from the Ministry of Justice budget that could contribute towards the Government-wide fiscal deficit. This research casts doubt on the ability of the proposals to deliver on this aim. Whilst uncertainty exists, the total knock-on costs predicted in this paper are in the region of £136 million compared to a gross saving of £228 million. It is important to remember that numerous costs could not be estimated due to a lack of data. Therefore despite uncertainties over the costs included in the research it is likely that the total knock-on cost is an underestimate of the true costs. These figures suggest a net saving in the region of £92 million per annum over the areas of law covered. At approximately 40% of the predicted savings, this level of saving would make an insignificant contribution to the total spending cuts of £81 billion per annum that the Government plans to implement by 2014–15.

In the context of wider policy changes these substantial changes to the legal aid system will generate insubstantial savings. For instance, the recent switch from index linking benefits and public sector pensions using the Retail Price Index (RPI) to the Consumer Price Index (CPI) is estimated to save £2.2 billion per annum from 2012–13. Further, using the average CPI for the six months to September 2011 rather than the CPI at the end of September 2011 could save £1.4 billion.[22] The impact would be worse in the short-run as the Government is budgeting additional spending during the transition period of £22 million, plus it will continue to fund the £27 million Financial Inclusion Fund for a further year. This paper focused on two broad areas of law but other areas of law will also be affected and will generate knock-on costs.

This research is based upon the results of a nationally representative household survey, a sample of the population, but there are limitations. Some of the responses used in this analysis relate to hypothetical questions, and in some cases the number of responses is low making the uncertainty quite large. Most of the costs used are also estimates or average costs. Therefore the findings in this report are subject to uncertainty. The Government's savings predictions are also uncertain. The net saving could be significantly less than half of the Government's prediction which undermines the Government's economic justification for the changes, especially given the numerous costs that could not be estimated in this study. Given this, it remains to be seen whether further cuts from the legal aid budget will be necessary for the Ministry of Justice to share in the burden of fiscal restraint.

A key finding of this analysis is the lack of robust data on numerous elements of the civil justice system, for example on the costs and productivity of the family courts. This has been remarked upon in the Family Justice Review and acknowledged by the Government. Better data on the civil justice system would be incredibly useful both for the justice system, researchers and to inform policymaking.

Acknowledgements

The analysis from which this article is prepared was originally funded by the Law Society of England & Wales and reported in Cookson, G. (2011) *Unintended Consequences: the costs of the government's legal aid reforms: a report for the Law Society of England & Wales*, King's College London, London: UK. The views expressed in this article are those of the author and not necessarily the Law Society. The author would also like to acknowledge the excellent research assistance of Mr Duncan McMillan. The usual disclaimers apply.

Notes

1. The £450 million savings are expected to come from scope changes (£270 million), fee reform (£160 million including £100 million from criminal, £50 million from civil/family and £10 million from expert fees), £10 million from eligibility changes, £7 million from the Supplementary Legal Aid Scheme, and £1–2 million from the new telephone advice service.
2. Social welfare law is expected to generate £58 million of savings across debt (£20 million), welfare (£25 million) and housing (£13 million) areas, and family law is expected to generate £170 million (less £10 million expected increase in mediation costs).
3. Margin of error is calculated as a 95% confidence interval for the proportion which is approximated by ± 2 x [p(1-p)/n-1].
4. As the sample size decreases in each of the subsamples considered, consequently the standard error and therefore the margin of error increases.
5. According to the 2010–11 annual report, Shelter spent £20.7 million on providing housing services and serviced 159,000 clients including 94,000 face-to-face, 60,000 over the telephone and 5000 via email. In addition, 1.1 million people visited their 'Get Advice' web pages. However based upon evidence from the Financial Inclusion Fund, providing face-to-face advice can cost five times as much as telephone-based advice.
6. The average cost is the total project cost divided by the number of people helped, while the average cost range for the 16 organisations delivering the advice was £201 to £377 per person. However, there were two phases to the project and average costs were £370 and £265 in each of the two phases.
7. Gift Aid is a matching system where charities are able to claim tax relief (at the base rate of 20%) on every donation from net (i.e. taxed) income. This equates to 25 pence in every £1.
8. It is also worth noting that higher rate taxpayers are entitled to claim back the difference between their tax rate and the base rate (as used in the Gift Aid programme) on the gross donation. For example, donating £100 will actually be a gross donation of £125 (at the 20% base rate) to the charity. A 40 (50)% taxpayer can then claim back tax relief of 20 (30)% on this £125 gross donation, or £25 i.e. 25 pence in every £1.
9. Although the Impact Assessment and related policy documents make no mention of mediation assessments, it is assumed that these will continue to be funded at the current rate of £87 (plus VAT) for one person and £130 (plus VAT) if the couple attend together.
10. This £1,200 cost was calculated by taking the £10 million identified as the additional cost of mediation in the Impact Assessment plus the £2 million saved from not performing 60,000 willingness tests, and dividing by 10,000 new cases. The Impact Assessment reported a range of 6–10,000. If we used 6000 as the number of additional cases, the per mediation cost would increase to £2167 (£500 + £1667).

11. Assuming that the legal aid fund will not provide the £150 of legal advice to the ineligible party and that the legal aid scheme pays the £200 to produce an order on the mediated agreement.
12. Rule 16.4 of the Family Procedure Rules 2010 available from: http://www.legislation.gov.uk/uksi/2010/2955/article/16.4/made
13. Published family court statistics are not useful for determining the average case cost. Cases involving adults are reported by the number of applications, while cases involving children are reported by the total number of children. To collapse the data into the number of cases all applications involving children will be divided by 1.9 – the average number of children per household. While this generates a crude measure of the total number of cases it does not help provide a very accurate measure of average cost as the court cost is usually determined by the length and complexity of case. For example, many applications for ancillary relief are uncontested and should take very little court time. Using the Family Matters statistics the estimated number of family law cases in 2009–10 was 310,529. Ministry of Justice. Family Matters – Annual Court Statistics, 2010.
14. According to the Family Justice Review the private family law courts cost £170 million per annum to run Family Justice Review. Final Report – November 2011. London: Ministry of Justice, 2011. Again, this is an estimate they calculated based upon the average case length and volume for public and private family law cases and the total family court costs. Together with the estimated total number of cases, this generates an average cost of £547 per case. A 50% knock-on cost would result in a £273.50 per person cost.
15. £120 million saving for family law/£150 million total legal representation saving.
16. Owing exclusively to housing cases.
17. Total family law expenditure reductions were calculated using the Ministry of Justice (MoJ Impact Assessment expenditure cuts restated in Table 4 as follows: (i) Total 2009–10 family expenditure: £609m=£50m/78% + £120m/22%, and (ii) Overall reduction: 28% = (£170m/£609m)*100.
18. Current LSC approved costs for a single client is £87 plus VAT. LSC 2010c.
19. Based upon an average client cost of £909 derived. This is the gross cost of the substantive mediations but the knock-on or net cost of these is £15.6 million as the Government has already made a provision of £26 million to fund 24,500 mediations – 14,500 already being funded plus a further 10,000 post reform.
20. One counterargument is that court fees could be increased to cover this additional expense. However, the recoverability of family court fees is notoriously low, circa 40%. Further, being legal aid eligible originally these clients are likely to be exempt from court fees.
21. Of these predicted 5290 people who 'give up' when legal aid is unavailable, the estimated knock-on cost of welfare benefits problems is £43.50 per person, for housing problems £144 and for debt problems £40. This generates a weighted average cost of £45 per person. The methodology applied in previous sections to calculate these costs has been repeated.
22. The IFS calculated that the sharp rise in inflation to 5.2% (CPI at September 2011) would add £1.8 billion to the welfare benefits budget in comparison to previous forecasts (CPI at September 2011). They estimated that freezing benefits would save £10 billion, increasing them in line with the average wage increase (of 2.5%) would save £5 billion, and using a six-month average CPI figure would save £1.4 billion (CPI at September 2011). This is not to suggest that this is a good policy nor that the Government is even considering this policy, but it provides a comparison that demonstrates that the savings generated by changing the scope of legal aid are relatively small. Further, the savings generated by averaging over the previous six months inflation figures is particularly large given the recent dramatic rise in the inflation rate. However, the substantial annual saving realised by switching from RPI to CPI is large and persistent.

References

Advice Services Alliance, 2011. *Proposal for the reform of legal aid in England and Wales: Ministry of Justice, consultation paper CP12/10: Advice Services Alliance response. Advice Services Alliance*, Available from: http://www.asauk.org.uk/fileLibrary/pdf/Propsals_for_the_Reform_of_Legal_Aid.pdf [Accessed 12 March 2013].

Association of Lawyers for Children, 2011. *Proposal for the reform of legal aid in England and Wales: Ministry of Justice, consultation paper CP12/10: Response of the Association of Lawyers for Children*. East Molesey: Association of Lawyers for Children, Available from: http://www.alc.org.uk/uploads/Reform_of_Legal_Aid_25_Jan_11[1].pdf [Accessed 12 March 2013].

Baksi, C., 2010. Family mediation pilot achieves mixed results. *Law society gazette*, Available from: http://www.lawgazette.co.uk/news/family-mediation-pilot-achieves-mixed-results [Accessed 12 March 2013].

Bowcott, O., 2011. Legal aid cuts will cause courts logjam, warn top judges. *The Guardian*, Available from: http://www.guardian.co.uk/law/2011/oct/25/legal-aid-cuts-courts-logjam. [Accessed 12 March 2013].

Bowles, R. and Perry, A., 2009. International comparison of publicly funded legal services and justice systems. *Ministry of Justice research series 14/09*, Available from: http://www.justice.gov.uk/publications/docs/comparison-public-fund-legal-services-justice-systems.pdf [Accessed 12 January 2012].

Citizens Advice Bureau, 2009. *Client and advice statistics: national issues*. London: CAB. [Accessed 12 March 2013].

Citizens Advice Bureau, 2010a. *Annual Reports and Accounts 2009/10*. London: Citizens Advice Bureau.

Citizens Advice Bureau, 2010b. Towards a business case for legal aid. *Legal Services research centre 8th international research conference*, Available from: http://www.citizensadvice.org.uk/towards_a_business_case_for_legal_aid.pdf [Accessed 12 March 2013].

Cookson, G., 2011. *Unintended consequences: the cost of the government's legal aid reforms*. London: King's College London.

Dewar, J., Smith, B.W. and Banks, C., 2000. *Litigants in person in the Family Court of Australia: Research report no. 20*, Family Court of Australia. Available from: http://www.austlii.edu.au/au/journals/FedJSchol/2000/1.pdf [Accessed 12 March 2013].

Doust, L.T., 2011. *Foundation for change: report of the Public Commission on Legal Aid in British Columbia*. Public Commission on Legal Aid in British Columbia, British Columbia, Canada.

Duoborg, R., and Hamed, J., 2005. *Estimates of the economic and social costs of crime in England and Wales: Costs of crime against individuals and households*, 2003–4. Home Office Online Report 30/05, London, UK.

Family Justice Review, 2011. Family Justice Review: interim report, Available from: http://www.justice.gov.uk/downloads/publications/moj/2011/family-justice-review-interim-rep.pdf [Accessed 12 March 2013].

Gingerbread, 2011. *Proposal for the reform of legal aid in England and Wales: Ministry of Justice, consultation paper CP12/10: Gingerbread response*. London, UK: Gingerbread.

HM Treasury, 2010. *Spending review 2010*. London: TSO.

Hunter, R., 2003. Adversarial mythologies: policy assumptions and research evidence in family law. *Journal of law and society*, 30 (1), 156–176.

Justice Select Committee, 2011. Government's proposed reform of legal aid: Third Report of Session 2010–2011, The Stationery Office, London, UK on behalf of Houses of Parliament.

Legal Services Commission, 2010a. *Family mediation contract guidance Q&A*. London: Legal Services Commission [Original accessed 17 October 2011. Visited again today 12 March 2013 but because the LSC has been closed the new weblink is via national archives: http://webarchive.nationalarchives.gov.uk/20121207044149/http://www.legalservices.gov.uk/-docs/archive/Statistical_information_pack_09-10.pdf].

Legal Services Commission, 2010b. Legal Services Commission: statistical information pack for financial year 2009–2010, Available from: http://www.legalservices.gov.uk/docs/archive/Statistical_information_pack_09-10.pdf

Legal Services Commission, 2010c. 2010 Standard Civil Contract - Family Mediation Specification, Available from: http://www.justice.gov.uk/downloads/legal-aid/civil-contracts/Family_Mediation_Specification-Dec_09.pdf [Accessed 12 March 2013].

Martin, J.R., 2011. *Proposal for the reform of legal aid in England and Wales: Ministry of Justice, consultation paper CP12/10: HH Judge Robert Martin, president of the Social Entitlement Chamber, response*, Available from: http://www.judiciary.gov.uk/media/media-releases/2011/responses-proposals-for-the-reform-of-legal-aid [Accessed 12 March 2013].

Master of Rolls, 2010. *Guideline hourly rates*, The Judiciary of England and Wales.

Matthews, S., 2011. *Making the case for the economic value of legal aid - briefing note*, The Canadian Bar Association (British Columbia branch).

Ministry of Justice, 2010a. Impact assessment: legal aid reform: provision of telephone advice, Available from: http://www.justice.gov.uk/downloads/consultations/ia-telephone-advice.pdf] [Accessed 12 March 2013].

Ministry of Justice, 2010b. *Proposal for the reform of legal aid in England and Wales: Ministry of Justice*, consultation paper CP12/10. Available from: http://webarchive.nationalarchives.gov.uk/20111121205348/http://www.justice.gov.uk/downloads/consultations/legal-aid-reform-consultation.pdf [Accessed 12 March 2013].

Ministry of Justice, 2011a. *Consultations on legal aid, Sentencing and Punishment of Offenders Bill – annex A: scope*. London: Ministry of Justice, Available from: http://www.justice.gov.uk/downloads/consultations/annex-a-scope.pdf [Accessed 12 March 2013].

Ministry of Justice, 2011b. *Government's response to Justice Committee's sixth report of session 2010–12: operation of the family courts*. London [Accessed 12 March 2013] .

Ministry of Justice, 2011c. *Government's response to Justice Committee's third report of session 2010/11: the government's proposed reform of legal aid*, Available from: http://www.official-documents.gov.uk/document/cm81/8111/8111.pdf [Accessed 12 March 2013].

Ministry of Justice, 2011d. Impact assessment: cumulative legal aid reform proposals, London: Ministry of Justice. Available from: http://webarchive.nationalarchives.gov.uk/20111121205348/http://www.justice.gov.uk/downloads/consultations/ia-cum-legal-aid-ref.pdf [Accessed 12 March 2013].

Moorhead, R., 2010. Litigants in person: what the research actually says. In: R. Moorhead, ed. *Lawyer watch*, (16 December 2011). Available from: http://lawyerwatch.wordpress.com/2010/12/16/litigants-in-person-what-the-research-actually-says/ [Last accessed 12 March 2013. Originally accessed 17 October 2011].

Moorhead, R., Sefton, M., 2005. *Litigants in person: unrepresented litigants in first instance proceedings*. London: Department for Constitutional Affairs.

National Audit Office, 2010. *Business, innovation and skills: helping over-indebted consumers*. London: House of Commons.

National Audit Office, 2011. *Proposal for the reform of legal aid in England and Wales: Ministry of Justice, consultation paper CP12/10: NAO response*. London: National Audit Office.

Norwich Union, 2006. Brits spend over £4 billion on divorce, 2011 (17 October). Available from: http://www.aviva.co.uk/media-centre/story/2935/brits-spend-over-4-billion-on-divorce/ [Originally accessed 17 October 2011. That's why there's a second date. Last accessed 12 March 2013] .

Pleasence, P., Balmer, N., Patel, A. and Denvir, C., 2010. *Civil justice in England and Wales 2009: report of the 2006–9 English and Welsh Civil and Social Justice Survey*. London: Legal Services Commission, Available from: http://www.justice.gov.uk/downloads/publications/research-and-analysis/lsrc/2010/2010CSJSAnnualReport.pdf [Accessed 12 March 2013].

Pleasence, P., Balmer, N., Buck, A., Smith, M. and Patel, A., 2007. Mounting Problems: further evidence of the social, economic and health consequences of civil justice problems. In: P. Pleasence, A. Buck and N. Balmer, eds. *Transforming lives: law and social process*. London: The Stationery Office.

PriceWaterhouseCoopers, 2009. *Economic value of legal aid: analysis in relation to Commonwealth funded matters with a focus on family law*, National Legal Aid. Available from: http://www.legalaidact.org.au/pdf/economic_value_of_legalaid.pdf [Accessed 12 March 2013].

Quartermain, S., 2011. Sustainability of mediation and legal representation in private family law cases: analysis of legal aid administrative datasets. *Ministry of Justice Research Series 8/11*.

Rosenbloom, J.D., 2002. Exploring methods to improve management and fairness in pro se cases: a study of the pro se docket in the southern district of New York. *Fordham urban law journal*, 35 (1): Article 19, 305–399.

Shelter, 2011. *Annual report 2010/11*. London: Shelter.

The Law Society, 2011. Report by the Law Society of England and Wales. Published by the Law Society of England and Wales, London, UK on 31 October 2011. Available from: http://www.lawsociety.org.uk/news/press-releases/law-society-launches-missing-millions-report-ahead-of-third-reading-of-the-laspo-bill/ [Accessed 12 March 2013].

Williams, K., 2011. Litigants in person: a literature review M. of Justice, ed., Available from: http://www.justice.gov.uk/downloads/publications/research-and-analysis/moj-research/litigants-in-person-literature-review.pdf [Accessed 12 March 2013.].

Self-represented litigants: the overlooked and unintended consequence of legal aid reform

Chris Bevan

Family Barrister, KCH Chambers, Nottingham, UK

The Legal Aid, Sentencing and Punishment of Offenders Act 2012 (LASPO) comes into force in April 2013 and is widely expected to lead to an increase in the number of self-representing litigants (SRLs) in the family courts. Taking a practitioner focus, this article considers the negative impact of this increase and considers possible measures for combating the practical pitfalls such a growth in SRLs presents.

Introduction

All too often overlooked in the debate that has encircled the Legal Aid, Sentencing and Punishment of Offenders Act 2012 (LASPO) is the inevitable increase in the number of litigants in person that are an unintended consequence of the legal aid reforms. According to Graham Cookson's (2011) report into the impact of these reforms, the scope changes in eligibility for legal aid introduced by the 2012 Act will reduce the volume of legal representation cases in the family courts by some 40%. Whilst the view of the Ministry of Justice in its *Impact assessment* (2011b) into the legal aid reforms was that, '... the overall implications [of reform] will depend on the behavioural responses of clients who no longer receive legal aid', it was conceded that there exists, 'a risk that outcomes may be worse' for those unable to pay privately for legal assistance (at para. 26(vi)).

From members of the legal profession and the bench, the reaction to LASPO has largely been more impassioned and critical with over 90% of responses to the Government's Consultation Paper, *Proposals for the reform of Legal Aid in England and Wales* (Ministry of Justice 2010) raising objections to the proposed changes. Such concerns were strongly echoed by the Civil Justice Council's (CJC) Report on *Access to justice for litigants in person (or self-represented litigants)* (2011) in which it recognised that:

> The forthcoming reductions and changes in legal aid will have the most serious consequences ... Every informed prediction is that ... the number of SRLs will increase, and on a considerable scale. (p. 8)

The CJC is not alone in drawing this conclusion and it thus appears somewhat unavoidable and uncontroversial that numbers of litigants in person or, more appropriately, self-represented litigants (SRLs) as they are now to be known following the CJC's report, are set to soar. The prevailing wind, desirable or otherwise, seems to be blowing in just one direction. What then will be these 'serious consequences' identified by the CJC? As has been recognised in the academic community, there is only a small volume of good quality empirical research into SRLs and that which does exist is rather limited in scope or addressed the issue of SRLs in a non-UK context. That said, the various obstacles, procedural and practical, faced by SRLs and simultaneously a court system charged with accommodating them have been explored most recently in an insightful article by Maclean and Eekelaar (2012), which draws on data from an observational study of family cases in the lower courts to provide a window into the dynamics of family cases involving SRLs.

This article intends to build on the current academic discourse in this area by Maclean and others in considering a related but arguably discrete issue; namely, the impact of an increase in SRLs from a distinctly family practitioner perspective. Taking a practitioner stance, this piece aims to cast a searching spotlight over the particular areas of concern likely to be experienced by practising family lawyers as a result of the swingeing cuts to family legal aid heralded by LASPO; highlighting some of the ways in which practitioners are likely to feel the full force of the legal aid reforms. Whilst research into the impact on SRLs of the removal of financial assistance in many family cases is insightful, the effect of LASPO on family practitioners has largely been passed over. In taking this practitioner approach, this article provides a unique contribution to the academic thinking in this field.

Before embarking on a consideration of the specific practitioner-based concerns that stem from this projected increase in SRLs, it is worth conducting an analysis of the current research literature that exist in this arena.

What the current research tells us

First, a note on the definition of a self-representing litigant. Research by Moorhead and Sefton (2005) found that the term 'litigant in person' or self-representing litigant covers a multitude of scenarios and the degree of involvement of such individuals ranges from a minority of 'active' self-representing participants to the majority who Moorhead and Sefton characterise as 'inactive'. Whatever the degree of participation, the label 'SRL' indicates an absence of a legal representative, including a solicitor or barrister, whether that be during conduct of any litigation or other forms of advice and representation. Some SRLs will have received a measure of legal advice, while others will undertake to navigate legal proceedings entirely unsupported.

Taken together, the body of empirical research that currently exists surrounding the experiences of SRLs generally can be distilled into several pertinent conclusions. It is suggested that three thematic categories emerge and each will be summarised briefly now.

Demographics of SRLs

A key theme in the research is the demographic of SRLs. The research around age and economic considerations indicates that SRLs tend to be younger individuals and on lower incomes (Beck *et al.* 2010). Moreover, work carried out in Australia's family court showed that SRLs are more likely to be male and rely on benefits or other welfare payments as their principal source of income (Hunter *et al.* 2002). Additionally, a study by Moorhead and Sefton (2005) provides evidence that a 'significant minority' of SRLs in family cases exhibited vulnerability indicators. Such indicators included histories of domestic violence, drug and alcohol dependencies, mental illness and incidence of young parenthood.

Motivations of SRLs

Individuals' motivations for conducting their own cases in court without professional legal assistance are, as can be imagined, manifold. Despite this article's chief concern being the likely increase in the number of SRLs in light of the reductions in legal aid funding, it must be stressed that certainly not all motivations to self-represent are financial. As identified by Moorhead and Sefton (2005), one example of non-financial motivation, was a sense among SRLs that legal professionals were simply not necessary; unwarranted given the perceived simplicity or straightforward nature of the proceedings. Such a conclusion is supported by research by Sales *et al.* (1993), which found that, in divorce cases, 45% of those unrepresented had chosen to self-represent as the case was regarded as simple. A further proportion of SRLs, it has been noted, refuse legal representation due to apathy or hostility towards the legal profession (Dewar *et al.* 2000); an attitude that most practitioners will doubtless have encountered.

In spite of this, the connection between finances and SRLs cannot be ignored and remains a significant motivation for many individuals to attend court without a lawyer. Dewar *et al.* (2000), Moorhead and Sefton (2005), and Hunter *et al.* (2003) have all identified the striking and self-explanatory correlation between the unavailability of legal aid and self-representation.

Case outcomes for SRLs

Research supports the finding that best outcomes are not achieved when parties are unrepresented. Studies by Engler (2010), Moorhead and Sefton (2005) and Citizens Advice (2009) have all concluded that outcomes are impacted unfavourably by an absence of legal representation. Of course, in the family courts, it is rightly regarded as inappropriate to talk of 'winners' and 'losers'. This point has been underlined recently in light of the Family Justice Review's Final Report and discussions surrounding reform of private law residence orders (Bevan 2012a). What is detectable from the research is a focus on how the incidence of SRLs affects the way cases are concluded. In one study (Hunter *et al.* 2002), it was found that cases involving unrepresented litigants were more likely to conclude with withdrawal or abandonment rather than a full trial of the issues and much less likely to result in compromise and settlement.

The thematic categorisation employed above is, furthermore, buttressed by a recently conducted Ministry of Justice literature review into the experience of SRLs (Williams 2011).

What the research does not tell us

Having analysed the key themes detectable in the research in this area and what it can usefully tell us of the experience of SRLs, it is of value to note what the research does not tell us. Thus, while it is clear that the research is informative as to the diversity of backgrounds from which SRLs originate; the motives discernible in self-representation and the varied case outcomes associated with these individuals, there exists a knowledge gap; a gap which embraces questions such as: what is the impact on legal practitioners when faced with SRLs? How does the role of instructed counsel and the presiding judge alter when adjudicating cases involving SRLs? What professional ethical issues do SRLs present for family practitioners? Finally, what can be done to avert a crisis of self-representation that many feel is imminent?

As the family justice system braces itself for sweeping cuts to legal aid provision under LASPO, the author suggests that these questions have acquired an added urgency and relevance; all the more so when we consider that concerns have been expressed that the legal aid reforms could result in the consequential loss of an entire generation of family lawyers (Wall 2012). It is, then, to these questions which this article will now turn.

Self-representing litigants – the practitioner perspective

The Family Bar and family justice system more widely has its firm roots in a common law adversarial system; albeit that it also exhibits many inquisitorial characteristics. As Baroness Hale (as she then was) observed in her paper at the Sir Henry Hodge Memorial Lecture in 2011: 'The adversarial procedure which we adopt is heavily dependent upon lawyers preparing, presenting and arguing the case.' This view was ratified most recently by Sir Nicholas Wall in his 2012 Resolution speech when he stated that, 'The common law adversarial legal system ... reflects the assumption that lawyers will be involved' (p. 4). Yet, for some time now, family practitioners, ultimately resigned to legal aid cuts, have been readying themselves for the forthcoming surge in SRLs. For these practitioners, the long-held assumption of lawyer involvement and legal representation in private law family cases now requires reassessment. Some of the practical challenges encountered by family practitioners when engaged in cases involving SRLs will now be explored. In so doing, the author suggests the following categories can be identified:

(1) Absence of early legal advice
(2) Procedural issues
(3) Role of judge in cases involving SRLs
(4) SRL presentational issues
(5) Ethical issues

Absence of early legal advice

First, it falls to be considered the extent to which the loss of legal aid in the majority of private children cases (except those where there is evidence of domestic violence, abuse towards children or exceptional circumstances such that there is a need for legal aid to prevent an actual or potential breach of ECHR) will impact upon the nature of those matters which do reach court (for an excellent review of LASPO's 'exceptional funding' scheme see Miles *et al.* 2012). The CJC in its 2011 report were keen to promote greater access to early advice on a fee-paying basis for SRLs who might be able to afford a single piece of advice but who would be unable to meet the cost of full legal representation at a forthcoming hearing. The aim here would be to provide greater information to SRLs about how and if to progress their legal claims. Whilst this may be possible, it is feared that the vast majority of those ineligible for legal aid under LASPO will simply not be in a position to pay for any advice whatsoever. Further, for those who do pay for such advice, they may be susceptible to exploitation. If this is right, then many individuals will simply embark upon their family case without any meaningful legal advice. Maclean and Eekelaar (2012) have drawn several insightful conclusions from their review of the current research on SRLs in this regard. Of direct relevance to practitioners is their observation that the lack of any legal advice prior to a court hearing will lead to more family matters actually reaching the courts which might otherwise have been resolved without the need for further action. Lawyers and family lawyers most especially are skilled in managing the expectations of their clients. This exercise is vital if emotions, doubtless riding high, are to be put aside, with the aim of attempting early settlement. Dewar (1998), referencing Beck and Beck-Gernsheim's (1995), *The normal chaos of love*, described how 'family law engages with areas of social life and feeling – namely love, passion, intimacy, commitment and betrayal – that are themselves riven with contradiction or paradox,' and that, 'family law engages the passions as no other part of our legal system does' (p. 484) It has to be queried how well SRLs unaccustomed to the containment and mastery of feelings in a courtroom setting, will fare in what is often a complex maelstrom of emotion as Dewar recounts.

Moreover, private children matters often involve much to-ing and fro-ing at the door of the court; a process of negotiation requiring often-difficult and hard-fought concessions from both parties before a final workable solution is reached. Mnookin and Kornhauser (1988) have underlined the importance of negotiation and bargaining between parties in family law disputes outside the courtroom and 'in the shadow of the law'. The fear for practitioners is that, without early legal advice, more self-representing individuals will arrive at the courthouse with unrealistic expectations, less willing or less able to engage in genuine compromise. In this way, the emotional distance provided by legal representation which provides a vital breathing space between the flurry of heightened passions and the legal quandary, will be lost. Put bluntly, an increase in the number of SRLs will mean more cases reaching court with fewer achieving settlement. This outcome is hard to square with the government's emphasis on mediation and creating workable agreements in an amicable and non-litigious manner (see *The government response to the family justice review: A system with children and families at its heart* (Ministry of Justice 2012).

Of those that do attain a compromise, this will only happen after a protracted and most likely more problematic process than would hitherto have been the case under the previous legal aid regime. Greater costs for the paying party will result from long-drawn-out proceedings in addition to the further resources needed for court staff and the damaging effects that 'fighting' family cases present for the children concerned. As the Family Justice Council emphasised in its Family Law Review Final Report (Ministry of Justice 2011a), 'Unrepresented litigants in person ... persist with these proceedings when they would not have done so had they had proper legal advice at the outset' (para. 4.176). Not only is this worrisome for practitioners but it will lead to less optimal outcomes for children; those who lose out most when proceedings are lengthy.

Procedural concerns

It is a common conception that it is practitioners' legal knowledge per se which is most influential and determinative inside the courtroom. However, in one study by Sandefur (2011) it was found that lawyers affected case outcomes not simply as a result of their greater knowledge of the law but rather as a result of their enhanced acquaintance with legal procedure. Thus while research carried out by Hunter *et al.* (2002) rightfully points out that there are SRLs who are able to conduct their cases confidently and competently, the majority of studies present SRLs as encountering serious problems in terms of understanding the procedural elements of family justice. What then will be the impact of such a lack of appreciation of procedural niceties on practitioners?

It is likely that practitioners conducting cases involving SRLs will be more than accustomed to the unfamiliarity of SRLs towards the evidential requirements of the family court. Such lack of understanding on the part of SRLs manifests itself in a number of ways. First, SRLs are often unaware of the correct court forms to be completed; secondly, they are more likely than represented clients to arrive at court unclear as to the nature of the proceedings or precisely what is at stake. In such cases, it can fall to the practitioner present to conduct a brief conference with the SRL prior to any hearing to explain the purpose and possible outcomes of the day. This raises very real concerns for practitioners who, being paid to represent their own client, are spending time explaining legal procedure to the non-paying party. Whilst many practitioners, of whom the author is one, meet happily with SRLs in order to facilitate the smooth running of proceedings, it would be entirely legitimate to query why these practitioners should engage in this exercise at all. Certainly, it would be understandable for the paying client to feel rather aggrieved at paying for his representative to impart legal advice to the opposing side.

Research by Kelly *et al.* (2006) and that carried out by the Family Law Council in Australia (2000) goes further in highlighting that many practitioners are undertaking additional work both inside and outside the courtroom in order to compensate for that not undertaken by the unrepresented party. By way of an example, in family cases there is an unwritten convention that 'the Applicant drafts'. This custom reflects the long-held position that the legal representative for the Applicant party will usually be the one to draft court orders or agreements reached between the parties. In cases where the Applicant to the proceedings is unrepresented, the convention is often seen to be broken and the practitioner can be called upon to prepare the documentation (Bevan 2012b). This task can take some considerable time in complex cases where court orders are finely balanced and detailed. Once again, the cost of this exercise will be borne by the paying party.

In addition, self-representing individuals' lack of knowledge as to procedure also poses a real concern for court staff and the judiciary. It has been shown that SRLs are less likely to file the appropriate court documents at the desired time and even attend hearings at all (Moorhead and Sefton 2005). Court staff and judges regularly express rightful frustration in this regard. For the practitioner who has prepared his or her client's case in readiness for the hearing and briefed the client, this is understandably exasperating; not to mention costly if the paying client is required to meet the cost of the redundant appointment and the follow-up adjourned hearing. This is supported by Maclean and Eekelaar (2012), who, in their observational study, noted the greater likelihood of adjournments and relisting of hearings in cases involving unrepresented parties as a consequence of SRL non-attendance.

The unavoidable corollary of the above-mentioned procedural concerns is greater delay. Of course, as family practitioners, we are all too cognizant of the adverse effects of delay; it being explicitly enshrined in the Children Act 1989 in section 1(2); commonly referred to as 'the no-delay principle'. It is an inescapable conclusion that with the increase in the number of SRLs, cases will take longer, resulting in more adjourned hearings and consequent delay. This will have a direct impact not only on the parties concerned but any relevant children and family practitioners who will be engaged in more protracted litigation. This has been explicitly emphasized by the CJC and is supported by a number of research studies (Dewar *et al.* 2000, Hunter 2003, Moorhead and Sefton 2005).

Having considered the pitfalls created by SRLs who lack early legal advice and those not equipped with knowledge of the appropriate legal procedure, we now turn to consider what could be termed the 'presentational issues' that family practitioners encounter when faced with a self-representing litigant in the courtroom.

SRL Presentational Issues

> ... the SRL who litigates will be the most intransigent. Sir Nicholas Wall, Resolution Speech (2012)

Of the utmost concern to many family practitioners when faced with conducting a hearing opposite a self-representing litigant is whether that individual possesses the skills to present their case fairly and thoughtfully. Naturally, there will be those SRLs who do hold these necessary skills to conduct legal proceedings in a just and effective manner, whether as a result of their employment or otherwise. Unfortunately, it is all too often the experience of family practitioners that SRLs simply are not endowed with the advocacy proficiency vital in an adversarial system such as that of England and Wales. Studies by Genn and Genn (1989), Baldwin (1997) and Hunter *et al.* (2002) have underlined that clients who are unrepresented are more likely to be overwhelmed by the advocacy demands of court hearings. Frequently SRLs express unease at the degree of formality of proceedings and bemusement at the legal jargon employed. In an enlightening article in the *Law gazette* by Hyde (2012), one SRL's experiences could scarcely have been made plainer, when he recollected that, 'looking back, I had no clue what I was doing in that building ... the whole thing was intimidating.' The consequences of this for legal practitioners will vary enormously from case to case; however, several commonly occurring issues will be considered below.

Some SRLs present as intimidated and overawed by the legal proceedings. Lack of representation here will not only reduce the chances of the SRL's viewpoint being heard fully but can also impact negatively on the represented client, whose lawyer may also not be able to participate as robustly as would have been the case had both sides been represented. As such, in cases of this nature, it is highly unlikely that a complete and effective adversarial hearing in the true tradition of our court system can be achieved. Additionally, there is evidence to suggest that judges sometimes change the order of proceedings and relax the rules surrounding the nature of witness questioning to assist those without representation. Circumstances can be therefore be foreseen in which such changes would disadvantage the represented client through no fault of his or her own.

Moreover, an SRL daunted and untrained in presentational skills will not, in many instances, be in a position to deliver sound legal submissions. Where this occurs, the represented client may find that their lawyer is held to a much higher professional standard than that of the other party or that their lawyer's role is even curtailed to accommodate the particular needs of the unqualified SRL. For practitioners, this could become a source of real frustration as they are forced to amend their questioning style and rigour, which could, ultimately, prove to be at odds with their paying client's interests.

One further area which troubles practitioners in particular is that of cross-examination in private family law proceedings. Whilst legal aid will still be available in cases where domestic violence is being or has historically been perpetrated, there will doubtless be cases where, short of domestic violence per se, threatening or aggressive behaviours have been exhibited by one or both of the parties. In such cases, under LASPO, there is the potential that SRLs will be in a position to engage in cross-examination of a party who has been the focus of such threatening or abusive behaviour in what may be a finely-balanced and delicate, emotionally-charged courtroom scenario. As underlined in the Family Justice Review's Final Report (Ministry of Justice 2011a), many individuals will enter the family courts, 'in the throes of relationship breakdown ... at crisis point in their lives' (at para. 4.176). This is all the more pressing when, as explored above, we recall that research indicates a 'significant minority' of SRLs display vulnerability indicators. Family proceedings thus have the potential to constitute some of the most emotionally sensitive and difficult times of the parties' lives (see Dewar 1998). The concern here for practitioners is that whilst they will be required to frame questions in a professional form, SRLs may be in a position to engage in unduly oppressive questioning or place the opposing client under immense pressure or stress; neither of which is conducive to achieving a workable resolution or effective court hearing.

As can be seen, presentational issues associated with SRLs present practitioners with perhaps the biggest challenge of all. From the verbose SRL whose rambling questioning technique extends proceedings to the detriment of the smooth running of justice, to the angry or controlling SRL who is unable to contain his or her nerves or flaring passions, and may exhibit an emotional block on settlement, it will likely, in some measure, come to rest on the shoulders of the instructed practitioner or the presiding judge to steer matters towards a just disposal. With this in mind, we turn to examine the ethical implications of a greater frequency of self-representation in the family court.

Ethical issues

Family practitioners are governed and guided by a series of professional codes of conduct, including the Bar Standards Board (2011) Code of Conduct. Practitioners are required to 'promote and protect fearlessly' their clients' interests and present their case robustly whilst, at the same time, not in any way misleading the court. Important then, is the question as to what impact the anticipated increase in SRLs under LASPO will have on professional ethics and how practitioners champion their clients' best interests.

This article has already touched on some of the ethical issues which SRLs pose for the family court service. Research into those who self-represent has also provided a useful insight in this regard. Studies by Moorhead and Sefton (2005) and Dewar *et al.* (2000) identified that where SRLs were involved in family proceedings, court staff felt the need to walk a fine line between providing appropriate assistance and, in fact, offering legal advice which falls outside their remit. Members of the judiciary have also shown themselves to be cognizant of this delicate balancing exercise (see Tugendhat J's comments in *O'Dwyer* v. *ITV plc* [2012] EWHC 3321 (QB) para. 55). Research by Goldschmidt *et al.* (1998) and Dewar *et al.* (2000) considered the ways in which judges tailored their role to assist SRLs, adapting their judicial approach to navigate SRLs through the court process. For practitioners and members of the judiciary this presents a potential concern; namely the perception of bias towards the unrepresented party. It would be most unfair if the party paying for legal representation lost out simply as a result of his or her having sought out expert legal advice.

Discussed above was the extent to which judges alter the course of proceedings to assist SRLs, yet some family judges have been found to go further in facilitating the courtroom experience of SRLs. By way of example, judges have been found to employ a more hands-on, interventionist approach in order to counteract a perceived imbalance between the unrepresented client and the practitioner advocate, including the judge perfecting the questioning technique of SRLs or extensively or wholly adopting the questioning of witnesses in place of the SRL. Other examples include members of the judiciary going to great lengths to explain various aspects of the proceedings and abandoning the more traditional structure of court hearings to suit the needs of the unrepresented party. Such approaches need not cause alarm in every case but there will be many instances in which, whilst done with only good intentions, these adjustments raise the suggestion of an erosion of impartiality on the part of the presiding judge; a worry which research has shown plays on the minds of members of the judiciary themselves (Goldschmidt *et al.* 1998).

Additionally, practitioners engaged in cases where one party is unrepresented are at risk of becoming 'counsel for all' in circumstances where the advocate is called upon, whether expressly or impliedly, to act in the best interests of the case as a whole or the court rather than principally in the best interest of their paying client. Beyond this, Maclean and Eekelaar (2012) have identified in their observational study that, in certain instances, particularly where both parties are unrepresented, the judge almost became 'advocate for both sides' trying to create a level playing field in the absence of skilled legal assistance. This has the potential to do very real harm to the impartiality or the perception of the impartiality of the judiciary and whilst undertaken with laudable motives, the means by which judiciary alter their behaviour in this way should, the author suggests, be disquieting to those who recognise that justice is best served when there is an equality of arms.

Where do we go from here?

In its 2011 report, the CJC noted that:

> The challenge is to protect the quality and values that underpin our system of justice while seeking to deliver, as far as possible, accessible and affordable procedures that promote accurate judicial determination on the merits. (p. 25)

There has been an air of inevitability and rather gloomy pessimism to the above discussion of the pitfalls encountered by legal practitioners facing an increase in the number of SRLs. However, it must be remembered that there will always be those unrepresented litigants who conduct proceedings thoroughly and effectively. That said, it is suggested that great problems await the family court service if reforms are not implemented. To take no action at all is plainly not an option. Rather, it is suggested that affirmative measures are needed to ameliorate the less than desirable situation that LASPO will herald.

The issue is thus how this not insignificant challenge can to be confronted. Writing in the *Guardian* newspaper, and in a powerful article, Jon Robins (2012) considered how the court system might be improved to reconcile the greater numbers of self-representing litigants. In particular, he criticised a scheme aimed at encouraging 'community legal companions' made up of largely unqualified law students, tasked with plugging the gap left by the removal of legal aid from the majority of private family law cases, by supporting SRLs at court hearings. It must be right to query the value of untrained legal companionship to unrepresented litigants engaged in family law proceedings. To expect untrained students unfamiliar with the rules of court, particularly those that relate to legal costs, to assist with hearings on behalf of SRLs must surely be to overstate their abilities and could possibly prove counterproductive if the judge is required to closely supervise these inexperienced legal novices at each stage. Others have suggested that greater use of Pro Bono services could assist following the coming into force of LASPO in April 2013. However it has to be doubted whether the family legal profession, already engaged in extensive Pro Bono work and feeling demoralized by budget cuts, has the appetite to undertake additional unpaid work to meet the increased demand for Pro Bono that may flow from LASPO.

This begs the very pressing question: what practically can be done and where do we go from here?

With the CJC concluding that SRLs 'will be the rule rather than the exception,' after 31 March of this year, it falls not to consider how the problems caused by SRLs can be avoided altogether but rather how they can be effectively managed and minimised. What is needed is simplification of the court system to accommodate SRLs. This appears to be an entirely defensible proposition having considered the significant problems that court procedures pose for self-representing individuals. It seems both justifiable and necessary that a wholesale cultural shift in the way the court system approaches SRLs is required if the 'disaster' of LASPO, as Robins describes it, is to be averted. If SRLs are to be assisted to enable them to present their cases more effectively and if legal practitioners are not to be overly burdened by the unintended consequences of government economic decisions as to legal aid, bold and practical steps must be taken to vastly simplify and strip back the court procedures. Such steps would need to include some or all of what follows. Complicated court forms must be scrapped; replacing the same with shorter, more streamlined, more accessible and readily comprehensible documents. Digital resources need to be developed and employed to their fullest potential which signpost would-be SRLs towards speedy and realistic internet advice; enabling them to monitor and, if required, limit their own expectations including when a claim should and, more importantly, should not be pursued. Detailed self-help schemes should be introduced to improve the presentational skills and procedural knowledge of SRLs whose cases do reach the door of the court. Finally, well-drafted advisory guides should be issued to all members of the family legal profession and judiciary which tackle how best to overcome the most common SRL-related issues (as explored in this article) including how to avoid any concerns as to judicial impartiality and overburdening of legal practitioners attending hearings at which SRLs are present. Some materials already exist to assist the legal profession in the form of books (such as *Family courts without a lawyer – a handbook for litigants in person*) and practice directions drafted for solicitors (available at: http://www.familylaw.co.uk/articles/law-society-practice-note-litigants-in-person). However, these alone will be insufficient to overcome the range of concerns that SRLs present and much more must be done.

At a time when the court service is already tasked with embracing Mr Justice Ryder's Judicial Proposals for the Modernisation of Family Justice (2011), effecting the cultural changes outlined above, will doubtless prove a difficult task; with the family court being pulled in many, often seemingly conflicting directions. However, in a system where SRLs are set to become the norm, there remains little choice but to take dramatic steps. After all, it was Lord Woolf's Access to Justice Report (1995) that noted, 'the true problem is the court system and its procedures which are still too often inaccessible and incomprehensible'. An unscrambling and clarification of some of the family justice system's more complex procedures and court documents must be the first step in any simplification process. This will aid SRLs, the judiciary and legal practitioners alike and is crucial if we are to prevent the family justice system becoming more inaccessible under LASPO.

Conclusion

> … good lawyers cost money, they also save it. Sir Nicholas Wall, Resolution Speech (2012,) p. 5)

Over a year has passed since the CJC issued its forceful report into access to justice and SRLs. Its conclusions were stark; namely that even in the event that all of their recommendations came to fruition, in many cases, there would still be a denial of justice. The CJC described English and Welsh justice as, 'a legal system that the world admires and which is the forum of choice for much international litigation … But … not a legal system designed with self-represented litigants in mind'. Sadly, nearly 18 months on with LASPO now on our doorstep, this portrayal appears all too accurate. It seems that good lawyers do cost money and there is very little money to go around.

This article has approached the LASPO reforms to legal aid from a practitioner perspective with a view to shining fresh light on the experiences of family lawyers and self-representing litigants. In so doing, it becomes readily apparent that an increase in the number of SRLs has an impact not only on the outcomes for the SRLs themselves but for the represented client and his instructed lawyer also. Moreover, in altering its practices to respond to the needs of unrepresented individuals, the judiciary inadvertently, though unintentional, risks compromising its impartiality and professional ethics. The time to act is very much upon us if we are to retain a gold standard legal system. SRLs must be assisted to improve their understanding of court procedures which must themselves be simplified; the judiciary must be supported so that equality and fairness in the justice system are fortified and not diminished and finally, practitioners must be advised and if need be, trained, as to how best to promote the efficacy of court hearings without jeopardizing their own professional or their client's personal and legal interests.

It seems essential to end on something of a hopeful tone. Family lawyers are perhaps dissimilar to many in the legal profession in that they have historically undertaken more work for less pay than most. As a family practitioner myself, I am of the view that the family court must now hold firm to its core values and have confidence that those who remain in practice will yet again rise to the occasion to meet head-on the great challenge that LASPO brings.

References

Baldwin, J., 1997. *Monitoring the rise of the small claims limit: litigants' experiences of different forms of adjudication*, Lord Chancellor's Department Research Series, No. 1/97.

Bar Standards Board, 2011. The Code of Conduct. Available from: https://www.barstandardsboard.org.uk/regulatory-requirements/the-code-of-conduct/

Beck, C.J.A., et al., 2010. Divorce mediation with and without legal representation: a focus on intimate partner violence and abuse. *Family court review*, 48 (4), 631–645.

Beck, U. and Beck-Gernsheim, E., 1995. *The normal chaos of love*. Oxford: Polity.

Bevan, C., 2012a. What's in a name? A practitioner's view on reform of residence orders. *Family law*, 42 (Jul), 862–864.

Bevan, C., 2012b. Modernisation of the family courts: litigants in peril? *Family law*, 42 (Nov), 1382–1384.

Citizens Advice, 2009. *Supporting justice: the case for publicly-funded legal representation before the Asylum Support Tribunal*. Citizens Advice Bureaux Evidence Briefing.

Civil Justice Council, 2011. *Access to justice for litigants in person (or self-represented litigants)*. Final Report November.

Cookson, G., 2011. Unintended consequences: the cost of the government's Legal Aid reforms, a report for the Law Society of England and Wales (Department of Management, King's College London). Available from: http://soundoffforjustice.org/wp-content/uploads/2012/01/Kings-College-report-into-costs-of-Govt-legal-aid-reforms1.pdf [Accessed 8 March 2013].

Dewar, J., 1998. The normal chaos of family law. *Modern law review*, 61 (4), 467–485.

Dewar, J., Smith, B.W. and Banks, C., 2000. *Litigants in person in the Family Court of Australia*. Family Court of Australia Research Report No. 20.

Engler, R., 2010. Connecting self-representation to civil Gideon: what existing data reveal about when counsel is most needed. *Fordham urban law journal*, 37. Available from: http://www.familycourt.gov.au/wps/wcm/resources/file/ebb87e04879610d/report20.pdf [Accessed 8 March 2013].

Family Law Council (Australia), 2000. *Litigants in person: a report to the Attorney General prepared by the Family Law Council*. Available from: http://www.lawcouncil.asn.au

Genn, H. and Genn, Y., 1989. *The effectiveness of representation at tribunals*. Lord Chancellor's Department.

Goldschmidt, J., et al., 1998. *Meeting the challenge of pro se litigation. A report and guidebook for judges and court managers*. American Judicature Society.

Hale, B., 2011. *Equal access to justice in the big society*. The Sir Henry Hodge Memorial Lecture.

Hunter, R., 2003. Adversarial mythologies: policy assumptions and research evidence in family law. *Journal of law and society*, 30 (1).

Hunter, R., et al., 2006. *Women and legal aid: identifying disadvantage*, Legal Aid Queensland.

Hunter, R., et al., 2002. *The changing face of litigation: unrepresented litigants in the Family Court of Australia*. Law and Justice Foundation of New South Wales.

Hunter, R., Giddings, J. and Chrzanowski, A., 2003. *Legal aid and self-representation in the family court of Australia*. National Legal Aid.

Hyde, J., 2012. Litigants in person 'need more support'. *The law gazette online*. Available at: http://www.lawgazette.co.uk/news/litigants-person-need-more-support [Accessed 8 March 2013].

Kelly, E., Cameron, C. and Chui, W.H., 2006. Litigants in person in civil proceedings: part IV barristers' perspectives. *Hong Kong law journal*, 36 (3), 519–552.

Lord Woolf, The Right Honourable., 1995. *Access to Justice: Interim Report to the Lord Chancellor on the civil justice system in England and Wales*.

Maclean, M. and Eekelaar, J., 2012. Legal representation in family matters and the reform of legal aid: a research note on current practice. *Child and family law quarterly*, 24 (2), 223–233.

Miles, J., Balmer, N.J. and Smith, M., 2012. When exceptional is the rule: mental health, family problems and the reform of legal aid in England and Wales. *Child and family law quarterly*, 24 (3), 320–332.

Ministry of Justice, 2010. *Proposals for the reform of Legal Aid in England and Wales*. Consultation Paper CP12/10, Cm 7967 (2010).

Ministry of Justice, 2011a. Family Law Review – Final Report (2011).

Ministry of Justice, 2011b. *Impact assessment annex a: scope to reform of Legal Aid in England and Wales: the government response*. London: TSO.

Ministry of Justice, 2011c. *Mr Justice Ryder's judicial proposals for the modernization of family justice*. Available at: http://www.judiciary.gov.uk/Resources/JCO/Documents/Reports/ryderj_recommendations_final.pdf [Accessed 8 March 2013].

Ministry of Justice, 2012. *The government response to the family justice review: a system with children and families at its heart*. Available at: https://www.education.gov.uk/publications/-standard/publicationDetail/Page1/CM-8273 [Accessed 8 March 2013].

Mnookin, R.H. and Kornhauser, L., 1988. Bargaining in the shadow of the law. *Yale law journal*, 950, 1978–1979.

Moorhead, R. and Sefton, M., 2005. *Litigants in person. Unrepresented litigants in first instance proceedings*, Department for Constitutional Affairs Research Series, 2/05.

Reed, L., 2011. *Family courts without a lawyer – a handbook for litigants in person*. Bath Publishing.

Robins, J., 2012. *The idea of law students filling the legal aid gap makes my heart sink*. Guardian Law online. Available at: http://www.guardian.co.uk/law/2012/dec/13/law-students-legal-aid-gap [Accessed 8 March 2013].

Sales, B., Beck, C.J. and Haan, R.K., 1993. Is self-representation a reasonable alternative to attorney representation in divorce cases? *Saint Louis university law journal*, 37, 553–605.

Sandefur, R., 2011. *Elements of expertise: lawyers' impact on civil trial and hearing outcomes*.

Wall, N., 2012. Resolution Speech. Available from: http://www.judiciary.gov.uk/Resources/JCO/Documents/Speeches/pfd-speech-resolution-annual-conference-240312.pdf. [Accessed 8 March 2013].

Williams, K., 2011. *Litigants in person: a literature review*, Research Summary 2/11. Available at: http://www.justice.gov.uk/downloads/publications/research-and-analysis/moj-research/litigants-in-person-literature-review.pdf [Accessed 8 March 2013].

Changing the immigration rules and withdrawing the 'currency' of legal aid: the impact of LASPO 2012 on migrants and their families

F. Meyler and S. Woodhouse

School of Law and Social Justice, University of Liverpool, Liverpool, UK

The provisions of the Legal Aid, Sentencing and Punishment of Offenders Act 2012 (LASPO 2012) will remove almost all immigration cases from the scope of legal aid with effect from 1 April 2013. Part One of this paper describes the expected changes LASPO 2012 will make and then explores their anticipated impact. It explains that large numbers of migrants and their family members are likely to be without legal advice and representation after April 2013, including in cases where the state-enforced removal or deportation from the UK of a parent is contemplated, with the consequence of separating parent from child. Part Two explores the possibility that an 'exceptional case determination' might provide a route back into legal aid funding, and finds that this is likely to be restricted, in immigration cases, to those making applications relying on Article 8 ECHR and who can demonstrate a particular and individual requirement for legal aid. Part Three explores the rationale for these changes, and concerns about access to justice for migrants and their family members in cases involving acute interference with rights to family and private life. It places these concerns in context, specifically the fundamental and restrictive amendments to the Immigration Rules relating to family migration introduced from July 2012. These amendments are enormously complex and their full legal implications have yet to be tested in the higher courts. Part Four questions whether the changes will in fact achieve their stated aim of cost savings or whether the costs will simply be transferred to other parts of the State (especially to the Tribunal system, in dealing with litigants in person). The paper additionally questions, in Part Five, whether the regulators are equipped to regulate the quality of the fee-charging immigration advice services to which at least some individuals will turn. The paper concludes that, at the very least, it is particularly harsh that the Government has removed the 'currency' of legal aid at this time, so that those with limited financial resources have neither access to legal aid advice about the meaning of those Rules nor legal aid representation to test their proper interpretation.

Introduction

The provisions of the Legal Aid, Sentencing and Punishment of Offenders Act 2012 (LASPO 2012) relating to legal aid will come into force on 1 April 2013.

At the time of writing (December 2012) the regulations that will implement LASPO 2012 were only available in draft form, and may be subject to amendment: some of the detail remains unclear. However, what is not debateable is that LASPO 2012 represents a seismic change in approach to the legal aid funding available to migrants and their family members.

The Legal Aid and Advice Act 1949 established a system of public funding for legal advice services for individuals without the means to pay for this: legal aid was seen as a key part of the welfare state (Elson 1946). Probate and conveyancing matters were excluded from the scope of the scheme, as was the drafting of wills, but all other areas of legal advice were included. It is unlikely that immigration advice was a large part of the services funded by legal aid in the early days, but during the 1960s and 1970s a sub-specialism of immigration and asylum advice began to emerge, especially amongst those practising in left-wing and radical legal practices and chambers. Practitioners were fuelled by political concerns about race discrimination, especially after the controversial imposition of immigration control on Commonwealth citizens in 1962.[1] The Joint Council for the Welfare of Immigrants, a key campaigning organisation offering help and assistance to many migrants, was set up in 1967. The key text used by immigration practitioners, *Macdonald's immigration law and practice*, was first published in 1983 (Macdonald 1983), and the Immigration Law Practitioners' Association (ILPA) was founded the following year. By the early 1980s there was a body of legal practitioners with specialist focus on asylum and immigration work.

At the same time, legal reforms were giving increased procedural protection to those affected by immigration control. Rights of appeal were accorded first to Commonwealth citizens by the Immigration Appeals Act 1969 in a move Macdonald and Toal (2010, p.1462) describe as 'calculated to ease the fears of racial discrimination' mentioned above). Appeal rights were then extended to aliens by the Immigration Act 1971 (although 'important gaps' in appeal rights remained) (Macdonald and Toal, 2010, p. 1462). However, although appeal rights were first created in 1969, it was not until 1 January 2000 (Macdonald and Toal, 2010, p. 520), over 20 years later, that the legal aid available for immigration advice was extended to include representation at appeal hearings. During the late 1990s and early 2000s, the system of legal aid for immigration and asylum cases was given a radical overhaul, and legal aid suppliers were given much greater autonomy in granting funding, and initial costs limits that applied to immigration cases were increased.

At this time, almost all immigration advice relating to UK immigration law fell within the scope of the legal aid scheme, regardless of the location of the applicant and the type of application they wished to make. The only real restriction was the requirement that there be sufficient benefit to the client or sufficient merit in the case to justify a grant of legal aid, and of course the requirement that the client pass the 'means test' by establishing a relatively low level of income.

In parallel to the various developments making the legal aid scheme more generous, the Legal Services Commission also made significant attempts to control the quality of advice it paid for, with the introduction of exclusive contracting with 'approved suppliers', 'peer review',[2] 'audit'[3] and the required 'accreditation'[4] of individual advisers. Later in this article we consider what impact LASPO 2012 might have on the quality of immigration advice available to those whose cases now fall out of scope.

The relative generosity of the late 1990s and early 2000s was short-lived. In 2004 the initial limits on what could be spent on a case were decreased. Representation at most asylum interviews was no longer funded, except where the applicant was a child or where there were special circumstances. The facility for 'staged billing' was withdrawn, which had allowed organisations to bill and be paid for work done as the case progressed, essential to ensure cash flow in a poorly remunerated and disbursement[5]-heavy area of practice, where cases could take years to conclude. In 2007 the Graduated Fee Scheme was introduced (effectively, in many cases, a fixed-fee system), followed by a 10% cut in all civil legal aid fees in October 2011. Both of the large not-for profit organisations supplying legal aid immigration and asylum advice went into administration at this time, Refugee and Migrant Justice[6] in June 2010 (BBC News 2010) and the Immigration Advisory Service in July 2011 (BBC News 2011), prompted by these changes,[7] together with the Government's refusal further financially to assist the organisations concerned.

Despite the significant retrenchments in the legal aid scheme which we have described above, LASPO 2012 nevertheless marks a new departure for immigration legal aid: it removes a whole tranche of immigration cases from the scope of legal aid altogether. Its impact on those affected will be profound. As will be seen later in this article, LASPO 2012 is being implemented in the context of fundamental and far reaching amendments to the Immigration Rules, particularly in the area of 'family migration'.

Alternatives to legal aid for those affected are more circumscribed in this area of legal services than in any other, because the provision of immigration services is highly regulated.[8] Charitable and voluntary groups will be prevented (with criminal sanctions as the penalty) from stepping in, unless both the organisation and individual immigration advisers are regulated by the Office for the Immigration Services Commissioner or by a 'qualifying regulator'.[9] Of course, even if charitable and voluntary organisations were permitted to provide immigration advice, it would not be a substitute for a properly funded legal aid service. Those charitable or not-for-profit organisations which are appropriately regulated will themselves be facing multiple funding cuts: law centres, for example, are facing cuts in funding from local authorities as well as in their legal aid funding, and are thus unable to provide pro bono immigration advice on anything like the scale required, if at all.

This paper is informed by the writers' past experience as practitioners specialising in immigration and asylum law. We have both conducted legally aided work on behalf of migrants and their families at a senior level. However, we both now work as lecturers at the University of Liverpool. Our paper also contains comments from current well-respected legal aid practitioners, from the Law Society, and from a member of the immigration judiciary who has provided personal views about the implications for the First Tier Tribunal. The article is therefore also shaped by the concerns and experience of those who are grappling at the present time with the implications of the changes for their professional practice, the organisations they work for and for their clients (or, in the terminology of the First Tier Tribunal, 'customers'). In this sense we have a particular professional perspective, and what we write is not purely scholarly. We hope our professional experience might add depth to what follows, and while we do not claim objectivity, we have tried to explain our thinking and our concerns in as balanced a way as possible. Perhaps our contribution might be seen as a sort of action research in retrospect?

Part One: Changes to the availability of legal aid for immigration cases

Impact

As explained in the introduction, at the current time immigration matters usually fall within the scope of the legal aid scheme. Once LASPO 2012 is implemented, it is estimated by the Government that 53,000 fewer cases will receive legal aid funding in the immigration category, representing a 92% reduction in the number of individuals receiving services in relation to an initial application, and 20% less in relation to preparation and representation for appeal hearings.[10]

LASPO 2012 and legal aid for immigration cases: an outline

LASPO 2012 will achieve the anticipated reduction in the numbers of immigration cases receiving funding through its requirement that 'civil legal services' will only be available if they are 'described in Part 1 Schedule 1',[11] which in turn sets out a restrictive list of applications or categories of applicants. Any immigration 'services' not 'described' in

Part 1 Schedule 1 are out of scope (unless they qualify for an Exceptional Cases Determination, which we explore in detail in Part 2).

Immigration services which remain in scope after 1 April 2013

The descriptors in Part 1 Schedule 1 are, for the most part, highly technical and detailed. What follows is, therefore, an abridged *simplified* version of the sorts of applications, legal issues and individual characteristics where immigration 'civil legal services' will continue to be available after 1 April 2013:[12]

- Asylum-type applications;[13]
- Immigration detention, including bail applications, temporary admission and release on residence and other restrictions;[14]
- Victims of domestic violence applying for indefinite leave to remain under the Immigration Rules[15] or for residence card applications on the basis of a retained right of residence arising from domestic violence;[16]
- Victims of trafficking;[17]
- Proceedings before the Special Immigration Appeals Commission (i.e. cases involving issues of national security);[18]
- Applications for asylum support where the application includes an application for accommodation[19,20]; and
- Judicial review applications (with significant restrictions, discussed in more detail below),[21] and applications for habeas corpus.[22]

Immigration services which fall out of scope after 1 April 2013

The result is that those making applications and appeals, and their family members, will have no clear eligibility for legal aid funding in the following sorts of cases (provided as examples and not by any means an exhaustive list):

- Family migration / family reunion where an individual is applying to join or remain with a family member in the UK,
- Deportation or removal from the UK (e.g. in the case of an individual who has been convicted of a criminal offence in the UK, or has breached the conditions of their stay),
- Article 8 ECHR (i.e. cases relying on the right to respect for family and private life), and
- Unaccompanied migrant children (non-asylum).

In some cases in the above categories what is in issue is state enforced removal or deportation from the UK, which will have the consequence of separating parent from child. In other cases, the issue is whether the state will allow parent and child to be reunited, by granting entry clearance. There is, in our view, a strong parallel with public law family cases. Other cases will not involve minor children, but might involve dependent, vulnerable or elderly family members. We set out in more detail in Part Three our argument that legal aid ought to be available in such circumstances if there is to be an even-handed approach across all areas of law, and if fairness is to be achieved.

Judicial review: special restrictions in immigration cases

A more extended discussion is warranted of the special provisions relating to legal aid for judicial review proceedings in immigration cases. As we have explained, most legal advice in relation to an initial application, and thereafter representation at an appeal hearing, will fall outside the scope of legal aid in non-asylum immigration cases after 1 April 2013. As a result, provisions restricting access to legal aid for immigration judicial review will have a particular impact: *those who are denied legal aid for judicial review may well not be eligible for any legal aid at any stage of domestic legal proceedings.*

Although in other areas of law all applications for judicial review will remain in scope after 1 April 2013, there are special restrictions that will be applied only in immigration and asylum cases.[23] The restrictions seem designed in part to prevent 'repetitious' judicial reviews: legal aid will not be available for judicial review where 'the same issue, or substantially the same issue, was the subject of a previous judicial review or an appeal to a court or tribunal',[24] 'the court, tribunal or other person hearing the case found against the applicant or appellant on that issue',[25] and 'the services in relation to the new judicial review are provided before the end of the period of 1 year beginning with the day of that determination'.[26] Fresh claims based on asylum grounds are preserved within scope, but not fresh submissions relating to Article 8 issues.

The second set of restrictions are aimed at judicial reviews of enforcement action where the enforcement action follows within 12 months of either an un-appealable decision, a decision that is not appealed, or the final determination of an appeal. Legal aid will not be available for judicial reviews challenging removal directions given 'not more than 1 year' after a decision was made to remove the individual or any appeal against such a decision was finally determined or withdrawn.[27]

So it might well be that an unrepresented appellant, whose appeal relating to family migration of some kind has been dismissed on Article 8 grounds as well as under the Immigration Rules, and who had no eligibility to legal aid in relation to that appeal, is ineligible for legal aid for a judicial review both of directions for their removal, and for the refusal of their fresh submissions. These restrictions will apply even to cases that meet the merits test, and we question why such restrictions are necessary. If the allegation is that practitioners are using powers devolved to them by the Legal Services Commission to grant legal aid in relation to judicial review proceedings in cases where this is unmerited, our view is that this should be picked up through audit and other LSC procedures to monitor contract compliance. If, on the other hand, there is 'merit'[28] in the proposed proceedings, then why should the fact that they are being initiated within a year of the determination of an appeal be a bar to the grant of funding?

Part Two: Exceptional funding

Exceptional case determination

For cases that fall outside the descriptions in Part 1, Schedule 1 (in the immigration context, the sorts of cases listed in Part One above under the heading 'Immigration Services which fall out of Scope after 1st April 2013') there is one final possibility which might provide access to legal aid. LASPO 2012 s 10 gives entitlement to legal aid where there has been an 'exceptional case determination' or ECD. An ECD *must* be made if failure to do so would be a breach of the person's 'Convention rights (within the meaning of the Human Rights Act 1998)', or their 'enforceable EU rights'. 'Any risk' that failure to make an ECD would be such a breach *may* also lead to an ECD if 'it is appropriate ... in the particular circumstances of the case'.[29]

Convention Rights: Article 6 ECHR

So when might failure to provide legal aid amount to a breach of a person's 'Convention Rights', so as to trigger an ECD, in the immigration context? Article 6(1) guarantees the right to a fair trial and, importantly, access to a court. Whether access to a court implies a right to state-funded legal assistance has been considered on several occasions by the European Court of Human Rights, and the general principles are now well established. The Court has held that the right to a fair trial, whether civil or criminal, implies that the litigant must have the opportunity to present his or her case effectively before the court, and if the litigant cannot pay for legal assistance then denial of legal aid can amount to a breach of the right of access to a court. The question of whether legal aid is necessary to give effect to this right is to be determined on the specific facts of each case, taking into account factors such as the complexity of the law or procedure, the capacity of the applicant to represent him or herself, and what is at stake for both sides. Complete equality of arms between the two sides is not required, provided both have a reasonable opportunity to present their case under conditions that do not place him or her at a substantial disadvantage vis-à-vis the adversary. Further, the right to legal aid or legal assistance from the State is not absolute, and proportionate restrictions that pursue a legitimate aim are lawful.

However, difficulties arise in the immigration context. Article 6(1) itself states that it applies to 'the determination of' a person's 'civil rights and obligations or of any criminal charge'. The European Court of Human Rights has held that 'civil rights' do not include disputes relating purely to public law rights.[30] In *Maaouia* v *France*[31] the Grand Chamber held that Article 6(1) was not applicable to decisions on entry, stay and deportation of aliens, since such decisions 'do not concern the determination of an applicant's civil rights or obligations or of a criminal charge against him, within the meaning of Article 6(1) of the Convention' (para. 40). The Grand Chamber explained, 'because of the substantial discretionary and public-order element in such decisions, proceedings relating to them are not to be seen as determining the civil rights of the person concerned, even if they inevitably but incidentally have major repercussions on his private and family life, prospects of employment, financial position and the like'.

Maaouia v *France* has since been applied in the UK,[32] but there is considerable confusion[33] about the distinction between a civil right (where Article 6 standards apply) and a public law right (where Article 6 standards do not), and the jurisprudence of the ECtHR about the proper scope of Article 6 is in a state of flux. In the meantime, domestic decisions have affirmed the distinction between civil and public law rights, clarifying that it is the 'the nature and purpose of the administrative action which determines whether its impact on private law rights is such that a legal challenge to it involves a determination of civil rights',[34] with some questioning, in the asylum context, whether the line between civil and public law has been drawn in the correct place by the European Court.[35]

Many immigration practitioners share the view that the decision in *Maaouia* v *France* needs rethinking, but would do so more generally, arguing that Article 6 protections to access the court should be extended to disputes concerning immigration as well as asylum. Whilst the jurisprudence of the European Court indicates that the gravity of the issues involved for the individual is not determinative of whether a right is characterised as a public or civil right,[36] many would argue that the seriousness of the impact on the individual of immigration decisions should be taken into account. Certainly, that the protections of Article 6 are enjoyed by those claiming a 'right to property', and other 'pecuniary rights'[37] strikes us as somewhat ironic, when these protections are denied to immigrants and asylum seekers. The other element is the increased specificity of the Immigration Rules, which perhaps make it incorrect to characterise immigration decisions as 'discretionary'[38] and suggest that the protections of Article 6 might be appropriate.

Convention Rights: Article 13 ECHR

Whatever the arguments about the proper scope of Article 6, we have explained why it does not, on the current jurisprudence of the domestic courts and European Court of Human Rights,[39] apply to immigration proceedings. It may be very difficult to use Article 6 in the immigration context to establish entitlement to a positive ECD for family migration cases, therefore, as to do so would probably require a change of approach by the European Court of Human Rights.[40]

However, Article 13 ECHR provides a right to an effective remedy for violations of other rights under the Convention: the inability to obtain a remedy before a national court for an infringement of a Convention right is itself an infringement of the Convention, and can be challenged as such. In the family migration context, those pleading Article 8 might be able to rely on Article 13 as the basis for an ECD. They might argue, for example, that an ECD should be made, since without it there would be a breach of their 'Convention rights' (Article 13, the right to an effective remedy), because legal aid is required to enable them to argue that their removal would breach Article 8 ECHR, and without legal aid there is no 'effective remedy'.

Article 13 will not help all those with whom we are concerned. It will probably not assist those whose applications rely on the Immigration Rules alone, as it requires another Convention right to be in play. In addition, the factors mentioned above in the discussion of Article 6 will need to be assessed to determine whether, on the particular facts of the case, refusal to grant legal aid in relation to an Article 8 claim might amount to a breach of Article 13. As a reminder, these factors include the complexity of the law or procedure, the capacity of the applicant to represent him or herself, and what is at stake for both sides. It is also worth noting that Article 13 was not implemented by the Human Rights Act, as it was assumed that the Act itself was the effective remedy.

EU Charter of Fundamental Rights

We have discussed above how an individual might establish that a failure to make an ECD would be a breach of their 'Convention rights'. However, an ECD must also be made if failure to do so would be a breach of 'enforceable EU rights'.

How might an 'enforceable EU right' to legal aid arise in the immigration context? The EU Charter of Fundamental Rights, Article 51, binds EU states to the provisions of the Charter when implementing EU law. Article 47 of the EU Charter sets out a right to an effective remedy and is based on Article 13 ECHR. However, Article 47 of the Charter is broader than Article 13 ECHR, and unique in its specific *mandatory* reference to legal aid where required to access justice meaningfully:

> Legal aid shall be made available to those who lack sufficient resources in so far as such aid is necessary to ensure effective access to justice.

Article 47 might therefore provide a right to legal aid where an immigration case is founded directly on EU law, but since the EU Charter largely imports ECHR concepts, the right to legal aid would not be absolute. This is also reflected in the wording of Article 47 (see above: 'in so far as such aid is necessary to ensure effective access to justice'). Individuals would need to demonstrate the particular reasons why a failure to grant legal aid would amount to a breach of Article 47, and why, in their particular circumstances, this is 'necessary'.

It is interesting to note the explanatory note to Article 47, which states:

> in Union law, the right to a fair hearing is not confined to disputes relating to civil law rights and obligations. That is one of the consequences of the fact that the Union is a community

based on the rule of law. Nevertheless, in all respects other than their scope, the guarantees afforded by the ECHR apply in a similar way to the Union.

Thus the reasoning in Maaouia v France falls away under the Charter. Disputes about issues the European Court of Human Rights has defined as concerning 'public law', such as immigration, fall squarely within the ambit of Article 47 as long as the member state is implementing EU law. A new line of authorities starting with *Zambrano*[42] raises the tantalising possibility of a wider conception of EU citizenship and its interplay with fundamental rights, which might, in the future, extend the reach of Article 47 to a broader category of cases. However this highly unstable and contradictory line of authorities has not yet reached its end point nor settled equilibrium.

Practical considerations

Unsurprisingly, there is much uncertainty about the operation of ECDs from all sides. The Government has indicated that it expects only a 'negligible' number of immigration cases to secure funding via an ECD.[44] However, it also acknowledges that 'administration costs might be higher than expected depending upon the cost of operating the new funding scheme for excluded cases'[45] (i.e. the scheme in relation to ECDs), and that 'the average cost of funding cases [via an ECD] might be higher than current case cost averages'.[46] Whilst the immigration practitioners we contacted did not seek to argue that all immigration cases raising Article 8 issues will qualify for a positive ECD, many consider the Government to have underestimated the numbers of cases where an ECD might be made. It seems likely, at least initially, wide arguments will be made (e.g. that all family migration cases, or all cases involving unaccompanied children, should qualify for an ECD). Richard Miller, Head of Legal Aid at the Law Society told us:

> we do believe that there may well be many more cases than the Government has calculated where representation is necessary to ensure ... effective access [to the Court as a litigant in person]. Cases where there is an interplay between family law and immigration law, which by definition will be more complex, are in my view more likely to be considered sufficiently difficult for a lay client that representation is required for effective access.

Decisions about whether to grant an ECD will have to be made on a case-by-case basis. If applications for ECDs are numerous, because large numbers qualify, there will be a large administrative burden on, and costs to, the Legal Aid Agency, and to legal aid suppliers, and this would be very inefficient for all concerned. It is likely that most applicants attempting to secure funding via an ECD on an exceptional basis will require the assistance of a legal representative: as is clear from the test, fairly sophisticated legal argument is required and an application is unlikely to be successful without such assistance. However, it is our view that there are strong disincentives for suppliers to make applications for ECDs. The work involved in taking relevant instructions from the client, perhaps marshalling evidence, and putting together an application for exceptional funding would be unremunerated by the Legal Aid Agency if the application were to be unsuccessful. The process of applying is likely to be onerous for legal aid suppliers in an area of work where rates of remuneration are low and where profit margins are extremely slim. The Law Society advises solicitor's firms:

> If you prepare an application for exceptional funding, there will be no payment for the work done on the application if it is not successful. Even if it is successful, you may find that the payment is inadequate. You should decide now if, and to what extent, you are going to spend time on such applications. You might opt for a blanket policy that you will always submit an application if the client requests it, or conversely that you will never do so. Most firms are likely to want to submit some applications. You may find it sensible to nominate one person,

> or a small group of people, who have the authority within your firm to decide that resources should be expended on an exceptional funding application, in order to control how much work your firm undertakes 'at risk'. (Law Society 2012)

Conclusions: exceptional cases

There will, no doubt, be judicial review challenges in the early stages of LASPO 2012's implementation of refusals to grant ECDs, since the outcome of applications will be critical for many applicants unable to pay their own legal fees. It may be that some cases will require reference to the ECJ for guidance, or litigation in the ECHR, given the criteria set out in s10 which makes explicit reference to 'Convention rights' and 'enforceable EU rights'. Our position is that it would be better for all concerned to have clear Article 13 compliant rules bringing within the scope of legal aid all immigration cases where Article 8 was in play, or at the very least those cases involving Article 8 where applicants met certain pre-determined criteria.

Part Three: Rationale

The Green Paper sets out the factors the Government asserts were taken into account in deciding what should be in and out of scope across the whole of the legal aid scheme: 'the importance of the issue, the litigant's ability to present their own case (including the venue before which the case is heard, the likely vulnerability of the litigant and the complexity of the law), the availability of alternative sources of funding and the availability of alternative routes to resolving the issue', as well as 'domestic, European and international legal obligations'.[47]

We have already examined (in Part Two, above) the UK's legal obligations in relation to family migration cases and legal aid, and argued why these obligations might suggest that at least some Article 8 cases should remain within scope. We have, in addition, explained why alternative sources of funding via charitable and voluntary sector organisations are an unrealistic option. Of course, Conditional Fee Agreements (*'no-win, no-fee'*) are not available in immigration cases. 'Alternative routes to resolving the issue' refers to other mechanisms of dispute resolution (e.g. family mediation), as well as to the use of complaints procedures and Ombudsmen services. Such 'alternatives' either have no place at all or do not have much to offer where family migration is concerned. We shall look at each of the remaining 'factors' in turn below, in considering whether, applying the Government's own decision-making matrix, family migration cases ought to have remained in scope.

Importance of the issue

A more detailed justification of the Government's position was set out in the Green Paper, and explains why asylum cases were considered to raise issues of sufficient importance to justify their remaining in scope, whereas immigration cases do not:

> these cases do not raise issues of such fundamental importance as asylum applications, where the issue at stake may be, literally, a matter of life and death. In contrast, to those cases, an individual involved in non-detention immigration cases will usually have made a *free and personal choice* to come to or remain in the UK, for example, where they wish to visit a family member in the UK, or to fulfil their desire to work or study here. We therefore consider that routine public funding is less likely to be justified.[48] (authors' emphasis)

While 'free and personal choice' may accurately characterise the position of those entering the UK to study, work or visit temporarily, such individuals would have been unlikely to qualify for legal aid in any event, either because the type of application they make is excluded from the scope of legal aid,[49] or because the financial requirements of the Immigration Rules mean that they would be unlikely to satisfy the means test for legal aid.[50]

In addition, it seems that 'personal choice', relevant to some immigration decisions, is being used to justify the denial of legal aid to a broader category of cases where it either has a limited role or no role at all. The Immigration Law Practitioners' Association's response to the Green Paper lists a number of examples of the types of immigration cases that will no longer qualify for legal aid after 1 April 2013, and which do not involve the individual making a 'free and personal choice' to live, work or study in the UK:

- Joining or remaining with a spouse, partner, child or parent;
- Whether a child/dependent who has lived in the UK for many years or even all his/her life must leave the UK as a result of the actions of a parent;
- ....
- The fate of unaccompanied asylum-seeking children (UASCs) who do not qualify for asylum but cannot be returned for reasons of welfare and safety;
- The fate of lone children who have been living in the UK once they turn 18; and
- Whether people who have lived in the UK for many years should be deported after serving their criminal sentence.[51]

A letter to the Immigration Law Practitioners' Association further explains the Government position:

> our proposals ... focus legal aid funding on circumstances where a person's life or liberty is at stake, where they are at risk of serious physical harm, or where they face immediate loss of their home. We do not consider that immigration cases fall into that category. Asylum cases, which remain in scope, do ...

It is our position that the Government has consistently underplayed the importance of family migration, involving as it does State decisions about whether husband and wife, partners, and / or parent and child should be allowed to join, reunite or remain with each other. Such decisions affecting the integrity of the family have a fundamental impact not only on each member of the family in question, but also on communities and society as a whole. There have been calls for the widespread problem of involuntary separation of families, the devastating impact it has on individuals and the long-term destructive impact it has on cultural groups and societies to receive increased attention as an issue of international human rights (Starr and Brilmayer 2003).

Family migration cases almost inevitably engage the fundamental right to private and family life protected by Article 8 of the European Convention on Human Rights (and the corresponding Article, Article 7 of the EU Charter of Fundamental Rights). They do so precisely because of the importance of such family bonds to the individuals concerned: Article 8 exists to protect a 'core value'.[52] As the House of Lords has acknowledged:

> Human beings are social animals. They depend on others. Their family, or extended family, is the group on which many people most heavily depend, socially, emotionally and often financially. There comes a point at which, for some, prolonged and unavoidable separation from this group seriously inhibits their ability to live full and fulfilling lives.[53]

However, Article 8 ECHR is not absolute.[54] Both domestically and in the European Court of Human Rights much attention has been paid to the articulation of Article 8(2) in immigration cases, and particularly the concept of 'proportionality'. It has been pointed out that, 'the case law of the UK courts prior to the decision of the House of Lords in

Huang reflected a much more conservative approach to Article 8 ECHR than that of the Strasbourg Court' (MacDonald and Toal 2010 p. 535) Since then, however, domestic decisions have realigned with those of the European Court of Human Rights. It is now well-settled that:

- there is no requirement of 'exceptionality' for an Article 8 family migration case to succeed;[55]
- the role of the court is not merely to review the decision of the UKBA, but to determine for itself the lawfulness of the decision[56] (in this respect the Government's recent attempt in July 2012 to circumscribe the scope and meaning of Article 8, and to prevent the court engaging in its own assessment of the proportionality of individual decisions,[57] has been ineffective[58]);
- Assuming the appellant's proposed removal would be disproportionate looking at the family unit as a whole, then each affected family member is to be regarded as a victim';[59]
- The 'ultimate question' by which the proportionality of the interference should be judged is 'whether the refusal of leave to enter or remain, in circumstances where the life of the family cannot reasonably be expected to be enjoyed elsewhere, taking full account of all considerations weighing in favour of the refusal, prejudices the family life of the applicant in a manner sufficiently serious to amount to a breach of the fundamental right protected by Article 8';
- The impact of removal on the 'rights attending' to the British citizenship of family members 'weigh heavily in the scales';[60]
- There is no requirement of 'insurmountable obstacles' to the enjoyment of family life elsewhere, the issue is whether it is it is 'reasonable' to expect the family members to leave with the appellant.[61]

The current legal position is perhaps best summarised in the following statement made by the Supreme Court:

> ... it will rarely be proportionate to uphold an order for removal of a spouse if there is a close and genuine bond with the other spouse and that spouse cannot reasonably be expected to follow the removed spouse to the country of removal, or if the effect of the order is to sever a genuine and subsisting relationship between parent and child.[62]

A high premium is thus placed by the Supreme Court on close and genuine bonds between spouses and between parent and child, regardless of the appellant's nationality, and this reflects the ECHR caselaw. It is clear, therefore, that judicially speaking the issue of family integrity in family migration cases is regarded as one of 'importance', and on many occasions will outweigh considerations such as the need for firm and fair immigration control.

One of the perplexing elements of the post-LASPO 2012 legal aid landscape is the disparity between areas of law, despite the Government's contention that it applied the same overarching factors to decisions about what would remain in scope and what would go out of scope. In the next section we contrast family migration cases with public law family cases: in public law family cases the concept of family integrity is a key element in the justification for the retention of legal aid.

Integrity of the family unit

Public family law cases remain in scope (although private family law cases do not). Typically public family law will involve the state intervening in a family to take children into care, where there are concerns about their safety or well-being. We think there are very significant parallels between some family migration cases (particularly those where separation of parent and child is contemplated) and public law family cases, since both involve state intervention in a family and the integrity of the family unit.

The Green Paper (MoJ 2010a, p.55) explains the rationale for retaining legal aid for public law family proceedings is as follows:

> In the Government's view, the issues at stake in these cases are extremely important, and the very emotional nature of the subject matter, and the personal circumstances of the individuals involved, will often make it difficult for them to present their own case. We recognise that families must have a practical means of taking part in proceedings brought by public authorities that affect the integrity of the family unit. We do not consider that there are viable alternatives to legal aid. We therefore consider that legal aid funding is justified ...

In our view, precisely the same factors apply in family migration cases. In family migration cases personal circumstances such as language barriers and cultural differences will make it difficult for the appellant to present their own case. The subject matter, if the integrity of the family unit is in issue, is likely to be equally emotional. The need for an investigation of the circumstances of the family, and for all relevant information to be before the decision-maker (whether the decision-maker is the Secretary of State or the court) will be similar. And importantly it is a public authority (the UKBA) whose intervention, via immigration control, is affecting the integrity of the family unit.

Public family law cases involve a consideration of 'the child's welfare' which is required to be 'the court's paramount consideration' by s 1(1) of the Children Act 1989. In immigration cases, there are similar statutory duties contained in the Borders, Citizenship and Immigration Act 2009, s 55(1) and (2). S 55 requires immigration authorities and the Secretary of State to discharge their functions 'having regard to the need to safeguard and promote the welfare of children who are in the United Kingdom'. There is statutory guidance regarding the implementation of these duties (UKBA and Department for Children, Schools and Families 2009), which must be followed unless there is good reason to depart from it (UKBA and Department for Children, Schools and Families 2009, s 55(3) and s 55(5).

In the important case of *ZH (Tanzania)* v *SSHD*,[63] the Supreme Court has held that the best interests of the child are to be taken into account as 'a primary consideration' in immigration cases concerning children who are in the UK. Contrasting s 1(1) Children Act 1989 and s 55 Borders, Citizenship and Immigration Act 2009, it held that there was a difference between, on the one hand, family cases which directly concern the child's upbringing, where the welfare of the child is the court's paramount consideration, and on the other hand, immigration decisions about where a child's parent is to live, which are not decisions which affects the child's upbringing '*directly*'[64] and where the best interests of the child can be outweighed by other factors. However, Lord Kerr made clear that in immigration cases, 'where the best interests of the child clearly favour a certain course, that course should be followed unless countervailing reasons of considerable force displace them'.

Looking forward to 1 April 2013, when family migration cases will go out of scope, how will the Secretary of State and her officials, and the courts, obtain the information they need to make s 55 compliant decisions, where families and unaccompanied minors are unrepresented? How far does the s 55 duty in relation to children place an obligation on the Secretary of State to consult with them and anyone else involved in their care, and investigate their circumstances, before making a decision? The statutory Guidance states that 'in order to safeguard and promote the welfare of individual children' children and young people should be 'listened to and what they have to say ... taken seriously and acted on' (UKBA and Department for Children, Schools and Families 2009, p. 11). Work with children and families should be 'child centred', 'rooted in child development'; 'multi and inter-agency in its approach' and 'informed by evidence' (UKBA and Department for Children, Schools and Families 2009, p. 11). The Guidance goes on to state,

> Children should be consulted and the wishes and feelings of children taken into account whenever practicable when decisions affecting them are made, even though it will not always be possible to reach decisions with which the child will agree. In instances where parents and carers are present they will have primary responsibility for the children's concerns. (UKBA and Department for Children, Schools and Families, 2009, p. 15)

Unaccompanied children

What is the position of lone/unaccompanied child migrants, who either have not made a claim for asylum, or whose claim has been unsuccessful? Any application they wish to make, other than a fresh claim for asylum, will fall out of scope for legal aid purposes after 1 April 2013; although some children in this position might be able to establish legal aid eligibility via an ECD if they were making an application relying on Article 8 ECHR (see Part Two). Simon Cliff, Legal Aid Policy Officer at the Law Society told us, 'Of particular concern are unaccompanied children who are not asylum seekers. Local authorities may have a duty to provide legal advice for some of those in care, but this is just a transfer of costs from central to local government.'

The Government appears to be considering exempting local authorities from the need to be regulated by OISC[65] so that they can provide immigration advice to children accommodated by them:

> The majority of unaccompanied children are asylum seekers and will continue to be eligible for legal aid. Where non-asylum immigration issues arise, children will rarely be applicants … and will normally be considered as part of their parents' application and these should generally be straightforward. A child's parent or guardian will be able to assist them in the practicalities of making an application. I understand your concerns that some non-asylum claims are brought by children on Article 8 grounds and that these may not always be as straightforward as other immigration cases. However, the government position remains that the applicant's life and liberty is not at stake in these cases and so they will not be eligible for legal aid.[66]

The letter continues:

> the Home Office will work with the OISC on how best to ensure that Local Authorities can assist children in their care with immigration applications. This could mean exempting Local Authorities from OISC regulation but this is only one of the options.[67]

We would be alarmed at the idea of Local Authorities acting as advisors to the children in their care, or even having the responsibility for paying for such advice. Quite apart from the obvious concerns about their expertise there is an arguable conflict of interest, since the local authority will be paying for the child's maintenance, but only if they remain in the UK (Valdez 2012). It seems that within the current legal aid system, the Legal Services Commission has accepted that there might be a conflict of interest between the local authority supporting an unaccompanied minor claiming asylum, and the minor, and that therefore the local authority should not be expected to meet the minor's legal costs (Legal Services Commission undated, Chapter 29, para. 29.11(2)).[68]

Consideration must be given to the need for the child's interests to be considered separately and for the views of the child to be represented adequately:[69]

> Questions may have to be asked about the situation of other family members, especially children, and about their views. It cannot be assumed that the interests of all the family members are

> identical. In particular, a child is not to be held responsible for the moral failures of either of his parents. Sometimes, further information may be required. If the Child and Family Court Advisory and Support Service or, more probably, the local children's services authority can be persuaded to help in difficult cases, then so much the better.[70]

Equally in the case of *ZH (Tanzania)* v *SSHD [2011] UKSC 4*, the Supreme Court countenanced the possibility that in some cases, the child might need to be separately represented:

> There are circumstances in which separate representation of a child in legal proceedings about her future is essential: in this country, this is so when a child is to be permanently removed from her family in her own best interests. There are other circumstances in which it may be desirable, as in some disputes between parents about a child's residence or contact. In most cases, however, it will be possible to obtain the necessary information about the child's welfare and views in other ways.[71]

It is at least possible that the UKBA and the courts will have to adopt a more investigative and inquisitorial approach in family migration cases involving children in order properly to comply with their s 55 duties. Where legal aid used to pay lawyers to investigate what evidence might be obtained in support of a family's case, and put this forward in a structured and intelligible format, other Government budgets may have to find resources to pay staff to perform a similar function. This would, of course, simply involve a transfer of costs to the UKBA and court system, and the net cost savings might be minimal or costs might increase. We will return to this theme in Part Four.

Litigants' ability to present their own cases

The Green Paper mentions 'the venue before which the case is heard', 'the likely vulnerability of the litigant' and 'the complexity of the law' as relevant issues.

Venue

The Immigration and Asylum Chamber remains a highly adversarial forum. It is therefore ill equipped to deal with high numbers of litigants in person. The procedure rules that govern the way the Tribunal operates[72] and supporting common law authorities do not allow Tribunal judges to investigate and obtain evidence, unlike other systems in Italy or Germany, or indeed other chambers of the Tribunal, such as the Social Entitlement Chamber.[73] Moreover a key imperative[74] of the Asylum and Immigration Chamber is the aim[75] to deliver swift decisions.

Vulnerability of the litigant

The personal circumstances of most migrants are such that they will be less able to present their case as a result of their background, socio-economic status and the fact that English will usually be their second language, at best. They may be vulnerable by reason of age (e.g. unaccompanied children or older people), or past experiences (e.g. a history of persecution, trauma, domestic violence, trafficking, enslavement or mental illness). Equality of arms is a very real concern; the family migrant is particularly disadvantaged by the disparity between their own resources and the resources and expertise at the Secretary of State's disposal.

Complexity of the law

Much of immigration law is rule-bound, highly complex and difficult to understand, even for judges and experienced practitioners. There is no consolidating legislation, and so many overlapping Acts of Parliament must be consulted, all potentially relevant and with an interrelationship that is, at best, obscure. It is also highly politicised, and involves fundamental human rights, thus the plethora of enactments, as well as litigation in the higher courts. Immigration law is arguably more susceptible to on-going development and reform than any other field of law. As Lord Taylor of Holbeach recently remarked in the House of Lords' 'no area is more complex than the whole business of the Immigration Rules and the procedures surrounding them' (Hansard, col. 1087).

If this were not enough, since the Green Paper' the Government has implemented far-reaching reforms to the Immigration Rules in relation to family migration cases. A UK-based sponsor wishing to sponsor a non-EEA partner is now required to have a minimum income of £18,600 per annum, rising to £22,400 per annum if a child is to accompany the partner, with an extra £2400 required for each additional child. There are complicated evidential requirements,[76] and fees for making applications are steep. There are rules of evidence which restrict, in certain circumstances, new evidence from being submitted in support of an appeal, so it is vital that applicants understand the documents they need to submit at the time they make their initial application.

It is clear from the documentation that accompanied the changes to the Immigration Rules that the government is targeting communities that practise 'chain migration'; it has been observed that:

> Immigration control has, for many years, separated families, using a variety of rationalisations ... Those most affected are families who operate an extended or 'corporate' family life, often, although not exclusively, of South Asian origin. (Wray 2009, p. 2)

Elderly dependent relatives, including parents, who wish to join their adult child in the UK must meet new requirements, and demonstrate firstly that they require a level of long term personal care as a result of age, illness disability, and secondly that this long term personal care can only be provided by their relative in the UK. There are, in addition, new rules governing the position of those facing deportation, which again are almost impossible for a lay person to comprehend.

The Government also attempted to oust the court's role in reviewing the proportionality of article 8 decisions (unsuccessfully it now appears), and created an 'exceptional' category for those applying on the basis of Article 8 ECHR in certain restricted circumstances.

These new Rules are in the early stages of examination by the courts, and their precise meaning and remit remains unclear. However, what is clear is that the minimum income threshold for partners will act as an insuperable barrier for many non-EEA spouses, civil partners and unmarried couples. Their only option will be to rely on Article 8 ECHR, which is complex to argue and evidentially laborious to prepare.

Part Four: Costs savings?

Since the principal motive for the legal aid reforms contained in LASPO 2012 is to make substantial savings in legal aid expenditure, in order to contribute to the government's deficit reduction target, this part of the paper will examine whether the changes are likely to achieve this.

It is more than a possibility that money spent on legal aid, and more particularly money spent on high quality legal advice (Gibb 2010),[77] produces a cost saving overall. We have already discussed the relevance of the duties imposed on the Secretary of State and other immigration authorities by s 55 (in Part Three above), and the additional costs that may occur from investigative duties in the absence of legal aid. The CAB has calculated that for every £1 of legal aid spent, money is saved overall, ranging from £2.34 per £1 of housing advice to £8.80 saved per £1 of benefits advice (Citizens Advice 2010). According to the All-Party Parliamentary Review on Migration, the legal aid reforms will result in an increased demand at MPs surgeries, higher numbers of litigants in person and a potential increase in the number of foreign nationals with irregular status (Immigration Advice, Regulation and the Legal Aid, Sentencing and Punishment of Offenders Bill 2012). The Ministry of Justice Impact Assessments concluded that the reforms will reduce access to justice, reduce fairness of dispute resolution and impose wide socio-economic costs such as an increase in crime, a reduction of social cohesion and reduced efficiency of other government services. (Legal Aid Reform 2010, para. 35). Simon Cliff, Law Society, told us 'There will certainly be knock-on costs, perhaps in relation to the NHS, education and perhaps the criminal justice system arising from the stresses and other problems that are experienced by divided families.'

We know that spending sufficient time to exercise knowledge and expertise and build a good relationship with the client is an essential ingredient to quality (James 2012; see also Trude and Gibbs 2010). The Early Legal Advice Pilot in Solihull concerned asylum cases, but its lessons have wide applicability in our view. A review of the project indicated that high quality early legal advice (Trude and Gibbs 2010), front-loading of cases and a high-level of participation on the part of legal representatives in the asylum application process leads to more sustainable decisions, a consequent reduction of allowed appeals and potential to make large savings on court time and on legal aid costs (Aspden 2008). There was a greater level of acceptance on the part of the loser where the decision-making process had been fair and transparent (Asylum Aid undated). The experience from the Early Legal Advice Pilot therefore shows that there are considerably wider costs savings to be made where there is good quality decision-making and representation early on in the process.

Self-represented Litigants and increased court time

Immigration practitioners, the Law Society and Judges are united in their opinion that litigants require more court time. Richard Miller, Head of Legal Aid at the Law Society, made the following points to us with reference to the effect of LASPO 2012 on family cases, and his remarks are equally applicable to immigration cases:

> We think that there will be significant knock-on costs to the Government as a result of these cuts... We think the impact of litigants in person is going to much worse than the Government has realised... We think the Government has misunderstood the role lawyers play in family cases. Key among the things lawyers do are persuading clients to focus only on relevant issues... presenting concise and pertinent arguments to the Court, explaining the procedures and the law to the client... When lawyers are removed from the system next April, what they do, which is presently largely invisible, will suddenly become apparent. We believe the impact on the Courts will be very problematic, and not just for the litigants in person and the judges. It will have a knock-on effect on privately-paying clients, whose hearings will be delayed or adjourned, and who will have to wait longer for hearing dates, because of the impact on Court time of the litigants in person.

Increased court time equates to higher costs, so higher numbers of self-represented litigants in the first and second tiers of the Immigration and Asylum Chamber will result in a more expensive tribunal system. Judges will have to call evidence that would otherwise have been elicited in the form of a witness statement by the appellant's legal representative.

It is notable that the impact on judicial time is far greater in immigration proceedings than in most other areas of law. Firstly appellants are less likely to understand the process and what is required of them in preparing their appeal as English may not be their first language. Secondly many, if not most, appellants require interpreters for the appeal hearing itself, which more than doubles the time taken to call evidence-in-chief. As Jawaid Luqmani, a solicitor practising at a senior level in the field of immigration and asylum, explains:

> ... it is possible that costs will end up being increased since the cost of judicial time spent considering an appeal is likely to be several times higher than the cost of a lawyer ensuring that the correct application is supported by the best evidence to optimise the greatest chance of an application succeeding.

The need for adjournments will probably also increase, as most appellants will not appreciate what type of evidence they need to gather in support of their appeal until the judge asks them if they have such evidence.

Mr Justice Blake, President of the Upper Tribunal of the Asylum and Immigration Chamber, has stated that judges of the upper tribunal need competent representatives for both parties to do their task and that targeted grounds of appeal enable them to do their task better.[78] Mr Justice Hodge, former President of the Immigration and Asylum Tribunal, stated, in 2006:

> The AIT and its judges ... value representation and we want as many people to be legally represented as possible ... The numbers of people who are unrepresented in front of immigration judges have gone up, largely because of the operation of the merits test. It causes particular problems for our judges in fast-track cases, in asylum cases, and *the hearings do extend as a result of that*.'[79] (authors' emphasis)

Richard Moorhead,[80] whose research was cited by the Ministry of Justice in the original Green Paper has stated:

> What the research essentially shows is not that litigants in person gum up the courts with vexatious cases and applications (though some do) but that most struggle to participate in their cases if they participate at all. Where they do participate, the evidence suggests they do so sporadically; they sometimes damage their own interests as a result; and they probably create more work for their opponents and the courts themselves. The main impact of reforms which reduce the number of represented litigants will be to reduce the number of cases that are brought or defended as Mr Clarke rightly identified, but where LiPs do not [sic.] participate they will increase the workload of opponents, court staff and judges. (Moorhead 2010)

Part Five: The regulation of the quality of advice

It is well recognised that at least some immigrants are particularly vulnerable to poor quality advice and ill-equipped to recognise it and to take action to protect themselves. This may be because of language problems and cultural differences, low levels of education or lack of legal literacy, or because of the nature of the advice needed (for example, those claiming asylum, or those with significant health problems). We have already discussed above the rather complex picture in terms of quality legal advice: although it may cost more in the short term, in the longer term costs savings may be procured.

Attempts to improve quality have not been entirely successful, and poor quality representation persists. It is a frequent complaint of judges at all levels regarding the quality of legal representatives who appear before them. Mr Justice Collins has stated, '... sadly, a lot of incompetent people ... deal with immigration cases, and some of them may be worse than incompetent'.[81] Where representation is poor, it can be more harmful than not having representation at all, especially considering that the errors of a legal adviser can be held against their client. As an experienced judge of the Immigration and Asylum Chamber told us anonymously:[82]

> a major issue as a judge is that representatives are often so poor it would be better not to have them as we are then constrained to listen to them and let them conduct the appeal and not to explore the case in our own way with the appellant.

At the current time, it is arguable that the Legal Services Commission acts as a *de facto* regulator of immigration and asylum advice where immigration services are funded by legal aid. It requires all advisers, whether they are qualified solicitors or unqualified caseworkers, to be 'accredited' if their work is to be remunerated by legal aid. It has other quality control mechanisms, including the auditing of organisations and of files and a system of peer review, which we described in our introduction. Whereas privately paid immigration representatives are not subject to these accreditation and supervision requirements.

We have explained that charitable and voluntary organisations are unlikely to step in to fill the legal aid gap, especially given the regulatory hurdles they would face. Thus it is likely that the thousands of individuals whose cases will fall out of scope after 1 April 2013 will have to pay for legal advice, if they are not to represent themselves. The Legal Services Board has expressed its concerns about the adequacy of the current regulators, chiefly the Bar Standards Board and the Solicitors Regulatory Authority, properly to regulate the quality of such privately paid immigration advice, and their 'seeming reliance on the Legal Services Commission (LSC) to manage the risks presented in the market, even though legal aid funds only a small and diminishing portion of the market' (Legal Services Board 2010). It was so concerned that it insisted that the regulators 'must identify what needs to be done to ensure satisfactory quality ... by all those who provide immigration advice and services' and, 'mechanisms for identifying and stopping advisers who provide unsatisfactory levels of quality'. It set out the minimum steps required in some detail, and made it clear that simply relying on their codes of conduct was insufficient to 'offer protection of all consumers, including those of immigration advice and services'. In addition, the Legal Services Board stated it would monitor progress and threatened enforcement action, including the possibility of removal of qualifying regulator status. It remains to be seen whether these steps are sufficient, and many are concerned that quality will suffer after April 2013.

Conclusion

Marshall's seminal theory included the proposition that the right to justice is a fundamental component of the welfare state, as without it, other rights are illusory (Marshall 1950, pp. 10–11). A social democratic state requires a system of empowering rights and obligations (Held 1995), concerned with respect for the dignity, integrity and equal moral worth of all persons and groups, enabled by substantive legal mechanisms which support the right to 'full participation' (Selznick 1999), or 'parity of recognition'.

As discussed, LASPO 2012 represents a significant dismantling of the system of public funding for legal advice services for those without the means to pay: for migrants requesting entry clearance, who are currently separated from their family, it may mean that reunification takes longer, or perhaps that it does not happen at all. For migrants facing deportation or removal, it may mean that they are separated from family members without a proper hearing of the factual and legal issues in their case. Given the introduction of extraordinarily complicated amendments to the Immigration Rules in July 2012, this is particularly harsh. Most such applicants will have no access to legal advice about the meaning of the Rules and their proper application to family circumstances, because they will not be able to pay for this. They will also not be eligible for legal aid representation to test the proper interpretation of the new Immigration Rules. When these changes are considered in the wider context of appeal lodgement fees making it expensive to bring appeals and the narrowing of the scope of appeal rights both leading to dwindling numbers of appeals, the abolition of appeal rights for family visitors in 2014 and the frequently poor quality of privately funded legal representation (the only alternative for funding such cases) it is clear that LASPO deals an all but fatal blow to family migrants' right to access justice and an effective remedy. Indeed, some characterise the dismantling of legal aid in such family migration cases as 'the unilateral forced disarmament' of the weakest side in a highly adversarial system.[83]

Notes

1. Commonwealth Immigrants Act 1962 (c.21).
2. Peer review is undertaken by experienced legal aid practitioners working for the Legal Services Commission. The peer reviewer assesses a random sample of case files, to measure the quality of advice and legal work carried out by a legal aid provider. The rating awarded by the peer reviewer is used to make decisions about future contracts, etc.
3. The Specialist Quality Mark audit involves the periodic attendance by employees of the Legal Services Commission to inspect not just individual files but also management and financial systems. Contract Compliance Audits require a certain (small) number of files to be sent to the Legal Services Commission, which are then reviewed. The accuracy of billing is minutely examined – and any over-billing extrapolated to calculate an amount to be 'recouped' from the organisation concerned.
4. The Law Society's Immigration and Asylum Law Accreditation Scheme is a scheme which accredits individual advisors. Only work done by those accredited via this scheme is remunerated by the Legal Services Commission, making it compulsory for legal aid immigration and asylum practitioners since 2005.
5. Typical disbursements in this area of work would be the professional fees of interpreters, medical experts, country experts, and barristers. These have to be met by legal practices as the case progresses, and once stage billing was removed would only be reimbursed at the end of the matter by the LSC. Many cases were long running due to Home Office delay, so payment could be delayed for years.
6. Formerly known as the 'Refugee Legal Centre'.
7. Killick and James (2009, p. 13) suggest that 'case workers find themselves caught in the middle, squeezed between increasing financial pressures and their ethical obligation to their clients', and that the tightening in the provision of legal aid threatened the continued existence of many of the UK's law centres and non-profit organisations.
8. The Immigration and Asylum Act 1999 set up the regulatory scheme, and created the post of Immigration Services Commissioner. Immigration 'advice' and 'services' in England and Wales may only be provided by those authorised by a 'qualifying regulator', by those regulated directly by the Office for the Immigration Services Commissioner or those exempted by ministerial order. The Immigration and Asylum Act 1999 also created new criminal offences. Providing any immigration 'advice' or 'services' not regulated amounts to a criminal offence if carried out in the 'course of a business' (which is defined to include the work of not-for-profit organisations).
9. Qualifying regulators are listed at Schedule 4 of the 2007 Act, and include the Law Society of England and Wales, the General Council of the Bar, and the Chartered Institute of Legal Executives. Their regulatory bodies, the Solicitors Regulation Authority, Bar Standards Board and Institute of Legal Executives Professional Standards, carry out the regulatory work.
10. Figures are relative to a 2009–2010 baseline, and appear to assume that the only immigration cases remaining in scope are challenges to immigration detention, and not to have taken into account changes to the LASPO 2012 scheme reintroducing legal aid for those making domestic violence applications and victims of trafficking. However, trafficking and domestic violence applications are likely to be small in number. (MoJ 2012, para. 10).
11. LASPO 2012, s 9.

12. Provided, *inter alia*, the applicant can locate a legal aid provider with capacity to take on their case, and provided the merits and the means tests are satisfied.
13. LASPO 2012 Part 1, Schedule 1, Part 1, paragraph 30: rights to enter and remain in the UK arising from the Convention relating to the Status of Refugees (UN General Assembly 1951); Articles 2 or 3 of the European Convention on Human Rights (Council of Europe 1950) Convention (Council of Europe, 1950); the Temporary Protection Directive (Council Directive 2001/55/EC); or the Qualification Directive (Council Directive 2004/83/EC).
14. LASPO 2012 Part 1, Schedule 1, Paras 25–27.
15. LASPO 2012 Part 1, Schedule 1, Para. 28.
16. Under regulation 10(5) of the Immigration (European Economic Area) Regulations 2006 (S.I. 2006/1003).
17. Restricted by LASPO 2012 schedule 1, Part 1 para. 32 (1) to applications for leave to enter or remain where 'there has been a conclusive determination that the individual is a victim of trafficking in human beings, or there are reasonable grounds to believe that the individual is such a victim and there has not yet been a conclusive determination that the individual is not such a victim'. Para. 32(6) and (7) further provide that the reference to 'determination' refers to a determination by a 'competent authority' under the Trafficking Convention (Council of Europe 2005), and that whether or not there are 'reasonable grounds to believe' is to be determined by a competent authority.
18. LASPO 2012, Part 1, Schedule 1, Para. 24.
19. LASPO 2012, Part 1, Schedule 1, Para. 31.
20. But, as was the case before April 2013, legal aid will not to be available for representation before the First Tier Tribunal (Asylum Support) in relation to appeals in such matters.
21. LASPO 2012, Part 1, Schedule 1, Para. 19.
22. LASPO 2012, Part 1, Schedule1, Para. 20.
23. Note that specific provisions ensure that judicial review remains in scope in asylum cases 'where there is no right of appeal to the First-tier Tribunal against the decision' (LASPO 2012, Part 1 Schedule 1, para.19(7)) (most likely to be fresh claims for asylum under para. 353 of the Immigration Rules) and 'of certification under section 94 or 96 of the Nationality, Immigration and Asylum Act 2002' (LASPO 2012, Part 1 Schedule 1, para. 19(7)(b)) (such certificates prevent appeals where an asylum or human rights claim is 'clearly unfounded', or where the decision could have been appealed against before).
24. LASPO 2012, Part 1, Schedule 1, Para. 19(5)(a).
25. LASPO 2012, Part 1, Schedule 1, Para. 19(5)(b).
26. LASPO 2012, Part 1, Schedule 1, Para. 19(5)(c).
27. LASPO 2012, Part 1, Schedule 1, Para. 19(6).
28. Which will be defined by the Civil Legal Aid (Merits Criteria) Regulations 2012, currently in draft form.
29. LASPO 2012, s 10.
30. *Steel and Morris* v *UK*, 68416/01 [2005] ECHR 103; *Alkan* v. *Turkey*, 17725/07 [2012] ECHR 233.
31. 39652/98 [2000] ECHR 455 (5 October 2000).
32. See, for example, the judgement of the Court of Appeal in ***R*** *(on the Application of) MK(Iran)* v *SSHD [2010]* EWCA Civ 115 (where, interestingly, Sedley LJ applied slightly different reasoning to the other members of the Court of Appeal, and thought perhaps *Maaouia* v *France* might not be applicable to asylum cases, and in any event should be re-examined by the ECtHR in light of the Qualification Directive (Council Directive 2004/83/EC).); and *MNM* v *Secretary of State for the Home Department* (2000) INLR 576 IAT.
33. See, for example, *Matfah* v *FCO* [2011] EWCA Civ 350, per Sedley LJ, para. 14: 'The only thing which is certain is that civil rights in article 6 have an autonomous meaning. The Strasbourg court has made this clear on more than one occasion. What is neither certain nor clear is what that meaning is.'
34. *Matfah* v *FCO* [2011] EWCA Civ 350, per Sedley LJ, para. 24, holding that the making or procuring of a freezing order is a discharge of public functions, albeit with a dramatic impact on the civil rights of individuals.
35. 'I agree that we have to dismiss this appeal, but I do so with considerable reluctance. Mr Bedford has advanced a formidable argument that article 13 of the Qualification Directive has introduced into EU law, and hence into the law of all EU member states, an affirmative right to

asylum. The obligation which the article spells out may be a public law duty, but it is an obligation which arguably generates a correlative individual right. In the domestic law of the United Kingdom and, I suspect, in civil law systems likewise, it is not easy to see how such a right, if it exists, can be anything but a civil right.' Sedley LJ in *MK (Iran)*, para. 70.

36. See, for example, 'I see no reason to depart from the constant case-law of the Commission that, because of the substantial discretionary and public-order element in such decisions, proceedings relating to them are not to be seen as determining the civil rights of the person concerned, even if they inevitably but incidentally have major repercussions on his private and family life, prospects of employment, financial position and the like ... ' (*Maaouia* v *France*, concurring opinion of Sir Nicolas Bratza).
37. Gearty (2004, pp. 111–112): 'the effect of this in many cases has been as insistence on due process which has had the effect of inhibiting the regulation of property by the state'.
38. In *Odelola* v *SSHD* [2009] UKHL 25, paras 6–7, per Lord Justice Hoffman, 'The status of the immigration rules is rather unusual. They are not subordinate legislation but detailed statements by a minister of the Crown as how the Crown proposes to exercises its executive power to control immigration. But they create legal rights: under section 84(1) of the Nationality, Immigration and Asylum Act 2002, one may appeal against an immigration decision on the ground that it is not in accordance with the immigration rules' per Lord Hoffman, paras 6–7.
39. With some limited exceptions: see, for example, its application in cases where an individual's removal would severely hamper their ability to bring civil proceedings in the UK, *R* v *Immigration Officer ex parte Quahquah* [2000] INLR 196.
40. *R (on the Application of) MK(Iran)* v *SSHD [2010]* EWCA Civ 115, where the Court of Appeal was unanimous that there was a strong imperative not to move ahead of Strasbourg's jurisprudence, citing Lord Bingham in Ahsan Ullah v Special Adjudicator; Thi Lien Do v Secretary of State for the Home Department [2002] EWCA Civ 185.
41. See European Parliament and Council Directive 2004/38/EC.
42. *Ruiz Zambrano (European citizenship)* [2011] EUECJ C-34/09 (08 March 2011).
43. *McCarthy (European citizenship)* [2011] EUECJ C-434/09 (05 May 2011).
44. Impact Assessment, Annex A: Scope, para. 10, Table 3.
45. Impact Assessment, Annex A: Scope, para. 37.
46. Impact Assessment, Annex A: Scope, para. 37.
47. Proposals for the Reform of Legal Aid in England and Wales, Consultation Paper CP12/10, Ministry of Justice, November 2010.
48. Para. 4.201, Green Paper.
49. Access to Justice Act 1999, Schedule 2.
50. ILPA Response to Ministry of Justice Consultation: Proposals for the Reform of Legal Aid in England and Wales, p. 7.
51. ILPA Consultation Response at p. 8.
52. *Huang* v *SSHD* [2007] UKHL 11, para. 18.
53. *Huang* v *SSHD* [2007] UKHL 11, para. 18. We might equally have quoted any nunber of academic sources: 'Families are the lifeblood of our communities – the place where dreams are born, children are nurtured, adults find purpose, and life challenges are weathered' (Rice 1994).
54. Article 8(2) ECHR.
55. *Huang* v *SSHD* [2007] UKHL 11, para. 20.
56. *Huang* v *SSHD* [2007] UKHL 11, paras 11 and 13.
57. HC 194, Statement of Changes to the Immigration Rules, 7/7/2012.
58. *MF (Article 8 – new rules) Nigeria* [2012] UKUT 00393(IAC).
59. *Beoku-Betts (FC) v Secretary of State for the Home Department* [2008] UKHL 39.
60. *VW (Uganda)* v *SSHD* [2009] EWCA Civ 5.
61. *EB (Kosovo) (FC) v Secretary of State for the Home Department* [2008] UKHL 4.
62. *EB (Kosovo) (FC) v Secretary of State for the Home Department* [2008] UKHL 41.
63. [2011] UKSC 4.
64. Baroness Hale, *ZH (Tanzania)* v *SSHD* [2011] UKSC 4.
65. See the introduction to this paper, where the regulation of immigration advice was discussed.
66. Letter from the Rt Hon the Lord Wallace of Tankerness QC to the Immigration Law Practitioner's Association, 26 March 2012.

67. Letter from the Rt Hon the Lord Wallace of Tankerness QC to the Immigration Law Practitioner's Association, 26 March 2012.
68. Note, that as Valdez (2012, p. 7) points out, this paragraph of the funding code is 'poorly drafted', and the reasoning is opaque.
69. *EM (Lebanon)* [2008] UKHL 64.
70. Per Lady Hale at para. 49.
71. Per Lady Hale at para. 35.
72. The Asylum and Immigration Tribunal (Procedure) Rules 2005 (as amended); SI 2005/230, hereinafter referred to as 'The Procedure Rules'.
73. The Tribunal Procedure (First-tier Tribunal) (Social Entitlement Chamber) Rules 2008 SI 2685/2008.
74. Rule 4 of the Procedure Rules.
75. Albeit one that is often not achieved.
76. Although 'UKBA case workers and decision makers must be aware of and give full effect to its "Evidential Flexibility" policy document. This requires due appreciation of the discretionary powers enshrined therein to request further information from applicants in any case and the exercise thereof in accordance with established legal principles viz the duties to appreciate the existence of and correctly understand and give effect to the policy; to act fairly and rationally; to take into account all material considerations; to disregard immaterial considerations; to observe the requirements of a procedurally fair decision making process; and to act compatibly with such ECHR rights as may be engaged in a particular case, in accordance with section 6 of the Human Rights Act 1998' (*Rodriguez (Flexibility Policy*) [2013] UKUT 00042 (IAC)).
77. This found in relation to asylum-seekers that although quality work costs, poor quality work costs more in the longer term both to the public purse and in human terms. In addition, quality work is more likely to achieve early resolution of the case, thus saving money in the long term. There is a correlation between cost and quality and between quality and successful outcomes.
78. Speaking at the Annual Conference of the OISC (Office of the Immigration Services Commissioner), on 6 December 2010.
79. Giving evidence before the Constitutional Affairs Committee, 21 March 2006 (Constitutional Affairs Committee 2006). http://www.publications.parliament.uk/pa/cm200506/cmselect/cmconst/1006/6032103.htm
80. Director of the Centre for Ethics and Law, Professor of Law and Professional Ethics at the Faculty of Laws, University College London.
81. Giving evidence before the Constitutional Affairs Committee, Tuesday 21 March 2006. http://www.publications.parliament.uk/pa/cm200506/cmselect/cmconst/1006/6032103.htm
82. On 17 October 2012.
83. Colin Yeo, immigration barrister at Rennaissance Chambers, speaking at a Refugee Law Initiative seminar in London on 14 March 2013.

References

All Party Parliamentary Group on Migration, 2012. *Immigration Advice, Regulation and the Legal Aid, Sentencing and Punishment of Offenders Bill* [online]. Available from: http://www.appgmigration.org.uk/sites/default/files/APPG_Migration-Legal_Aid_BP-Feb_2012.pdf [Accessed 15 November 2012].

Aspden, J., 2008. Evaluation of the Solihull Pilot for the UKBA and the LSC, commissioned by the LSC and the UKBA [online], Available from: http://www.asylumaid.org.uk/data/files/publications/137/Solihull_Pilot.pdf [Accessed 15 November 2012].

Asylum Aid, undated. *Asylum Aid policy Briefing. Early legal advice for asylum seekers* [online]. Available from: http://www.asylumaid.org.uk/data/files/ELAPbrief.pdf [Accessed 15 November 2012].

BBC News, 2010. *Migrant charity in administration amid cash problems* [online]. Available from: http://www.bbc.co.uk/news/10324774 [Accessed 15 November 2012].

BBC News, 2011. *Immigration Advisory Service goes into administration* [online]. Available from: http://www.bbc.co.uk/news/uk-14105065 [Accessed 15 November 2012].

Citizens Advice Bureau, 2010. *Towards a Business Case for Legal Aid* [online]. Available from: http://www.citizensadvice.org.uk/towards_a_business_case_for_legal_aid.pdf [Accessed 15 November 2012].

Civil Legal Aid (Merits Criteria) Regulations 2012 (draft).

Constitutional Affairs Committee, 2006. *Asylum and Immigration* [online]. Available from: http://www.publications.parliament.uk/pa/cm200506/cmselect/cmconst/1006/6032103.htm [Accessed 7 January 2013].

Council Directive 2001/55/EC of 20 July 2001 on minimum standards for giving temporary protection in the event of a mass influx of displaced persons and on measures promoting a balance of efforts between Member States in receiving such persons and bearing the consequences thereof.

Council Directive 2004/83/EC of 29 April 2004 on minimum standards for the qualification and status of third country nationals or stateless persons as refugees or as persons who otherwise need international protection and the content of the protection granted.

Council of Europe, 1950. European Convention on Human Rights, as amended by Protocols Nos. 11 and 14, ETS 5.

Council of Europe, 2005. *Council of Europe Convention on Action Against Trafficking in Human Beings*, CETS 197.

Elson, A., 1946. The Rushcliffe Report. *The University of Chicago Law Review*, 13 (2), 131–144.

Fraser, N., 1995. From Redistribution to Recognition? Dilemmas of Justice in the 'Post-Socialist' Age. *New Left Review*, 212, 68–94.

Gearty, C., 2004. *Principles of Human Rights Adjudication*. Oxford: Oxford University Press.

Gibb, J., June 2010. *Justice at Risk: quality and value for money in asylum legal aid. Interim Report* [online]. Available from: http://www.asylumaid.org.uk/data/files/publications/135/Justice_at_Risk.pdf [Accessed 15 November 2012].

Held, D., 1995. *Democracy and the Global Order*. Cambridge: Polity Press.

House of Lords, 2012. *Hansard*, 12 December, Column 1087 [online] Available from: http://www.publications.parliament.uk/pa/ld201213/ldhansrd/text/121212-0001.htm [Accessed 15 November 2012].

Immigration (European Economic Area) Regulations, 2006. SI 2006/1003.

Immigration Law Practitioners' Association, 2010. *ILPA briefing for adjournment debate on legal aid 15 December 2010* [online]. Available from: http://www.ilpa.org.uk/data/resources/12850/10-12-15-ILPA-Briefing-Adjournment-debate-legal-aid-_2_.pdf [Accessed 15 November 2012].

Immigration Law Practitioners' Association, 2011. *ILPA Response to Ministry of Justice Consultation: Proposals for the Reform of Legal Aid in England and Wales* [online]. Available from: http://www.ilpa.org.uk/data/resources/4121/11.02.503.pdf [Accessed 15 November 2012].

James, D., 2012. Empathy and Expertise: Case Workers and Immigration / Asylum Applicants in London. *Law & Social Inquiry*, 37 (2), 430–455.

Killick, E. and James, D., 2009. Ethical dilemmas? UK immigration, legal aid funding reform and caseworkers. *Anthropology Today*, 26 (1), 13–15.

Law Society, 2012. *Preparing for LASPO: things you should be doing today* [online]. Available at: http://www.lawsociety.org.uk/advice/articles/preparing-for-laspo–things-you-should-be-doing-today/ [Accessed 7 January 2012].

Legal Services Board, 2012. *Regulation of immigration advice and services - Summary of responses to consultation and LSB response* [online]. Available from: http://www.legalservicesboard.org.uk/what_we_do/consultations/closed/pdf/20120727_reg_if_imm_advice_to_publish.pdf [Accessed 7 January 2012].

Legal Services Commission, undated. *The Funding Code, Chapter 29*. Available at: http://www.justice.gov.uk/downloads/legal-aid/funding-code/Funding_Code_Chapter_29_Immigration_Nov_2010.pdf [Accessed 15 November 2012].

Macdonald, I., 1983. *Macdonald's Immigration Law and Practice*. First Edition. London: Butterworths.

Macdonald, I. and Toal, R., 2010. *Macdonald's Immigration Law and Practice in the United Kingdom*. Eighth Edition. Vol. 1. London: LexisNexis.

Marshall, T.H., 1950. *Citizenship and Social Class*. Cambridge: Cambridge University Press.

MoJ, 2010a. *Proposals for the Reform of Legal Aid in England and Wales. Consultation Paper CP 12/10* [online]. Available from: http://www.justice.gov.uk/downloads/consultations/legal-aid-reform-consultation.pdf [Accessed 15 November 2012].

MoJ, 2010b. *Legal Aid Reform: Scope Changes* [online]. Available from: http://www.justice.gov.uk/downloads/consultations/ia-scope-changes.pdf [Accessed 15 November 2012].
MoJ, 2012. *Royal Assent Stage - Impact Assessments and Equality Impact Assessments, Annex A: Scope* [online]. Available from: http://www.justice.gov.uk/legislation/bills-and-acts/acts/legal-aid-and-sentencing-act/laspo-background-information [Accessed 7 January 2013].
Moorhead, R., 2010. Litigants in Person: what the research actually says. *Lawyer Watch* [online]. http://lawyerwatch.wordpress.com/2010/12/16/litigants-in-person-what-the-research-actually-says/ [Accessed 7 January 2013].
Rice, N., 1994. Local Initiatives in Support of Families. In: S. Kagan and B. Weissbourd, eds. *Putting Families First: America's family support movement and the challenge of change*. San Francisco: Jossey-Bass.
Selznick, P., 1999. Legal Cultures and the Rule of Law. In: M. Krygier and A. Czarnota, eds. *The Rule of Law after Communism: Problems and Prospects in East-Central Europe*. Aldershot: Ashgate.
Starr, S. and Brilmayer, L., 2003. Family Separation as a Violation of International Law. *Berkley Journal of International Law*, 21 (2), 213–287.
Trude, A. and Gibbs, J., 2010. *Review of quality issues in legal advice: measuring and costing quality in asylum work*, [online]. Available from: http://www.asylumaid.org.uk/data/files/publications/136/Cost_of_Quality_Legal_Advice_Review_March2010.pdf [Accessed 7 January 2013].
UKBA and Department for Children, Schools and Families, 2009. *Every Child Matters: Change for Children* [online]. Available from: http://www.ukba.homeoffice.gov.uk/sitecontent/documents/policyandlaw/legislation/bci-act1/change-for-children.pdf?view=Binary [Accessed 7 January 2013].
UN General Assembly, 1951. *Convention relating to the Status of Refugees*, United Nations, Treaty Series, 189, 137.
Valdez, S., 2012. *Separated Children and Legal Aid Provision*. London: ILPA.
Wray, H., 2009. Moulding the migrant family. *Legal Studies*, 29 (4), 592–618.

The impact of cuts in legal aid funding on charities

Debra Morris and Warren Barr

Charity Law & Policy Unit, School of Law and Social Justice, University of Liverpool, UK

This article focusses on the specific impact of the cuts in legal aid funding on the charitable sector. The sector plays a significant role in advice giving. Some charities have the provision of legal advice as their sole purpose, whilst the work of other charities includes the giving of legal advice. Funding comes via a number of sources including legal aid, local authorities and charitable trusts. Whilst this volume highlights the legal aid reforms that will lead to significant cuts in funding, this article notes that charitable providers of legal advice have also suffered major cuts from their other traditional funding sources. Against this background, the article considers the serious and often unforeseen consequences for charities of the legal aid reforms, which go far beyond the impact on the high street law firm and access to justice for claimants.

Introduction

This article will focus on one particular aspect of the legal aid reforms that form the subject of this special volume and this concerns the specific impact of the cuts in legal aid funding on the charitable sector.

Before turning to look at some of the specific impacts of the implementation of the Legal Aid, Sentencing and Punishment of Offenders Act 2012 (LASPO) for charities, the first section of this article provides some context in which to place this discussion. In particular, it considers the composition and regulation of the charitable sector, the sector's role in advice giving and the funding of this charitable work. It briefly sets out how both the legal aid reforms and other funding cuts are affecting charities and their regulator. Having set the scene, the main section of the article considers the effect of the legal aid reforms on charities. It will be seen that the consequences for charities are significant and, arguably, largely unforeseen. They have certainly not been high on the agenda for policy makers who have been focussed on the impacts of the reforms on private law firms and on concerns for access to justice for claimants. The article concludes by suggesting that charities will survive the reforms. Charities will gain some assistance from Government by way of transitional funding but they will mainly survive by relying on their time-honoured characteristics of resilience and innovation.

The context

The charitable sector

The Charity Commission's latest facts and figures reveal that there are 162,624 registered charities, whose total annual income is £58.578 billion (Charity Commission 2012). Over 75% of these charities have annual income of less than £100,000 and nearly 43% have annual income of less than £10,000. It is important to identify what charities are, as compared to other third sector organisations, as this article deals with charities in the strictest sense. Charitable bodies are distinct from the voluntary sector at large. They are registered with and regulated by the Charity Commission and enjoy the fiscal and other advantages associated with charitable status. To be eligible for registration, such organisations must be of charitable character: they must have as their object a recognised charitable purpose, must be for the benefit of the public and be wholly and exclusively charitable (Charities Act 2011, s 2). The National Council for Voluntary Organisations (NCVO) *UK Voluntary Sector Almanac* (2012) reports that the voluntary sector, of which the charitable sector forms part, receives income from two main sources: individuals and statutory bodies. Whilst individuals are still the sector's main source, providing £14.3 billion in 2009/10 (39% of total income) via donations and purchases, contracts and grants from statutory bodies, worth £13.9 billion, generate almost as much of the sector's income (38%). Together, statutory bodies and individuals account for just over three-quarters of the voluntary sector's income. The proportion of the sector's income that comes from statutory sources has steadily increased from 32% in 2004/05 to 38% in 2009/10.

The Charity Commission is the regulator of charities in England and Wales. Since the 1990s, the Commission has developed into a modern regulator, significantly increasing its activities to include conducting a wholesale review of the charities on the Register, publishing a wide range of guidance for trustees, and carrying out a programme of charity visits and investigations. It has also gone fully online, with all its information published on its website, together with the Register of charities. Its statutory objectives (Charities Act 2011, s 14) include: the increasing of public trust and confidence in charities; the promotion of compliance by charity trustees with their legal obligations in exercising control and management of the administration of their charities; and, the promotion of the effective use of charitable resources. One of its statutory general functions (Charities Act 2011, s 15) is to encourage and facilitate the better administration of charities and in connection with this function, the Commission may give such advice or guidance with respect to the administration of charities as it considers appropriate. Such advice or guidance may be in any appropriate form and may relate to charities generally, or a class or a particular charity.

The sector's role in the provision of advice

One element of the charity sector comprises bodies that provide legal and related advice. Charitable purposes are now codified in section 2 the Charities Act 2011 and include (a) the prevention or relief of poverty and (j) the relief of those in need because of youth, age, ill-health, disability, financial hardship or other disadvantage. The provision of money management and debt counselling advice are examples of the ways in which charities might help prevent poverty. Charitable purposes that are directed towards the relief of those in need, by reason of youth, age, ill-health, disability, financial or other disadvantage include the relief of financial hardship by the provision of free legal advice and assistance to persons who, through lack of means, would otherwise be unable to obtain such advice.

Most of the charitable advice providers are community-based charities, some of which exclusively provide advice, whilst others provide a number of services including advice (Cabinet Office 2012, p. 6). Some of these charities are part of a network of national organisations. A Cabinet Office report on the advice-providing charitable sector found that, in addition to some national charities (including Shelter and Age UK) that have traditionally provided advice, the sector it is made up of Citizens Advice Bureaux (CABx),

Law Centres and members of the AdviceUK network (Cabinet Office 2012, p. 6). CABx deliver advice services from over 3500 community locations in England and Wales, run by 382 individual charities (Citizens Advice Bureaux 2011). Citizens Advice itself is also a registered charity, as well as being the membership organisation for bureaux. The income of CABx totalled £178 million in 2010/11, and this came from local authorities, the Legal Services Commission, Lottery funds, primary care trusts, charitable trusts, companies and individuals (Citizens Advice Bureaux 2011). In addition, there are around 50 local independent Law Centres (Cabinet Office 2012), which are registered charities specialising in social welfare law, offering free legal advice, casework and representation to individuals and groups. The previously mentioned AdviceUK is the largest network of independent advice agencies in the UK. It is itself a charity that supports around 860 community based organisations that give free advice to members of the public (House of Commons Justice Committee 2011, Ev W 77).

Many of these charitable bodies have been funded in the past to provide legal advice, including legal aid, which is not the sole province of private law firm providers. CABx are one of the main providers of legal aid-funded advice, as well as other types of advice that in some circumstances might be an alternative to legal advice. In 2009–2010, the Legal Services Commission (LSC) provided around 15% of income for CABx, providing £27 million funding (House of Commons Justice Committee 2011, Ev 95). As an example of an individual charity funded to provide legal aid, Shelter is a leading national provider of specialist social welfare law advice, which has helped over 25,000 people each year under legal aid contracts and which has employed over 200 advisers and 40 solicitors to give legal aid advice to the public (House of Commons Justice Committee 2011, Ev 104).

The nature of the legal aid reforms

The reforms are discussed in detail elsewhere in this volume, but, for present purposes, from April 2013, LASPO 2012, s 8 and Schedule 1 mean that legal aid advice will be abolished for all welfare benefit matters (para. 15, Part 2), debt, employment (except discrimination cases under para. 43(1) and (3), Part 1) and all housing cases except those that involve disrepair issues that pose a serious threat to health (para. 35(1) Part 1) or where a person's home is classified at being at 'immediate risk' such as eviction proceedings (para. 33(1) Part 1) or assistance with homelessness (para. 34(1) Part 1). The charitable sector will be heavily hit by these reforms. The Ministry of Justice's own initial impact assessment revealed that the reforms were likely to result in a massive 92% reduction in legal aid income for charities (Ministry of Justice 2010, Table G). Compared to private law firms, a larger proportion of charities' advice work is taken 'out of scope' due to the categories of law in which they are more likely to work, for example, welfare benefits. This partly explains the disproportionate impact on the sector. It is also because charity providers currently undertake very little representation and so would not benefit from the exceptional case funding mechanism (Ministry of Justice 2010, p. 15).

Funding cuts affecting charities

These are not the only cuts in funding that charities are currently experiencing, as they are not immune from the impacts of the recession. Like private organisations, charities have administration and staffing costs, including the management and training of a volunteer workforce alongside paid staff, and, despite some limited tax reliefs and exemptions, the sector make a significant contribution to public finances, estimated at £1.35 billion for the year 2007/8 (NCVO 2009). Unlike many private companies, however, they have few or limited cash reserves to weather economic adversity, as 'most charities live hand to mouth' (NCVO 2011, p. 29). Funding comes from a variety of sources, including fund-raising by private donation, but charities cannot simply 'fundraise' themselves out of financial trouble – money raised from individual donations fell by nearly £1 billion between 2008 and 2009 (Wilding 2010) and there are no signs of a recovery to date (NCVO 2011, p. 29).

Typically, a significant source of funding for advice-providing charities has come from local authorities. As a result of deep cuts to local authority budgets and the tough funding environment generally, charities are now suffering from significant reductions in local authority funding and a decline in grants from national government sources and other funders. Combined with cuts to legal aid funding, such charities are suffering a 'double whammy'. Financial support is being decimated, whilst the demand for services increases as a result of the impacts of the recession on the general public. In addition, local authority cuts are also affecting general charities for whom advice provision is one part of their service, again leading to extra demand on the charitable advice sector. A survey of London's voluntary and community sector found that the services most commonly reported to have seen an increase in demand in 2011–2012 were advice services (LVSC 2012). This repeats the findings from an online survey of advice charities by Justice for All (2012), which reported increased demand for advice from 86% of respondents. In fact, current demand is likely to increase as changes to benefits entitlements (including the introduction of universal credit) are implemented: 'As unemployment continues to rise and with major changes in the benefits system and employment rights in the foreseeable future, the need for advice is continuing to increase. This puts additional pressure on advice providers who are struggling to sustain and maintain their current (or reduced level) of service as a result of government policies' (LVSC 2012, p. 40). The Justice for All (2012) survey found local authority funding to be the biggest source of income for half of advice charities, usually funding core running costs and generalist advice. Following cuts, nearly one quarter of respondents were facing closure and most were making major cutbacks to frontline services.

The NCVO (2011) estimates that the UK voluntary and community sector will lose around £911 million per year in public funding. This means voluntary and community sector stands to lose £2.8 billion from Government over the current spending review period running from 2011–2016. Service providing charities, including those providing advice services are already suffering as a result of general funding cuts. Recent research (Compact Voice 2012) into the extent of spending from local authorities to the voluntary and community sector through grants and contracts, including changes to levels of funding, found that around half of local authorities are continuing to see the voluntary sector as a soft target for spending cuts, with disproportionate cuts common. This is in line with an earlier report produced by the Association of Chief Executives of Voluntary Organisations (ACEVO), based on data provided by 1725 organisations that applied to the Office for Civil Society Transition Fund, intended to support civil society organisations facing public spending cuts. This suggested that it is highly likely that public sector agencies are passing on disproportionate cuts to charities (i.e. higher cuts to charities than they themselves are facing) (ACEVO 2011, p. 3). Another more recent survey, commissioned by the Charities Aid Foundation, found that one in six charities believe they could face closure in the coming year (Charities Aid Foundation 2012).

The 'Voluntary Sector Cuts' website (Voluntary Sector Cuts 2013), maintained by the NCVO on the impact of these public sector cuts, makes for grim reading. Of the 530 reported cuts (as at 20 January 2013), 80 relate to the provision of advice services directly, with the result that many services are being decommissioned as alternative funding is not available.

Changing role of the charity commission

Charitable organisations are not the only ones feeling the pinch. Their regulator, the Charity Commission, has also had its budget significantly decreased. As a result of a 33% budget cut over the current spending period, the Charity Commission, which will lose about 140 staff, is reducing its one-to-one advice to charities and its interventions in individual cases, as it focuses on its key regulatory priorities (Charity Commission 2011). This new strategy will see charities becoming heavily reliant on professional advisors and, perhaps, their own umbrella bodies. In fact, the Charity Commission now has as one of its two strategic priorities ‘developing the self-reliance of the sector’, moving to a position where ‘the Commission is not seen as the first or only point of call for those who need tailored advice’ (Charity Commission 2011b, p. 4).

Clearly, charities will not have the luxury in the future of seeking advice and reassurance from the Charity Commission as they deal with governance and other issues. They will either have to muddle through themselves or incur expense in the acquisition of specialist advice.

Demands of the Big Society

At the same time that they must contend with straitened financial circumstances, charities are also under pressure to become fully fledged members of the Big Society by being commissioned to deliver public services. Earlier research has shown (Morris 2012) that whilst this may be beneficial and appropriate for some charities, the legal and regulatory framework within which charities operate impedes their role in some of the key planks of the Big Society. Specifically, certain legal constraints, which are inherent characteristics of charities, such as the need to maintain their independence and to act in line with their objects, suggest that there could be significant difficulties for many charities, especially smaller ones that lack capacity to engage with the Big Society ideals.

Adapting and surviving

A characteristic of the charity sector is its ability to innovate and be flexible and it is expected that charities providing advice will find ways through their current funding difficulties. The recent London Voluntary Service Council (LVSC) survey found that, every year between 2009–2012, the majority of surveyed bodies continued to take action to adapt to changes, affirming the flexibility and innovation of the sector in striving to ensure that it can continue to provide services and better meet the needs of the most disadvantaged (LVSC 2012, p. 45). The changes in legal aid funding are the latest in a long line of reductions in funding with which charities have had to contend. Crisis management is often the norm, when, for example, within the contract culture, charities have often received little or no notice of non-renewal of contracts despite efforts in the past to ensure that government funders did not act in this way (see HM Government 2010, para. 4.4 which requires a minimum of three months’ notice in writing when changing or ending a funding relationship).

It is important that charities providing advice do survive. Those people approaching them for advice, whether that be legal or other advice, are often already in crisis and rely on charities to assist them when they have exhausted all other possibilities. It is in the general public interest that charities find the means to continue to carry on this important work.

It has already been noted that the legal aid reforms are only one part of a package of tripartite cuts that impact on charities giving legal (and other) advice; the removal of direct financial support through the swingeing Public Sector cuts and the withdrawal of supportive activities for charities by the Charity Commission, in its refocused role as regulator, together forming the other two elements. Such charities are not also enjoying a commensurate reduction in the demand for their services. In fact, the general economic climate, coupled with the introduction of the welfare reform programme with its cap on benefits, mean that the demand for charities to provide advice services is likely to increase. It is within this context that the specific impact of the implementation of LASPO on charities must be considered.

Effect of legal aid reform on charities

In addition to the direct loss of funding for the provision of social welfare services, the sharp divisions made in the new funding regime are difficult to explain and may lead to creating more extreme need, rather than helping meet existing need. A good example lies in the housing sector, with the distinction between legal aid being available to contest possession proceedings but not for welfare benefit or debt advice.

One of the key triggers for a landlord to start an eviction action is rent arrears, and for those within social housing through poverty, the principle cause of rent arrears is problems with Housing Benefit payments (Barr 2007). It is an accepted fact that the administration of Housing Benefit is both slow and unreliable, and that it can be very difficult either to challenge an incorrect, initial assessment or to resolve difficulties in a timely manner before or at the time of possession proceedings (Hunter *et al.* 2005). The complexity of benefit issues means that this requires specialist advice to resolve, given by appropriately trained staff and this is expensive to provide. It is here that CABx and charities such as Shelter have provided such advice in the past, assisted by the legal aid funding which will now be removed from this area of work. It is darkly ironic that, should the Housing Benefit issue remain unresolved and lead to a possession claim, aid for advice and support becomes available, at the point where costs, both financial and human, increase and, by which time it may be too late to resolve the issues. Prevention here would be better than cure, yet the new funding regime does not support this. Similarly, taking legal aid funding away from general advice on debt management may lead to more individuals falling prey to the consequences of mismanaged debt, such as losing their home through the build-up of mortgage or rent arrears. Legal aid now only responds at the point of crisis.

A failure to fund preventative measures is already evident in the sector, as a result of the general cuts in charity funding. The LVSC survey showed that preventative services are being disproportionately cut compared with curative or crisis services, and that this is expected to continue in 2012–2013 (LVSC 2012, p. 56). Whilst investment is diverted from more preventative services to achieve short-term solutions to funding cuts, the risk is that the demand to address complex longer-term problems that are more expensive to resolve will continue to increase. Research on the impact of spending cuts on communities across Greater Manchester came to the same conclusion: 'Austerity dictates that scarce resources are dedicated to the ongoing crisis, thereby directing resources away from preventative services. According to many of our respondents, this means that increasingly people are being allowed to drift towards crisis before qualifying for services' (GMCVO 2012, p. 4).

The most obvious impact of the cuts will be a severe reduction in the private solicitor's legal aid work portfolio. Inevitably, whatever role charities seek to play, these cuts will mean that individuals in crisis cannot get legal advice and/or representation. This will lead to more individuals, some of whom are the most vulnerable in our society and who may well lack the capacity to engage effectively with the justice system, seeking to represent themselves. These citizens often have complex lives, with inter-connected legal problems (Cabinet Office 2012, p. 7). For example, marital breakdown can lead to debt problems, which, if not tackled early enough, can lead to homelessness. This will lead to poor quality litigation in complex areas (such as welfare benefits or employment law). A report from the Civil Justice Council (2011, p. 8) predicts that self-represented litigants will become 'the rule rather than the exception'. This is clearly going to require significant changes to the way that litigation is currently undertaken so as to ensure some kind of equality of arms between the represented and unrepresented party. As Baroness Hale recently put it: 'The adversarial procedure which we adopt is heavily dependent upon lawyers preparing, presenting and arguing the case' (Hale 2011, p. 12).

It is clear that CABx or other advice charities may no longer be able to meet increasing need as the services are supported by the same funding stream as for legal professionals. The direct impact of the loss of funding from legal services is estimated at over £20 million per annum (Citizens Advice Bureau 2012). The need is also great – in 2010–2011, CABx dealt with 2.3 million debt-related advice problems, serving 550,000 clients across their network. Housing disputes, already served by other specialist advice providers such as Shelter, still saw CABx dealing with over 270,000 clients in the same period to resolve some 500,000 issues. Demand is increasing, as the social welfare issues now excluded from legal aid provision 'tend to 'cluster' around vulnerable people with multiple problems, leading to adverse consequences such as . . . debt and loss of employment – the compounding issues of poverty and exclusion' (CABx, 2012).

There are a number of more specific consequences that arise from the changes to legal aid as they affect charities. These are considered below.

Nature and quality of advice changes

One response to the withdrawal of funding for advice through legal aid for social welfare issues is for charities to provide a different type of advice than is available through current services, such as a move to a more general advice service. This would be cheaper to administer than a more specialist service and would seem to be a sensible response to maintaining service rather than simply disestablishing advice services altogether. The direct result would be that charities would not be giving the advice they previously gave, either in nature or quality.

This is entirely understandable. Dealing with complex issues in employment disputes, for example, or solving difficult questions about the legal status of an occupation agreement and the rights arising from that agreement (Barr 2007) require legal expertise, and appropriately trained staff. The package of cuts facing charities means that training budgets for staff are already under threat. Research undertaken by Lasa (a provider of services to the charity sector, including advice and training on welfare rights and the use of technology) found that, of those 446 charity sector professionals surveyed, 76% felt that training and professional development were absolutely necessary to discharge the requirements of their jobs, yet 49% of those surveyed said charities did not have the budget for staff training, with 34% unsure whether resource was available (Lasa 2012). The key finding of the research was that 86% felt the quality of support and advice given by charities would deteriorate, with 61% suggesting that charities would not be able to help as many people due to a shortage of suitably qualified staff.

If the advice provided by charities to those in need is not of sufficient quality, or is perceived not to be, this could harm charities. Charities trade on trust as a major component of the charity brand – the NCVO has called public trust 'the voluntary sector exchange rate' (NCVO 1998). Advice is often sought by those most in need and they approach charities, often as a last resort, for answers. Such people will be disappointed if they are sent elsewhere for specialist advice, or, worse still, find that no advice is forthcoming. Similarly, the public tend to trust legal advice given by specialists – it is unlikely that this would extend to untrained volunteers attempting to provide such advice. Charities may damage their reputation in trying to give advice that they are seen not to be qualified to provide. If such issues are sustained, ultimately they could have adverse consequences on fundraising by charities following from the damage caused to reputation by media interest in such failings. This may set up a vicious circle, as any reduction of funding would necessarily impact on the ability of the relevant organisation to carry out its charitable purposes. Any change in the nature of advice services therefore needs to be carefully managed, and hard decisions will have to be made following careful planning of the potential impact of such choices.

Increased use of ADR

It is not only advice services that charities may have to reconfigure as a result of the legal aid cuts. If funding is not available to private legal professionals to fund legal action on social welfare issues for people in crisis, then it is unlikely that charities will be able to make up the shortfall to do so.

Many charities already have recourse to methods of Alternative Dispute Resolution (ADR) as a means to assist claimants, with the aim either to resolve issues of dispute without the expense in time and money of the court system or to find a less expensive alternative to full legal action (Morris 2003). It may be that the constraints of funding will lead to increased use of ADR and a seemingly welcome boost in the accessibility of such services.

ADR has its limits, and it is not always as effective as might be expected. The quality of the service is variable; specialist services may not be available in the necessary quantity or in the relevant locality and some disputes, by their nature, are not suitable for ADR methods because they require the exercise of legal power to resolve (Morris and Warburton 2006).

Even where ADR is successfully employed, it has one significant weakness compared to full legal suit; it addresses the particular issue at hand but creates no binding precedent by which similar issues can be decided in the future. This could ultimately lead to a lack of clarity in the law around pressing social welfare issues, such as the calculation or availability of welfare benefit schemes. It highlights, again, the latent unfairness in the nature of the legal aid reforms. A charity or other body might be able to assist someone in contesting an eviction claim through legal aid, but would not be able to help a claimant who has been evicted with questions about entitlement to social housing under a local authorities' homelessness duties, or about whether they are eligible within the new listing scheme exclusions under the Localism Act 2011 (through amendment to Part 6 of the

Housing Act 1996). Such questions need legal answers, to clarify interpretations of complex statutory provisions and duties. In the absence of funding from legal aid, the threatened lack of clarity around important issues of social welfare law is a pressing concern, not a distant possibility.

Losing their voice

Charities may also lose the ability to challenge public bodies on the execution of social welfare duties through legal action, viewed as a significant check on the public sector and benefit of the operation of the charitable sector (Blackmore 2004). Indeed, the Charity Commission permits charities to take reasonable steps to apply pressure to secure additional funding for services where they are inadequately provided (Charity Commission 2007, p. 26); a painful irony in the context of the legal aid cuts. The loss of legal aid thus has both a direct and indirect impact on the ability of charities to assist potential litigants with social welfare disputes.

Pro bono support as an alternative

If charities cannot carry out advice work themselves, due to lack of funding, one option might be to direct individuals to pro bono support. The pro bono activity of law firms (and others) has increased in recent years. The legal profession is giving this area of activity much more prominence. Both the solicitors' branch of the profession (LawWorks) and barristers (Bar Pro Bono Unit) have their own pro bono groups that aim to provide free legal help to those who cannot afford to pay for it and who are unable to access legal aid. One problem in accessing such services might be lack of knowledge on the part of the front-facing charities, whom members of the public approach for advice. Charities that have not hitherto been used to dealing with advice provision may not know of the availability of pro bono support or how to access it. As would be expected, the charitable advice sector already enjoys a close partnership with pro bono providers (see, e.g., ProBonoUK.net 2012, p. 12). The converse problem here may be that, whilst there is widespread *knowledge* of such support, the current *supply* of pro bono work is unlikely to satisfy the need. A recent LawWorks survey found 'widespread concern about the impact of the legal aid, Sentencing and Punishment of Offenders Act 2012 but almost no planning or appetite for moving into new areas of pro bono work to fill the gaps' (LawWorks 2012, p. 3).

Planning for change

Adaptability is a key asset of charitable bodies and, historically, a major response to changes in funding regimes has been for organisations to reorganise to meet the new demands created. In the social housing sector, for example, charities moved from being the only providers of housing services, to partners in helping housing associations discharge social housing, either through providing housing itself or specialist services to bolster general housing services (Glover Thomas and Barr 2009). Hence, charities may decide, either individually or through discussion with local partner organisations, to change the nature of the service that they provide and to address the lack of legal aid funding for welfare in this way.

There are a number of pitfalls in doing so. It is important that a charity is appropriately governed, and two key hallmarks of effective charities are they are 'clear about their purpose and direction' as well as 'fit for purpose' (Charity Commission 2008). Changes in activity should not be undertaken lightly, whatever the perceived need, and a charity has a responsibility to make sure that any change contemplated is sustainable, so risk must be a relevant consideration in making a major change of direction. Similarly, to meet the needs of fitness for purpose in governance, an organisation must give due consideration to 'protect its reputation in all aspects of its work' (Charity Commission 2008, p. 8).

One real risk in changing to provision of advice in social welfare issues is that, as already discussed, it requires appropriately trained and qualified staff. This may well provide a significant stumbling block for charities in seeking to provide this type of assistance. Addressing staffing needs will require time and money, and until they are met a charity runs a dual risk of creating a significant backlog of work and a loss of reputation in failing to give appropriate, high quality advice. One feeds the other, so that the reputation of the charity may be damaged. In addition, unless other organisations are quick to fill the gaps left by the charity changing focus, there will be gaps in underlying provision that will potentially damage the reputation of all charities working in the area, thus undermining the charity brand. A lack of performance indicators, such as charity league tables, means that any loss of service becomes the focus of damage to the brand (Hankinson and Rochester 2005).

Charitable bodies reorganising in this way are also working against a background of uncertainty, not just in predicting the scale of need and the scope of change necessary to meet it effectively, but also in terms of legal compliance. The Charity Commission, as regulator, is no longer providing individual advice about the legal compliance issues relating to changes of purpose or mission, so charities are either acting on their own, or relying on advice from charities who support the sector, such as NCVO or having to pay private organisations (such as legal professionals) to assist. Those umbrella bodies that support the sector have to step up to the changing needs, but due to the general funding crisis, they are themselves short of money and may not have the resources to provide the services that they would like to provide at best, or, at worst, cannot provide appropriate support services.

The potential risks, both in changing to an effective service without damaging reputation and in making sure that changes are legally compliant, mean that fundamental changes to the activity of the charity will need to be carefully considered and managed, and should not be taken lightly.

Changing activity through drift

Conversely, changes in the nature of the activity of a charity may instead happen in practice, without being planned or managed in any accepted sense. The increased demand on advice services, and the potential loss of services elsewhere in the sector, mean that the core business of many charities might change. A housing provider, for example, whose focus was on providing housing to those in need, might find that they are giving ever more advice to people who approach them due to their expertise as housing practitioners, in the absence of free access to advice from the legal profession. They may also be giving advice to other charities, for similar reasons of the benefit of their experience. While at the start this may be a distraction from core activity, over time it could become the core activity of the charity. This is a form of 'mission drift', and it comes with an inherent danger. Charities are constrained by their stated charitable purposes, and, if they act outside those purposes, may find themselves in breach of their legal obligations, which could lead to investigation by the Charity Commission. If these matters are not resolved, serious consequences for the charity and, ultimately, the loss of charitable status, may ensue. Also, the issues already identified in the potential damage to the charity brand with unplanned change are likely to have a greater impact here, as staff roles, for example, change through necessity rather than through a supported transition. Such unplanned changes in service delivery could have consequent impacts on attracting funding; a funder is unlikely to continue funding for the 'core' work of a charity that is instead carrying out purposes that should be ancillary as its primary function.

Such changes in activity are not a theoretical concern. They are already happening. The recently conducted Greater Manchester Centre for Voluntary Organisations (GMCVO) survey found as follows: 'The survey evidence overwhelmingly suggests that a gap is beginning to open up in advice and advocacy services. It is worth noting that the evidence does not primarily come from organisations such as Citizens Advice Bureaux, whose main remit is advice, but also from other types of organisations, such as community centres, specialist infrastructure organisations and service providers. There is an indication that in view of general advice services having been cut and/or being in a transition due to the legal aid reform, people are increasingly turning for advice to any organisation that they happen to know, many of them community centres.' (GMCVO 2012, p. 14). As one respondent wrote: 'Services cut [elsewhere] ... have increased demand for services from the community centre as they have nowhere to go to for these services.'

It is also possible to envisage an advice charity becoming a service provider in order to survive, as funding for the advice has been removed with the legal aid cuts, or to imagine a charity removing advice from the range of activities carried on by the organisation. Many organisations may, in the face of adversity in funding, reduce services to the very core, which will, in most cases, be the relief of those in need. This is also 'mission drift', as the change is one driven by what is perceived as necessity, and it will have an impact on the quality and availability of provision for those in need.

Even if mission drift does not occur, it is likely that charities will see increased demand to offer a full suite of services. This has already happened in the health sector on the basis of changes to the funding regime. An infrastructure organisation in the health sector commented on the increase in demand for advice and advocacy despite not being a service provider: 'We have seen an increased demand on us for information, advice, signposting, support to challenge decisions' (GMCVO 2012, p. 15).

Charities changing legal structure

Another response to the difficulties of changing activity is that charities are considering reconstituting with different legal structures. For example, the Advisory Centre for Education was a charity that helped needy parents to navigate the complex changing landscape of education law surrounding exclusion from school, bullying, special educational needs and school admission appeals. After operating for over 50 years, it closed in 2012 having lost its Department for Education grant (Third Sector 2012b). In its place, a new community interest company (CIC) and a limited liability partnership have been formed with the intention, ultimately, to provide the same kind of services as those previously provided by the charity. As a CIC (which is not a charity) the entity will be able to charge fees without having the same concerns that charities have in relation to the provision of public benefit (see e.g. *Independent Schools Council* v *Charity Commission* [2011] UKUT 421). The CIC was introduced as a new hybrid legal form in July 2005. Whilst it is a type of non-charitable company, it is nevertheless designed for social enterprises that want to use their profits and assets for the public good. The two main features that distinguish CICs from 'normal' companies are the asset lock (Companies (Audit, Investigations and Community Enterprise) Act 2004, s 30 and SI 2005 No. 1788, regs 17–25) and the requirement to satisfy the community interest test (Companies (Audit, Investigations and Community Enterprise) Act 2004, s 35. See also SI 2005 No. 1788, regs 26–29).

Another example of a charity restructuring its affairs as a result of cuts in advice funding and again using the CIC format is the charity, RAD (formerly the Royal Association for Deaf People, established in 1841) which runs a Deaf Law Centre. It provides deaf-friendly advice for the deaf community. The charity has seen a 'dramatic increase' in claims since the economic crisis and has lost its funding from the Equality and Human Rights Commission (*Law Society Gazette* 2012a). As well as delivering legal advice in the traditional areas of law usually associated with Law Centres, RAD Deaf Law Centre also provides legal advice in relation to will-writing, conveyancing, family law, business support, employment and HR services through its sister company RAD Deaf Legal Enterprise CIC. In doing so, the charity is addressing the gap in the provision of affordable professional mainstream legal advice directed at deaf people. In addition, income generated through fees paid to RAD Deaf Legal Enterprise CIC will go back to RAD Deaf Law Centre to fund its pro bono activities (Royal Association for Deaf People 2012). This seems like a good option that will provide a specialist service to a particular user group and will hopefully provide some funds to the connected charity so that it can continue to provide legal advice without cost.

The LVSC survey found evidence of much strategic planning in response to the cuts, such as developing new business models, diversifying funding sources, redesigning services, making greater use of ICT or social media and working in collaboration, including with the private sector, funders and commissioners (LVSC 2012, p. 50). In the most recent survey, 10% of respondents had merged and one other organisation was seriously considering merger, while in the previous year's survey, of the 3% of organisations that mentioned mergers, none mentioned concrete plans to take this forward (LVSC 2012, p. 50). A number of CABx have merged in recent years as a result of tighter funding regimes. The Charity Commission register of mergers (which lists certain charity mergers since 2007) lists 14 CAB mergers. Mergers are a complex and often costly business for charities and are not to be entered into without careful consideration (Morris 2001).

As a result of the funding crisis, some law centres are considering whether it would be appropriate for them to charge those clients who can afford to pay something towards the cost of their legal advice, whilst continuing to provide free legal aid advice to those who cannot afford to pay. In some cases, restrictions on such activities are imposed by the bodies themselves or their umbrella organisations. There have also been some regulatory restrictions that prohibit charging. For example, the Solicitors Regulation Authority (SRA) does not currently allow solicitors in special bodies/non-commercial organisations to charge for advice, but this is likely to change in the future (Legal Services Board 2012). Islington Law Centre in London has applied to the SRA for alternative business structure (ABS) status to enable it to charge clients for some legal services (*Law Society Gazette* 2012b). The ABS for law firms, introduced in the Legal Services Act 2007, allow non-lawyers to own or invest in law firms, subject to regulatory approval. The first licences were granted in 2012. Rochdale law centre has set up a CIC to provide fixed fee services for immigration and employment work (*Law Society Gazette* 2012b). The law centre in London's Tower Hamlets has formed a co-operative with other organisations in the borough (*Law Society Gazette* 2012b). The idea of using arms' length paid-for legal services to cross-subsidise free legal advice has been recommended by the Cabinet Office

(2012, p. 14), which referred to the Islington centre's funding model as an example of 'innovation and entrepreneurship'.

Many charities, including those giving advice, are getting involved in multi-agency working. This way of working can provide many benefits for beneficiaries, including the potential for improved quality of service. CABx are already heavily involved in collaborative working (see the examples in New Philanthropy Capital (2011) for ways in which CABx participate in 'impact networks'). This model works particularly well with people with multiple or complex needs, which will often be the case for those people who need to seek legal advice. However, these arrangements do make for a more complex funding environment for advice-providing charities that are trying to survive and at least maintain some level of provision. This complexity can make sustainability of services difficult, as the interdependency between the various agencies can be fragile; something that charities working in housing the mentally vulnerable are well aware of (Glover-Thomas and Barr 2008).

Closure of charities

The most extreme and visible impact of the cuts in the funding of legal advice provision for advice-giving charities is that some bodies may no longer be able to carry on operating. The homeless charity, Shelter, has concerns that it may need to close eight offices as a result of the cuts, which will cause a 50% reduction in its face-to-face advice services (Third Sector 2012a). Shelter offices provide independent advice on housing, debt and benefits and largely rely on legal aid funding to undertake their work. One of the locations in which closure is likely is Gloucester, where the chief executive of a local homelessness charity noted that 'Shelter is the only place that provides some kind of legal services to people who are having problems with housing' (*Gloucestershire Echo* 2012). The same report noted that the county council had recently remodelled its homeless provision so that there were now 13 fewer emergency beds available in Gloucester. Hence, as the demand for advice and protection of welfare rights grows, its availability shrinks.

Birmingham CABx have been hit particularly hard. In 2011, as a result of cuts to local authority funding, one branch closed and the opening hours of the four others were reduced. In October 2012, it was announced that Birmingham CABx may have to close two of its four remaining branches in the city (BBC 2012). The picture is likely to extend nationwide, given the severity of the operating environment for charities. With the closure of these services, there is nothing to replace them. This is not an argument of commercial economies of scale, but a reduction in the ability to meet very real and increasing need.

Conclusions

It is almost trite to suggest that these are very challenging times for charities. It was always going to be difficult to be positive about the exclusion of most social welfare issues from legal aid funding, but it has been demonstrated that there are many serious and unforeseen consequences that go far beyond the impact on the high street law firm and access to justice for claimants. Despite legal aid funding only being one stream of funding for charities, its importance cannot be under-estimated, and it is simply not realistic to believe that charities have limitless reserves to call upon through beneficent donors to weather the storm.

The issues raised in this article are not scaremongering. It is very likely that many of the suggested consequences will materialise. Earlier changes to the funding of legal aid gave rise to similar outcomes for some charities. For example, reforms to legal aid in 2007 introducing fixed fee payments and then payment only on completion of case stages led to a cash flow crisis for many advice-giving charities, in areas where they had previously been paid for giving legal advice on account and on an hourly rate. The well-established and respected charity Refugee and Migrant Justice (formerly Refugee Legal Centre), which was the UK's largest specialist provider of legal assistance for immigration and asylum seekers, was forced into administration with a backlog of payments of £1.8 m owed by the Legal Services Commission (Third Sector 2010). Its demise was followed one year later by the Immigration Advisory Service, a legal advice charity for immigrants and asylum seekers that employed about 250 people, facing the same fate (Third Sector 2011). Whilst changes to the funding of legal aid affect all providers, late payment has had an unequal impact on charities because they generally do not have large reserves and cannot get bank loans to finance the cash gap.

The Government is not entirely blind to the financial issues raised in this article. In October 2012, the Cabinet Office and Big Lottery Fund announced a £65 m transition fund for advice charities affected by cuts to legal aid and other advice service budgets (Big Lottery Fund 2013). The Advice Services Transition Fund will provide funding for two years from 2013/14 and will require applicants to modernise, collaborate with other organisations and form partnerships to ensure their long-term sustainability. They must have plans in place to 'improve efficiency, resilience and quality of service over the long term'. The launch of the Transition Fund was accompanied by the publication of a review of not-for-profit advice services in England. The report concludes that the Government has a role to play in supporting the sector to adapt to the new funding realities, but advice providers will also need to take the initiative and change the way they work. The report recommends that advice organisations should: collaborate more; take early action to prevent the problems which cause people to seek advice; diversify their funding streams and service provision; demonstrate their impact more effectively; and, use all appropriate channels to reach those in need of support (Cabinet Office 2012, p. 16). These tenets are easy to state, but difficult to follow, not least due to the damaging cuts to funding across the charity sector and, as demonstrated in this article, the various factors that can impinge upon a charity's ability to plan mean that they may not have either the capacity or the interest to bid for such funds.

The advice-giving charities of the kind discussed in this article epitomise the Big Society ideals: localism, community, volunteering (Morris 2012). Yet their position is being made untenable by funding changes and it is tempting to count what is happening as further evidence of the failure of the concept of local communities and local organisations working together to find the best solutions for those in need. At the very least, it suggests that the removal of social welfare issues from the legal aid funding pot has been ill-thought through, though it is unlikely to be reversed given the continuing impact of the financial crisis in Britain, Europe and the Western World.

Hope comes from the fact that, as stated, facing adversity and finding solutions to overcome it is what charities do best. Solutions may well be found that address or avoid some of the key concerns about the quality of provision and diminution in the charity brand identified in this article, but the legal aid reforms have exacerbated difficulties for those in need, rather than helped to resolve it. The fact that the interpretation and clarity of law in this country in relation to social welfare provision may well suffer as a result of these changes to legal aid, by removing the ability for issues to be contested and developed through precedent, may, perhaps, be the most damning and unforeseen legacy of the alterations in the practice of advice-giving charities. Time will tell.

References

ACEVO, 2011. *Cuts to the third sector: what can we learn from Transition Fund applications?* London: ACEVO.

Barr, W., 2007. Leases: rethinking possession against vulnerable groups. In: E. Cooke, ed. *Modern studies in property law: volume 4*, Oxford: Hart, 119–142.

BBC, 2012. Birmingham CAB may close two branches. Available from: http://www.bbc.co.uk/news/uk-england-birmingham-20110872 [Accessed 11 March 2013].

Big Lottery Fund, 2013. Advice Services Transition Fund. Helping the not-for-profit advice sector. Available from: http://sc01.biglotteryfund.org.uk/global-content/programmes/england/advice-services-transition-fund [Accessed 11 March 2013].

Blackmore, A., 2004. *Standing apart, working together: a study of the myths and realities of voluntary and community sector independence*. London: NCVO.

Cabinet Office, 2012. *Not-for-profit advice services in England*. London: Cabinet Office.

Charities Aid Foundation, 2012. One in six charities fear closure as crisis hits, say charity chiefs, CAF Press Release, 9 December.

Charity Commission, 2007. *CC37: charities and public service delivery – an introduction and overview*. London: Charity Commission.

Charity Commission, 2008. *CC10: the hallmarks of an effective charity* (updated February 2010). London: Charity Commission.

Charity Commission, 2011a. *Commission calls on charities to become more independent*, 28 June. London: Charity Commission.

Charity Commission, 2011b. *Strategic plan 2012–2015*. London: Charity Commission.

Charity Commission, 2012. Facts and figures. Available form: http://www.charitycommission.gov.uk/About_us/About_charities/factfigures.aspx [Accessed 11 March 2013].

Citizens Advice Bureaux, 2011. Key facts about the citizens advice service. Available from: http://www.citizensadvice.org.uk/index/aboutus/factsheets/cab_key_facts.htm [Accessed 11 March 2013].

Citizens Advice Bureau, 2012. Briefing: Legal aid Sentencing and Punishment of Offenders Bill, March.

Civil Justice Council, 2011. Access to justice for litigants in person (or self-represented litigants), A report and series of recommendations to the Lord Chancellor and to the Lord Chief Justice. Available from Civil Justice Website: http://www.judiciary.gov.uk/about-the-judiciary/advisory-bodies/cjc/ [Accessed 11 March 2013].

Compact Voice, 2012. *Local authorities and the voluntary and community sector: investigating funding and engagement*. London: Compact Voice (NCVO).

Gloucestershire Echo, 2012. Future of county branch of homeless charity Shelter hangs in balance, 4 October, p. 17.

Glover-Thomas, N. and Barr, W., 2008. Re-examining the benefits of charitable involvement in housing the mentally vulnerable, *Northern Ireland Legal Quarterly*, 59 (2), 177–200.

Glover-Thomas, N. and Barr, W., 2009. Enabling or disabling? increasing involvement of charities in social housing, *Conveyancer*, 73 (3), 209–235.

GMCVO, 2012. *An ounce of prevention is worth a pound of cuts*, Findings from a GMCVO survey on the impact of spending cuts on communities across Greater Manchester. Manchester: GMCVO.

Hale, B., 2011. Equal access to justice in the big society, Sir Henry Hodge Memorial Lecture. Available from Supreme Court Speeches Website: http://www.supremecourt.gov.uk/news/speeches-archive.html [Accessed 11 March 2013].

Hankinson, P. and Rochester, C., 2005. The face and voice of volunteering: a suitable case for branding? *International Journal of Nonprofit and Voluntary Sector Marketing*, 10 (2), 93–105.

HM Government, 2010. Compact. London: Cabinet Office.

House of Commons Justice Committee, 2011. *Government's proposed reform of legal aid, third report of session 2010–11, Volume 1-III*. London: The Stationery Office.

Hunter, C., et al., 2005. *DCA Research Series 6/05.The exercise of judicial discretion in rent arrears cases*, October. London: Department for Constitutional Affairs..

Justice for All, 2012. *Advice needs: what local advice charities need to continue serving their communities*. London: Justice for All.

Lasa, 2012. *Third sector learning and development survey results February 2012*. London: Lasa.

LawWorks, 2012. *LawWorks Pro Bono Survey 2012*, Summary report. Available from LawWorks Website: http://www.lawworks.org.uk/lawworksprobonosurvey2012 [Accessed 11 March 2013].

Law Society Gazette, 2012a. Deaf Law Centre hits out at discrimination 'scandal', 8 June, p. 4.

Law Society Gazette, 2012b. Law centres ponder structure switch, 8 November, p. 2.

Legal Services Board, 2012. *Regulation of special bodies/non-commercial bodies. Consultation paper on the regulation of special bodies/non-commercial bodies that provide reserved legal activities.* London: LSB.

LVSC, 2012. The big squeeze 2012: surviving not thriving. London: LVSC.

Ministry of Justice, 2010. Impact assessment, cumulative legal aid reform proposals. London: Ministry of Justice.

Morris, D., 2001. Legal issues in charity mergers. Liverpool: Charity Law Unit.

Morris, D., 2003. Disputes in the charitable sector. Liverpool: Charity Law Unit.

Morris, D., 2012. Charities and the big society: a doomed coalition? *Legal Studies*, 32 (1), 132–153.

Morris, D. and Warburton, J., 2006. Mediation and charities; frustrated desires. *Charity law & practice review*, 9 (1), 1–21.

NCVO, 1998. Blurred Vision: public trust in charities. *Research quarterly*, January, p. 1.

NCVO, 2009. The state and the voluntary sector. London: NCVO.

NCVO, 2011. Counting the cuts: the impact of spending cuts on the UK voluntary and community sector. London: NCVO.

NCVO, 2012. UK voluntary sector Almanac. London: NCVO.

New Philanthropy Capital, 2011. Impact networks, Charities working together to improve outcomes. London: New Philanthropy Capital.

ProBonoUK.net, 2012. *The Pro Bono yearbook of England and Wales 2012*. London: ProbonoUK.net.

Royal Association for Deaf People, 2012. Making the law work for Deaf people. Available from: http://www.deaflawcentre.org.uk/2012/09/making-the-law-work-for-deaf-people/ [Accessed 11 March 2013].

Third Sector, 2010. Refugee and migrant justice goes into administration, 15 June.

Third Sector, 2011. Immigration Advisory Service goes into administration, 11 July.

Third Sector, 2012a. Shelter says eight of its offices could close because of cuts in legal aid, 5 October.

Third Sector, 2012b. Fifty-year-old charity the Advisory Centre for Education closes after loss of central grant, 10 October.

Voluntary Sector Cuts, 2013. Voluntary Sector Cuts Website. Available from: www.voluntarysectorcuts.org.uk [Accessed 11 March 2013].

Wilding, K., 2010. Voluntary organisations and the recession. *Voluntary Sector Review*, 1 (1), 97–101.

Back for the future: a client centred analysis of social welfare and family law provision

Alexy Buck and Marisol Smith

Legal Services Research Centre, Legal Services Commission, Petty France, London

The landscape of legal advice provision is entering a period of significant change in England and Wales. Whilst there is a great deal of uncertainty about how the future landscape of advice service provision will evolve, there are lessons to be drawn from past delivery models.

This article first looks back at the period following the Access to Justice Act 1999, setting out a range of delivery models initiated following the Act, as well as research and evaluation conducted in the millennium decade. Findings are then presented from a comprehensive qualitative study on how people experience and deal with social welfare and family problems, and on facilitators and barriers to integrated advice provision, including inter-organisational working. This is explored through the lens of a delivery model which emphasised partnership and the pooling of resources and specialisms to meet client needs: the Community Legal Advice Centre model.

Introduction

The landscape of legal advice provision is entering a period of significant change in England and Wales. The Legal Aid Sentencing and Punishment of Offenders Act will, from April 2013, remove much of social welfare[1] and private family law from the scope of the legal aid scheme. Elsewhere, fiscal pressures have impacted on the budgets of local authorities (Local Government Association 2012, Crawford and Phillips 2012), threatening the funding for services which local authorities have no legal obligation to provide, such as legal advice. With recessions leading to an increased demand for legal services (e.g. Pleasence and Balmer 2010, 2012, Ministry of Justice 2009, Edwards 2003), central government has acknowledged the squeeze on advice providers, particularly for those in the not-for-profit sector (Cabinet Office 2012, p. 3).

This reduced funding environment appears to contrast with the period following the enactment of the Access to Justice Act 1999, which introduced the Community Legal Service (CLS). The aim of the CLS was in part, to revolutionise 'ordinary people's access to information about their rights, and promote new avenues to good quality legal services, particularly for those who are disadvantaged or socially excluded' (Lord Chancellor's Department 1998, p. 3). The decade which followed saw the development of new forms of legal advice delivery, the targeting of vulnerable groups and a growing emphasis on integrated services which addressed multiple needs.

A range of initiatives to support forward-looking approaches to the delivery of legal advice and information were funded through the then Lord Chancellor's Department Partnership Innovation Budget, launched in 2000. These included projects in primary health care settings, services delivered using videolink technology, and services targeted towards specific clients constituencies, such as those with mental health problems and those not accessing mainstream advice. All these projects were required to attract match funding from other sources, although core funding was administered by the Legal Services Commission (LSC).[2] Later developments included the establishment of the Community Legal Advice (CLA) telephone services and advances in digital access to information through the Community Legal Advice (formerly JustAsk!) website. Other examples of exploring different delivery models included the Money Advice Outreach Pilots, funded by the Financial Inclusion Fund (HM Treasury 2004) and targeted towards 'hard-to-reach' groups.

Integrated approaches to legal service delivery were pioneered by Community Legal Service Partnerships (CLSPs) (see Legal Services Commission 2000). Established under the Access to Justice Act, CLSPs were tasked with developing a strategic approach to the planning and delivery of civil legal advice and information services in local authority areas. They brought together the main funders and providers of legal advice and information to map current patterns of supply and need, to identify priority needs, to develop local referral networks among providers, and to agree a joint strategic plan to address gaps in provision.

Meanwhile, integrated advice delivery was piloted through the Family Advice and Information Networks (FAInS) in selected areas of England and Wales (Legal Services Commission 2001). The aim was to encourage family law practitioners to adopt a more holistic role in providing information, advice and guidance to publicly funded private family law clients, and to enable clients to access a range of services through a single gateway. This required practitioners to have good local knowledge of specialist advice services to enable them to signpost and refer clients appropriately. The LSC anticipated that FAInS providers would develop interdisciplinary working and local partnerships across services (e.g. debt advice and relationship counselling).

The last major policy development, with an expectation of national roll-out, and drawing on many of the themes that characterized the early years of the decade, were Community Legal Advice Centres (CLACs) and Networks (CLANs) (Legal Services Commission 2006). In one delivery model, partnership working, joint funding, integrated advice, and outreach advice for particularly vulnerable groups, was to be realised.

In parallel to these policy and delivery developments in access to justice, the new Millennium saw an unprecedented decade of research and evaluation in the legal services field in England and Wales; with an increased interest among policy makers in 'law in the real world' (Genn *et al.* 2006). Interest was driven by a focus on people's experience of the law, by viewing people as 'consumers' of the justice process and, more generally, by the importance attached to research and analysis as a way of making informed policy decisions (Buck 2007). It encompassed bespoke research and evaluation on the initiatives set out above, as well as strategic quantitative and qualitative research on people's experience of legal problems.

Service evaluations included reports published on projects funded by the Partnership Innovation Budget (Legal Services Commission 2005) and telephone advice (Hobson and Jones 2003). Research on the Money Advice Outreach Pilots demonstrated the success of outreach in reaching socially and financially excluded people who had not sought advice before, building new partnerships and delivering advice in new locations. It also highlighted the importance of 'trust transfer' (Buck *et al.* 2009), as well as the unavoidable overhead or fixed costs associated with outreach services (Smith and Patel 2008). Research evaluating the success of integrated programs such as CLSPs (Matrix Research 2004) and FAInS (Walker *et al.* 2007) suggested that some benefits from a more coordinated approach were possible, but that there were significant challenges to integrating provision across individual providers.

More generally, research on the experience of civil justice problems demonstrated how legal and social problems intersect with each other (e.g. Pleasence *et al.* 2004, Moorhead *et al.* 2006, Smith *et al.* 2013) and how different vulnerable groups experience civil justice problems (e.g. Williams 2004, Mason *et al.* 2009, Buck *et al.* 2005). Research on advice-seeking behaviour (e.g. Genn 1999, Pleasence 2006, De Simone and Hunter 2009) and capability (Buck *et al.* 2007, Buck *et al.* 2008, Balmer *et al.* 2010, Denvir *et al.* 2012) showed marked differences among problem solving strategies and client ability to take action.

Whilst there is a great deal of uncertainty about how the future landscape of advice service provision will evolve, there are lessons to be drawn from past delivery models. Much of the research and evaluation highlighted above remains relevant. Early indications for social welfare law from the Cabinet Office through the Advice Services Transition Fund[3] (Cabinet Office 2012) highlight a continuing desire to bring together providers in partnerships and to use different channels to reach vulnerable people in need of support: 'Non-for-profit advice providers will need to come together as partnerships with plans for collaborative ways of working to address local needs' (Cabinet Office 2012, p. 16) and 'The shared ambition of both the government and the advice sector is to ensure that particularly the most vulnerable clients continue receiving relevant, free advice and effective support' (Cabinet Office 2012, p. 4).

In an environment of limited resources for the provision of social welfare law, an understanding of problem experience and client behaviour therefore continues to be important in informing the development of service design. Much can be learnt from the past. This article presents findings from a comprehensive qualitative study on how people experience and deal with social welfare problems, and on facilitators and barriers to integrated advice provision, including inter-organisational working. This is explored through the lens of a delivery model which emphasised partnership and the pooling of resources and specialisms to meet client needs: the CLAC model.

The CLAC delivery model

CLACs were commissioned and funded jointly between the LSC and local authorities. They were a controversial initiative (see, e.g., Griffiths 2008) because they concentrated LSC and local authority funding for services in social welfare law into one contract; thereby reducing the number of outlets offering publicly funded legal advice. Contracts were normally let for a period of three years and had delivery targets in respect of volumes of clients and cases. CLACs, the focus of this article, pulled together key services in a geographical area into a single entity. CLANs consisted of a consortium of providers supplying complementary services.

The aim of CLACs was to provide clients with an 'integrated and seamless' advice service for social welfare and family law problems. The services were intended to offer a 'one-stop shop' for clients with multiple legal needs. They were also supposed to meet legal needs from diagnosis and information through to advice and assistance and legal representation in complex court proceedings. Depending on their needs, clients were therefore routed through a system which potentially included: a short diagnostic advice session provided by a generalist adviser; a generalist, often one-off, advice session; and referral to one or more specialist advisors for more complex problems.[4] The aim was for clients to enjoy a smooth and seamless 'advice journey' starting from first contact with the service through to appropriate aftercare.

CLAC services were targeted toward disadvantaged groups, especially those who did not access mainstream services, such as certain Black and Minority Ethnic (BME) groups and clients with mental health problems. For the more in-depth specialist legal advice, as opposed to the one-off generalist advice, legal aid eligibility tended to be a prerequisite and a means test to establish eligibility needed to be conducted by the CLAC. At the time of the research study five CLACs were open and delivering services to clients. These were located in Gateshead, Portsmouth, Leicester, Derby and Hull. At the height of the CLAC and CLAN initiative in autumn 2010, there were eight CLACs and two CLANs. The reforms set out in LASPO will remove around 75 per cent of their legal aid funded work from scope. All contracts for CLAC and CLAN services will come to an end in March 2013 and joint contracts with local authorities will no longer exist in those geographical areas.

Methodology

The study reported here adopted a triangulated qualitative research design, including advice session observations and first and follow-up interviews with both clients and advisors. Together these data elements provide a comprehensive and detailed account of the advice process. This qualitative approach is uniquely suited to enabling an in-depth examination of problem experience, advice seeking and problem disclosure. By incorporating the perspectives of both clients and advisors, the qualitative approach reveals the dynamics of advice provision. Follow-up interviews capture additional problem experience and changing perceptions.

Over the last decades qualitative research has been increasingly recognised as a valuable tool in applied social policy research (e.g. Ritchie and Spencer 1994, Srivastava and Thomson 2009). It can 'offer policy makers information about decision making, experiences and behaviour grounded in the experiences and world view of those likely to be affected by a policy decision' (Molloy *et al.* 2002, p. 1). The capture of data which are detailed, rich and complex enables 'how?' and 'why?' questions to be answered. Qualitative research is used in policy research and evaluation to, among other purposes, identify the factors that contribute to successful or unsuccessful delivery, identify outcomes and how they occur, and examine the nature of requirements of different groups within the target population (see Spencer *et al.* 2003).

Fieldwork was carried out in three of the centres, chosen to reflect the diversity across them in respect of a number of criteria, including geography, type of organisation running the centre (i.e. private firms or not-for-profit provision), subcontracting arrangements and length of time the centre had been operational.[5]

The fieldwork stages of the research took place in 2009, starting with three-day familiarisation and logistical visits to the CLACs. Subsequently, two researchers were embedded for one week in each selected CLAC, observing advice sessions and conducting first interviews with clients and advisors. The researchers returned two weeks after the first visit, and carried out in-depth interviews with clients who had been observed and consented to a second interview. Subsequent in-depth interviews were also conducted with a sample of advisors who had been observed. Together these data elements resulted in 169 separate data units.

A total of 42 advice sessions were observed with observation sessions covering all advice levels: diagnostic, generalist and specialist and encompassing the full range of areas of law in which CLACs were delivering services. The length of advice sessions varied between around 10 minutes to two hours. Each session was observed by two researchers to allow for added robustness with both recording their notes separately on a pro forma. Information captured details on clients and their demeanour, advisor demographics, physical environment, as well details of the client-advisor interaction such as the opening discussion, raising and exploring of issues, courses of action and explaining, and the concluding talk.

Client and advisor interviews were carried out for the advice sessions observed. The total number of clients who agreed to first interview was 41. First stage interviews took place immediately after the advice session, with one researcher interviewing the client, and the other the advisor. All interviews were exploratory and interactive in form and were based on a topic guide, which outlined the themes to be addressed. The purpose of the first client interview was to examine: client's motivations for attending the CLAC and how they prepared for the advice session; client perceptions of interacting and communicating with the advisor; client perceptions of the extent to which the session went as expected and the extent to which they felt it met their needs.

First advisor interviews explored: perceptions of interacting and communicating with the client; making decisions about raising, discussing and prioritising needs; shaping client expectations; deciding on courses of action; barriers to communication; advisor's sense of the client's understanding of their explanations and advice; perceptions of any other stated or unstated client advice needs; and factors which might have hindered or eased identification of other problems.

Clients who completed a first interview were invited to take part in a second interview. The total number of second client interviews was 29.[6] Second interviews were all conducted away from the advice centres under study, either in clients' own homes or at a community venue.

The interviews explored the social and economic circumstances of the client and their routes and pathways to the CLAC. They covered clients' expectations of the service and how these were formed. Clients were asked to recap on their presenting problem and asked about progress on it. The interview also explored any additional problems clients were experiencing, the relationship between problems, and reasons why any additional problems were or were not raised at the time of the advice session.

Second interviews were also carried out with a purposive (non-probability) sample of 15 advisors designed to include a range of demographics, experience and specialisms. Interviews covered the advisor's work history in the advice sector, their training, and experience of the pre- and current CLAC environments. Advisors were asked to describe the factors which made it easy or difficult to work with clients and to identify their problems, and about the use of referrals and signposting. They were also asked to describe what they saw to be the aims of CLACs, and barriers and facilitators to achieving these. The final part of the interview sought views on how the service could be improved and built upon.

All interviews with clients and advisors were digitally recorded with permission and later transcribed verbatim.

Extensive qualitative data were generated through the research, enabling wide-ranging analysis. The data gathered via observation and interview were analysed using the 'framework' method, an approach to qualitative data analysis developed during the 1980s at the National Centre for Social Research in London (Ritchie and Spencer 1994) and later incorporated into a standalone Computer Aided Qualitative Data Analysis Software (CAQDAS) package. The central component of the method is the thematic framework which is used to classify and organise the data according to key themes, concepts and subtopics. In this approach, each main theme is displayed, or 'charted' in its own matrix.

Rows within the matrix are used for cases and the columns are used for subtopics within the themes (Ritchie *et al.* 2003). Data management requires the identification of the initial themes in the data, the indexing of the data against these themes, and the systematic summarizing, sifting and sorting of the verbatim material.

The data were analysed by theme and by case. Each row within the matrix represented a client's case to which were attached a number of specific pieces of data, including the observation record, the first client interview, the first advisor interview and the second client interview, where an interview had been conducted. The significance of managing the data in this way was that all of the accounts related to each client's case, such as data from observations, first interviews and in-depth interviews, could be analysed together. This holistic approach to case analysis, enabling the integration of both client and advisor accounts, allowed cross checking and verification.

Using the 'framework' method, the transcripts and observation records from this study were subjected to a rigorous content analysis. The data were explored using descriptive accounts and explanatory accounts. Further classificatory and interpretative analyses were carried out and these form the basis of the findings reported here. The findings are illustrated with the use of quotations. The key themes to emerge from the analysis which are reported here are an introductory section on the profile of service users, followed by sections on accessibility, integration and the tailoring of services.

Results

Service users

The clients themselves were of a variety of ages ranging from around 18 to the mid-sixties and were divided almost equally between men and women. Some were from BME groups and some were from other European countries.

Clients presented at their advice session with a wide range of problems. The most common problems were associated with welfare benefits and these were often presented as mistakes on the part of benefits offices – as refusals or reductions in benefits or as overpayments. In several cases clients sought help with the completion of benefit application forms: '*... just glad these places exist. I'd be stuck without them. When you're scared of forms you're in the dark a bit.*'

The next most common were debt and employment problems. Several clients presented with family and housing problems. Clients presented with problem clusters, but often wanted help with a particular aspect of the cluster. Several clients were already being seen by the CLAC service about other issues.

One of the most noticeable client characteristics was the prevalence of health problems. In some cases these were associated with the presenting problem, for example in relation to benefits claims; for others their ability to cope with their problem was affected by their physical or mental health.

Importantly, clients' ongoing health problems impacted on their ability to participate in the advice sessions. Memory problems due to substance misuse, chronic brain disorders such as epilepsy, and earlier brain injury such as stroke sometimes interfered with clients' recall of facts and detail. For example, one client described his memory as '*hopeless*' and highlighted how he had '*really got to think*' in the advice session. Working around these health issues could therefore be challenging for advisors.

Members of a client's support network often accompanied clients to advice sessions. They were observed fulfilling a variety of functions, such as translation, morale support, information and confirmation providers, and a 'voice' when clients were very vulnerable.

Accessibility

Motivation to seek advice

Clients' reports of what motivated them to seek advice showed marked similarities. Clients needed assistance with routine paperwork or form filling. Clients with learning difficulties, health problems, language and literacy problems struggled with understanding paperwork and correspondence. Other clients had reached a crisis point in their management of an ongoing legal problem for which urgent assistance was needed. Typically, clients had attempted to manage the problem themselves but felt they could no longer cope on their own. These clients were at imminent risk of losing something significant in their lives. Some were at the point of losing their home while others were in fear of losing contact with their children following marital separation. Others were about to lose or have to repay money they did not have. Clients were also motivated to get help in response to action by another party, such as receiving a letter from a creditor or receiving court papers. All felt they had reached the stage of needing external, professional help: '*We didn't know where to go to get it from but we knew we needed to find somewhere to go*'. There was a general sense among the interviewees that their decision to visit the CLAC had been quite impulsive and motivated by an increasing sense of despair:

> Just spur of the moment decision I just decided I've had enough, I can't take it anymore ...

Seeking advice at the CLAC was often considered to be a '*last resort*':

> I thought 'Oh God this couldn't, you know, this is about the worst scenario'. And it was that that made me pick up the phone.
>
> This for me is the last solution, I have tried all my best.

Routes into the service

Clients came to the CLAC through a number of routes – including attending the drop-in service, contacting the CLAC by telephone, through the CLACs' outreach services or on the basis of a signpost from family, friends and acquaintances or from other external services or agencies.

Drop-in was greatly valued by clients as it enabled them to access services quickly following a decision to seek advice. Advisors also highlighted the advantages of drop-in for the type of clients using the services, given the seriousness and urgency of problems and client vulnerability.

> I think it's more flexible for [clients] because the kind of people that are coming through aren't the types to keep an eye on the time for appointments. Or some of them aren't willing to wait two weeks to get an appointment, they want something done that day when they're ready to get advice. Some people literally can't risk the time for an appointment... because it's urgent or it's going to be to their detriment. I think it works really well for the clients that we get, for example, people who are going to get kicked out in the next couple of days from their home.

However, there were disadvantages to drop-in services, especially where demand for advisors led to long waiting times and in some cases to clients being turned away.

The telephone was used both for making initial contact with reception services and for getting advice for those repeat clients who had been given direct dial numbers for advisors. Both clients and advisors talked about the role that telephone could play in service provision. Advisors felt that telephone could streamline the process of advice seeking for clients and widen the service for clients who were less able to come in person. Clients suggested telephone advice lines as an alternative to having to wait at the drop-in service, as a way of identifying their needs and making specialist appointments.

However, clients and advisors recognised the potential limitations to telephone provision as part of CLAC delivery. For example, one advisor stated:

> But we've got to think about what resources do the clients have; some people don't even have a phone in their property.

And clients felt it might not be suitable:

> I didn't know whether I could put my case forward on the phone, I didn't think I could explain it really well so I just decided to come down really.

Both clients and advisors spoke about the telephone as complementary to face-to-face provision rather than as a substitute. It was a component part of the advice process which offered potential that was not currently being harnessed.

None of the clients interviewed at the CLAC reported difficulties in getting to the advice centre. Nevertheless, advisors were aware that there were other people in need of legal advice who, for various reasons, would find it difficult getting to the CLAC. For those clients, outreach services were designed to offer access to legal advice.

Interviewees reported that they had gone to the CLAC on the basis of recommendations from a variety of people including friends, family and work colleagues:

> A friend of mine advised me to go and see them regarding my particular matter. She kind of had the same problem as me.
>
> My mum set it all up for me to come here and that.

Once clients had been for advice, they in turn 'spread the word' of the existence of the CLAC, so that others in their social network could also profit from the advice on offer.

People also attended the centres because they had been signposted there by other services or agencies. These recommendations came mainly from other local advice or support services, including the local Citizens Advice Bureau, private law firms, the local council and other community services.

The importance of 'word of mouth' recommendations and signposting from networks and local organisations in the community are therefore apparent. However, the location of the Centres, situated within the community, was also relevant. Interviewees reported that they had gone to the CLAC for logistical reasons – because of its proximity to their home or work.

Seamlessness

Seamless working was being achieved in CLACs, although not all the time and not for every client. Key factors that could facilitate or hinder seamless working included how reception operated; how diagnostics (also referred to as triage or gateway) were used; the relationship between generalist and specialist advisers; and the organisation of paperwork. Seamless working took on a particular significance in the CLAC delivery model, because most services involved some form of consortium arrangement to deliver the necessary range of legal specialisms as well as generalist and specialist tiers of advice. Partnership working had to be established in order for generalist and specialist tiers to work effectively and closely together, and it was crucial that the interface of processes between them supported that working.

Pathways through the services

Despite not being advisors themselves, receptionists could impede or facilitate an effective advice journey. Reception was the point at which initial filtering took place as the client was signposted on; asked to return at a less busy time; or invited to wait to see an advisor. Receptionists could contribute to an effective service by alerting the client on first contact to bring in all necessary paperwork. Indeed, clients who came unprepared sometimes found themselves being turned away or not being able to access the advice they needed, as this advisor points out:

> The problem sometimes happens, if it's a debt problem, they don't always bring their letters which means that if they've not brought their letters we then have to say that 'You're going to have to bring your letters back before we can take this any further'.

Receptionists were also described as helping to identify language needs for clients who had difficulty with English, and checking any forms which clients might bring in for completion to make sure it was something the CLAC could help with and to assess the likely time it would take.

Several advisors stressed the importance of reception and the need for the training of receptionists, especially as receptionists needed to be able to recognise urgent cases and filter them to an advisor in order to avoid delay or sending such clients away. Advisors were also aware of the importance to vulnerable clients of coming into a friendly and welcoming environment.

Diagnostic assessments were used in two of the CLACs during the research period, and were conducted by generalist advisors, both volunteer and paid. Advisors saw the key purpose of diagnostics as finding out enough information to be able to decide on the most appropriate source of advice and referral route for the client. However, there was ambiguity among the CLAC advisors interviewed about how long diagnostics were supposed to last. The timeframe for diagnostics was seen as challenging, especially for volunteers.

There were clients who were clear on the remit of the diagnostic interview, but others found it too short and had hoped for and expected immediate advice, as this client highlights:

> I didn't expect it to be sort of filling out the form, then somebody taking me into a room, looking at this and saying 'Right, just a minute' leaving the room, coming back and then 'There's your appointment. Bye bye'.

Diagnostic assessments were also used to establish client vulnerability and fast-tracking such clients to generalist or specialist advice. Fast-tracking was also used where the diagnostic advisor had established that a case was '*blisteringly urgent*'. Some advisors regarded the diagnostic system as a '*better model*' for routing clients through the system and filtering out those clients the CLAC could not help. It saved clients an unnecessary wait and it enabled the urgent cases to be separated out.

The dividing line between a diagnostic and a generalist session could be blurred for advisors, but the interview style was different in a diagnostic session. The latter left little room for exploration or probing for additional advice needs. However, generalists, in particular volunteers, wanted to spend time on interesting cases and feared deskilling if they did not get the chance to do this in diagnostic assessments.

Generalist advice was provided either at a drop-in session or by means of a full appointment and was regarded as '*more intense than triage.*' The length of generalist advice sessions varied depending on the nature of the client's problem and the action required, with the average length of generalist appointments across all three CLACs lasting 32 minutes.

In all the CLACs observed, the pressure of client numbers placed strains upon the generalist service and this factor was frequently mentioned in the advisor in-depth interviews. The lack of advisors at busy times was a common theme and was reflected in sometimes long waiting times for clients attending generalist drop-in and, in one CLAC, the early closure of drop-in sessions.

In this context, the difficulty of attracting and retaining volunteer advisors assumes an importance for the aim of seamlessness. The ability to work flexibly and as many hours as wanted was attractive to volunteers, but was difficult to reconcile with the demands of advice provision. One specialist spoke about the importance of avoiding a '*feast or famine*' situation where there were either too many or not enough volunteers on duty at any one time. In the CLACs with salaried generalist advisors, this issue did not arise. Evidence from one CLAC showed that volunteer time could be managed effectively to smooth advisor availability.

The generalist advice session was often the key session for determining the client's advice journey, and how seamless that journey would be. The role of the generalist included determining whether to help the client then and there or refer them on. Decisions about referral were generally taken in discussion with a supervisor or a relevant specialist.

The feeding in of higher-level supervisory support to generalists contributed to seamlessness by avoiding moving the client to another appointment. Where a CLAC involved volunteers, the role of the paid and experienced supervisor was seen as crucial in deciding the trajectory of a case and supporting the work of unpaid advisors. While this role provided structure for the volunteers, the need for consultation could confuse some clients or undermine their confidence in the advisor, if the process was not explained.

Through specialist advisors supporting generalists with expertise, clients benefitted from specialist knowledge without the need for a specialist appointment. This exchange worked particularly well when there was good integration between the service tiers, as highlighted by this quote from a generalist advisor:

> It's informal, for example, if you've got an appointment and you need advice on a particularly complex area, you just go to their room and have a chat with them there, often. I mean they are always... happy to talk to you if they are there... they wouldn't say they are busy.

Generalists also referred clients to specialists, although they were not always happy to do this, preferring to hold on to cases, especially where the integration of CLAC generalists and specialists was not particularly successful in logistical and cultural terms. In these cases, difficulties were also caused for specialists by inappropriate referrals and inadequate paperwork. High client numbers were thought to exacerbate these problems.

Waiting times from the generalist advice level for specialist appointments varied across CLACs and subject areas. Lack of available appointments could act as a barrier to the movement of clients from generalist to specialist and impede seamlessness.

At the time of research fieldwork there were four different routes for the client's journey to specialists. The most common was for the generalist CLAC advisor to make an appointment with a CLAC specialist advisor. Some clients also went directly from a diagnostic appointment to a specialist appointment. Other clients self-referred, in particular when they were repeat clients. Finally, clients with multiple problems were referred by one specialist to another CLAC specialist in a different area of law.

Enablers for a seamless advice journey

A key enabler for seamless advice journeys was a clear definition of roles and responsibilities among CLAC advisors of different tiers and organisations. Confusion was caused if the division of tasks was not well specified. This ranged from an understanding of the responsibilities for 'mundane' tasks, such as who made appointments and told clients what paperwork to bring, to who had responsibility for probing for additional problems.

Many of the clients observed during fieldwork were repeat clients. They presented particular challenges for CLAC services and how the CLAC dealt with these types of clients was a good indicator of how seamless or otherwise CLAC processes were. Repeat clients could be frequent visitors to the CLAC, they were often particularly vulnerable and their cases generated new information at each contact. The arrival of new forms, correspondence and decisions – especially those from public bodies concerning benefits, tax credits and similar – induced clients to return to the CLAC specialists. One of the specific challenges when dealing with repeat clients was therefore the sharing and accessing of information and paperwork across service tiers.

Well-organised paperwork processes were crucial in enabling a seamless advice journey for the client, including paperwork related to the case and service eligibility. All of the CLACs had procedures for passing case information between advisers across the service. Exchange of information could be hampered by the difficulty of data transfer between two service providers using different IT systems. Lack of clarity about the protocols governing data exchange could compound these difficulties.

Information sharing should enable subsequent advisors to deal with clients' problems in a continuous manner. The research findings indicated however that some form of 'story telling' to subsequent advisors may be important to clients, to establish trust with a new advisor. The research revealed a potential conflict between the emphasis in CLAC services on eliminating the need for clients to tell their story more than once, and the role of story telling for the building of trust between clients and advisors.

Integration

One of the key aims of the CLAC initiative was to address problem clusters through the provision of integrated advice, in other words, to detect and assist people with multiple problems. The research found clear evidence of problem clusters. In the words of one advisor:

> It's like a can of worms. When you open it, you pour a little bit and it all comes out.

Problems with debt, welfare benefits and employment were at the heart of the clusters observed. For most clients who were experiencing three or more problems, at least two of debt, welfare benefits or employment formed part of the problem cluster.[7] Family problems clustered with employment and housing. More unusual problem clusters included neighbours' problems, discrimination, immigration and problems with clinical negligence.

Clients themselves reported the triggering of inter-related cluster experience. As one client put it pertinently:

> That's when my whole life changed. My whole life changed, so there you go. Just the loss of a job, and that's it. It just tumbles and tumbles and tumbles after that.

The data show that advisors had mixed success in identifying problems beyond the presenting problems with which clients initially attended. Advisors were most successful at identifying all client problems when these were related to the presenting problem. Advisors were aware of common patterns of problem clusters, as one advisor commented '*welfare benefits and debt is usually quite interlinked,*' and so routinely checked for these additional problems. In some cases clients also raised additional problems themselves during the course of the advice session. There were instances where the advisor identified additional problems, noted them on case sheets, but did not raise them with the client. This was a strategy adopted by advisors when an issue which might arise in the future had been identified and the advisor knew that the client was already scheduled to return to the service.

Instances where clients' additional advice needs were not identified included cases where advisors had identified additional problems but where the client revealed even more problems during the research interviews. Typically, these cases were those in which the advisor had explored related problems but had not detected other unrelated advice needs. For example, a female client who visited the CLAC for help with a welfare benefits problem later revealed to researchers that she had a problem with an ex-partner over the division of property and money. When interviewed, the advisor explained that he only routinely checked for related problems such as debt.

There were a smaller number of cases where there had been no observable attempt to identify additional advice needs during the advice session but where clients spoke about multiple problems during the second research interview.

The research explored in detail the numerous challenges associated with problem identification. As set out below, these spanned issues originating with clients, including their demographic characteristics, their knowledge and their willingness to disclose problems, factors originating in the interaction between clients and advisors, the experience and training of advisors themselves and the advice environment.

A number of demographic characteristics were highlighted by advisors and clients as potential barriers to communication and therefore to problem identification. Significant among these were the health status of clients.

The health conditions of clients affected advisors' ability to manage sessions and probe for clients' advice needs. Poor physical health meant advisors had to ensure that sessions were not too lengthy. Advisors could be reluctant to ask too many questions of clients with poor mental health.

A consistent theme emerging from the research interviews with clients and advisors was that client knowledge about service scope and expectations often shaped the advice session and impacted on clients' willingness to raise additional issues. Some clients were well informed; however, there were many clients who had no, or limited, knowledge on what the CLACs were able to offer and as a consequence did not ask about additional issues. Expectations were also affected by experiences with other services. For example, one client explained that she had been told at another service '*we can only deal with one issue, so if you want to talk about something else you make another appointment so I think that stayed in my mind*'.

Clients generally arrived at advice sessions with a clear focus on the problem on which they were seeking help. This meant that they could be reluctant to engage in discussion about additional issues: '*I didn't feel comfortable discussing everything else and I would rather not have done*'. Advisors were well aware of the tendency for many clients to be set on sorting out one problem, not realising the gravity of other issues, and as advisors pointed out clients were not always best placed to identify which was the '*most important*' issue.

Client confidence in advisors was also crucial to a client's willingness to provide information. The confidence of clients in specialist advisors was largely very positive. Confidence in generalist advisors was more muted at times and was shaped by the pattern of such advisors leaving the session, either to consult with supervisors and/or specialists, or to look up information using the Internet or to photocopy materials. Confidence was also affected by clients' sometimes unrealistic expectations of what the advisor could do.

As one client described: '*I was just hoping someone would make it go away and take over from me and just leave me alone.*'

The research identified five key stages in the advice interview which affected how effectively advisors were able to engage clients and explore for a range of problems. These included the building of trust, allowing clients to tell their story, probing and exploring, checking of understanding and inviting other issues.

The trust between client and advisor was forged in a number of ways. The appropriate use of language was important to clients, especially for those whose first language was not English and those with learning difficulties. Clients also placed great emphasis on being treated with respect and on advisors being non-judgemental. Being non-judgemental made it easier for clients to talk to advisors revealing details about their lives, which were sometimes chaotic and unstructured.

Clients used eye contact and other non-verbal communication to determine if advisors were listening to them. Trust could be broken or depleted over time. The primary causes of this were weakness in client aftercare and a belated dissatisfaction with the service. In some cases this was because clients had found it difficult to carry out the tasks that advisors had suggested. In others it was rooted in a growing realisation that their expectations about the service had not been fulfilled; or that they had not had the outcome for which they had been hoping.

A key component of the interaction between clients and advisors was allowing clients to 'tell their story'. Clients used a variety of clues to check if advisors listened to them, including eye contact, appropriate pauses and the ability of advisors to repeat back what the client had been saying. The need for advisors to take notes could get in the way of good listening skills, and clients had mixed views about advisors' use of laptops.

A critical phase of the advice interview occurred when advisors tried to open up the session and explore additional issues with clients. Probing was used by advisors to gather detail and context on the presenting problem and potential additional problems. Very experienced advisors used both direct and subtle approaches to exploring additional problems. The way questions were asked affected whether clients felt able and willing to elaborate on their responses. A series of closed questions was not always a successful strategy with clients. There were limits to probing, especially where clients did not wish to discuss an issue.

Clients viewed the advice session positively when advisors checked their understanding of the advice and any next steps. A number of clients and advisors talked about the need to break problems into small and manageable chunks to aid understanding. One client said he needed an advisor to '*break it down a bit easier so it's easy to understand*'. Clients wanted the opportunity to clarify explanations and next steps as the following quote illustrates:

> I understood everything he was saying but just to make sure I got the information that I needed to give was, to go over it again just to make sure that I've got everything. You know because sometimes you can't take everything all in at once so you need to ask again too.

Clients were often invited to raise other issues at the end of a session, usually with an open question. This approach had mixed success in getting clients to reveal additional problems. For this strategy to work, clients needed both to recognise that an invitation was being extended and to be prepared to respond. When asked at their research interview, some clients had no recollection of being invited to raise additional issues, even though the research observers recorded that an invitation had been extended. More worryingly, even in those cases where clients knew that they had the opportunity they were sometimes reluctant to take it. A striking finding of the research was the impact of perceived time limits on client behaviour. Conscious of the pressure of demand for services, clients effectively restricted their use of services by limiting the number of issues raised with advisors. As one client described:

> I didn't bring it up because I just thought I've spent half an hour of her time and there's other people waiting so it's not fair if I bring 2 things up in one go.

Beyond the interaction they had with clients, advisor experience and training were also relevant to their ability to identify multiple problems that clients could be facing. Advisors emphasised that experience enabled them to understand the interlinked nature of particular problems and talked about '*being alert*' to issues. Training could substitute for experience where it was focussed on providing enough basics in different areas of law to enable advisors to pick up on clues.

The amount of time spent in sessions of differing types varied across the CLACs, which were operating different intake and appointment systems at the time of the research fieldwork. Time constraints could affect the ability of advisors to identify additional problems and make clients feel '*rushed*'. However, the ability of advisors to manage the time pressure made a big difference to the perception of clients about being hurried.

Both clients and advisors suggested that the advice environment could affect the dynamic of the interaction between them. Comfort, privacy and safety in the physical environment were important for both advisors and clients.

Cramped interview rooms were problematic when clients were accompanied by others. Advisors did not always regard clients being accompanied positively, as it could make it hard for them to focus on the '*real*' client and inhibit advisor questioning.

Tailoring services

In providing advice to CLAC clients, advisors made judgements about a client's capability to follow the course of action they suggested, and judgements on how the steps to be taken in furthering the case should be divided between themselves and the client. Health factors and any medication which might affect a client's abilities also had to be taken into account when tailoring services, because of their effect on client capacity. Some clients were very forthcoming about their conditions, enabling advisors to adjust next steps accordingly.

Some vulnerable clients were looking for, and needed, intensive support from the service. This presented a challenge in terms of tailoring service delivery – such support was time consuming and required specialist skills. Advisors picked up on vulnerability to varying degrees. This was easier when the clients were repeat clients whose situation was known in the CLAC concerned.

Advisors had to routinely make judgements about where to focus their efforts when tailoring CLAC services. One advisor felt that a client had wanted more help with a consumer problem than could be provided, and that his son could provide assistance if needed. She felt that where clients could do things then they should be encouraged to do so:

> . . . we do ask clients to, if they're able to do things like this themselves, you know, if they are more than capable of doing so, then we stress that they do it because we run a drop-in centre, so we want to avoid people coming back with the same problem . . .

Some advisors implied that client capability could be fostered or improved, and mentioned the notion of empowerment. A specialist advisor felt that it '*empowered*' the client to do things for themselves and that if a client was not vulnerable, then an advisor could say '*it's your problem*'.

Advisors recognised the advantages to the organisation of tailoring services in this way. It offered an opportunity to maximise the outputs of the CLACs because, by encouraging those clients who were judged able to take on tasks for themselves, the burden on the whole service could be reduced. The most capable clients also recognised the benefits of this division of labour:

> ... because, you know, the thing is, like simple things I can do it myself, you know. Why burden them, give them so much work when you can do it yourself? You know, help them and help yourself at the same time. You know. It's like I said, I'm not that educated but I can still write simple letters, you know, and do my own things.

When tailoring, advisors needed to be mindful of clients' access to other resources. An apparently straightforward next step could present a practical obstacle to a client. One client felt confident about undertaking the next steps which included a phone call to the Department for Work and Pensions. But during the second research interview it was apparent that, although she had done this, she had no income and was concerned about the cost of the call:

> ... because it's like they keep you on hold all the time and it's all, you know, I mean me and my partner have both got mobiles but to be quite honest to you, I've got no credit on them because we can't afford to, you know; with the money he gets he has been keeping the two of us. So you are having to use like public phones and it's just, it costs so much to get in touch with them.

Language was also linked to capability and tailoring. Even with a family member to translate, such cases demanded patience and extra effort from the advisor and could generate incomprehension and frustration on the part of clients. In none of the cases observed were external professional translators considered and advisors referred to the expense of such services as an impediment to their use.

When tailoring services, the wider context in which clients lived had to be considered. Dealing with clients' non-legal problems required advisors to have relationships with local health services or the police. Brokering these kinds of relationships was also important when it came to encouraging effective signposting into and out of the CLAC. One generalist advisor noted how the CLAC was being used as a default place of last resort:

> If the [local authority] can't handle what's going on they say 'go across the road to the [centre], you know, they'll sort you out.' The same with the police. [They] will send them here regardless of whatever the problem is.....the Job Centre will say 'oh we don't know what to do, go and see the [Centre].

Conclusions

This article has presented results from a comprehensive study of advice provision, detailing the advice process from the perspective of both advisors and clients. The research has demonstrated that the population of clients who came to the CLACs for advice showed a range of vulnerabilities, including learning and language difficulties, complex physical and mental health needs and cultural issues. This meant that for many clients there were potential intellectual barriers to accessing advice, such as difficulties in completing paperwork, accessing the information and advice needed, understanding the advice given and carrying out the actions given to them by advisors. Tailoring services across the range of client capabilities was a crucial aspect of service provision because it allowed more intensive support for the most vulnerable clients. Advisors tried to shape services to client capabilities, but determining the division of responsibilities was not always straightforward. Misjudgements about capability had resource implications because clients might simply have to return to the service, or could not follow the advice provided.

Given the vulnerability displayed by some clients, face-to-face advice appeared a critical mode of delivery, although both advisors and clients recognised the benefits that telephone services could provide as a complementary part of advice provision. The research showed that maintaining service access via drop-in was important, particularly for those clients who had reached a crisis point in managing their problem and needed urgent assistance. However, the research also highlighted the challenges for service providers of managing bulges of clients, especially for those services reliant on volunteers.

The research confirms that clients experience clusters of problems, but also identified the many challenges associated with problem identification. The research sheds light on why clients do not raise additional problems, adding a new dimension to research on problem clusters (Pleasence *et al.* 2004, Moorhead and Robinson 2006). The desire to postpone other problems, to concentrate only on the one uppermost in their minds, or to focus their limited energy on the problem that was causing the most immediate difficulty were identified as factors which inhibited disclosure. Clear barriers and facilitators to problem identification emerged from the research, taking both client and advisor perspectives into account (Smith *et al.* 2013). Understanding the advice dynamic is a pre-condition for integrated advice provision.

The findings highlight the benefits of an integrated advice service model for clients. Bringing together generalist (including diagnostic) and specialist advice in one service has important benefits for clients beyond the chance of being referred. It is advantageous for them as higher-level expertise moves along the advice chain, with specialist advice feeding into generalist advice sessions. This knowledge transfer helps to reduce the need for further appointments, with their potential for 'no-shows' and other resource use implications. However, it is crucial that generalist and specialist tiers work effectively and closely together in order to achieve this benefit, and that the interface of processes between them supports that working. Co-location of services offers a number of potential benefits here; though it is not in itself sufficient for co-working and delivery. The research data suggest that what is key is that services communicate with each other and that the boundaries between different parts of the service, whether defined by areas of work, by levels or by task, are clearly defined and understood in the same way by all staff. Where CLAC services were delivered by more than one organisation, agreements needed to be reached about protocols for data sharing.

On the eve of the implementation of LASPO, there is a great deal of uncertainty about what the future for social welfare law provision will hold. As discussed in the introduction, the Advice Services Transition Fund has been established to help the not-for-profit sector transform and adapt to the new funding environment. The early indications are that partnership working and a focus on vulnerable clients will continue to be important, as will be a search for new ways of delivering services. Given this, the experiences of clients receiving advice in the CLAC setting has continued applicability, shedding light on both client behaviour and the challenges specific to a partnership delivery model. Much can also be learnt from a separate process evaluation on CLACs and CLANs (Fox *et al.* 2010, Fox *et al.* 2011) which identified in detail factors of practical relevance to partnership working and joint funding. The challenge in the post-LASPO environment will be how to adapt service models and forge partnerships when public funding, as well as the high cost of the initiative for social welfare law provision has fallen significantly. Our article aims to make a contribution by looking back, to inform thinking for the future.

Acknowledgements

The authors would like to thank Judith Sidaway and Lesley Scanlan for their work on this project. We would also like to acknowledge the contributions of Ashish Patel and Catrina Denvir to the success of the project fieldwork.

Notes

1. Debt, employment, welfare benefits, housing and community care.
2. The LSC is a non-departmental public body sponsored by the Ministry of Justice, brought into being under the Access to Justice Act 1999 and thereby replacing the Legal Aid Board. The LSC will in turn be replaced by the Legal Aid Agency in April 2013, becoming an Executive Agency of the Ministry of Justice.
3. The Advice Services Transition Fund, a big Lottery Fund programme, will provide funding in 2013/14 and in 2014/15 to help not-for-profit advice organisations in England to adapt and develop new ways to meet local needs. The Cabinet Office will contribute £35m to the overall £65m budget.
4. There is no universally accepted definition of generalist advice, though it usually refers to basic or initial, often one-off, advice, provided by advisors who do not specialise in a particular area of law. Broadly speaking, specialist legal advice includes taking action on behalf of clients in order to move the case on, with the advisor taking responsibility for further action. This may include negotiation with third parties and liaising with third parties on behalf of the client, either by telephone, in writing, or face-to-face. It can also include the use of experts and interpreters, where appropriate. Specialist advisors should be able to provide complex legal advice in specific areas of law, including representation in legal proceedings.
5. For reasons of confidentiality and anonymity of research participants, the CLACs in which fieldwork took place are not named in this paper. However, they encompassed the range of provider type, the variation in subcontracting arrangements for the different tiers of service delivery, the length of time the services had been open and a range of contract values and volumes.
6. Three clients were not invited for second interviews because they were regarded by researchers as particularly vulnerable and unable to give fully informed consent. Three clients did not wish to participate in the second interview. There were no second depth interviews conducted with a further six clients although they were scheduled. One client could not attend because of illness, the interview of a second client was suspended because the interviewers felt that the client was no longer able to provide informed consent (this client had mental health problems), and in a further four cases the clients did not arrive at the scheduled interview time and could not be traced for rescheduling.
7. Of the 30 clients who experienced more than one problem, 17 had two problems, 10 experienced three problems, and the remaining three clients had four identified problems.

References

Balmer, N.J., et al., 2010. *Knowledge, capability and the experience of rights problems.* London: PLENET/LSRC Research Report.

Balmer, N.J., Pleasence, P. and Buck, A., 2010. Psychiatric morbidity and people's experience of and response to social problems involving rights. *Health and social care in the community*, 18 (6), 588–597.

Buck, A., 2007. The policy-demand for social research in civil justice: the UK perspective. *Zeitschrift für Rechtssoziologie/The German journal of law and society*, 2 (2), 165–178.

Buck, A., Balmer, N. and Pleasence, P., 2005. Social exclusion and civil law: experience of civil justice problems among vulnerable groups. *Social policy and administration*, 39 (3), 302–322.

Buck, A., et al., 2008. Do citizens know how to deal with legal issues? Some empirical insights. *Journal of social policy*, 37 (4), 661–681.

Buck, A., et al., 2009. *Outreach advice for debt problems: research and evaluation of outreach services for financially excluded people.* London: Legal Services Research Centre.

Cabinet Office, 2012. *Not for profit advice services in England.* London: Cabinet Office.

Crawford, R. and Phillips, D., 2012. Local government spending: where is the axe falling? In: C. Emmerson, P. Johnson and H. Miller, eds. *The IFS green budget 2012*. London: Institute for Fiscal Studies, 124–141.

Denvir, C., Balmer, N.J. and Buck, A., 2012. Informed citizens? Knowledge of rights and the resolution of civil justice problems. *Journal of social policy*, 41 (3), 591–614.

De Simone, T. and Hunter, R., 2009. Causes of inaction: barriers to accessing legal aid services. *Alternative law journal*, 34 (4), 265–269.

Edwards, S., 2003. *In too deep: CAB clients' experience of debt/.* London: Citizens Advice.

Fox, C., Moorhead, R., Sefton, M. and Wong, K., 2010. *Community Legal Advice Centres and Networks: a process evaluation*. London: Legal Services Research Centre.

Fox, C., Moorhead, R., Sefton, M. and Wong, K., 2011. Community Legal Advice Centres and Networks: A Process Evaluation, *Civil Justice Quarterly*, 30 (2), 204–22.

Genn, H., 1999. *Paths to justice*. Oxford: Hart.

Genn, H., Partington, M. and Wheeler, S., 2006. *Law in the real world: improving our understanding of how law works*. London: Nuffield Foundation.

Griffiths, A., 2008. *CLACs – are they worth it?* London: Advice Services Alliance.

HM Treasury, 2004. *Promoting financial inclusion*. London: HM Treasury.

Hobson, J. and Jones, P., 2003. *Methods of delivery: telephone advice pilot evaluation report*. London: Legal Services Commission.

Legal Services Commission, 2000. *Guidance and information for CLSPs*. London: Legal Services Commission.

Legal Services Commission, 2001. *Family advice and information networks consultation paper*. London: Legal Services Commission.

Legal Services Commission, 2005. *Innovation in the Community Legal Service: a review of 22 projects supported through the Partnership Initiative Budget*. London: Legal Services Commission.

Legal Services Commission, 2006. *Making legal rights a reality: the Legal Services Commission's strategy for the Community Legal Service*. London: Legal Services Commission.

Local Government Association, 2012. *Funding outlook for councils from 2012/11 to 2019/20*. Available from: http://www.local.gov.uk/c/document_library/get_file?uuid=c98405b7-b4a6-4b25-aebf-a63b5bcfa5c1&groupId=10171 [Accessed: 18 December 2012].

Lord Chancellors Department, 1998. *Modernising justice: the government's plans for reforming legal services and the courts*. London: Lord Chancellor's Department.

Mason, P., Hughes, N., with Hek, R., Spalek, B. and Ward, N., 2009. *Access to justice: evidence of the experiences of minority groups based on ethnicity, identity and sexuality*. Institute of Applied Social Studies, University of Birmingham and Allan Norman Celtic Knot, Birmingham. Ministry of Justice Research Series 7/09 May.

Matrix Research and Consultancy, 2004. *Independent review of the community legal service*. London: Department for Constitutional Affairs.

Ministry of Justice, 2009. *Study of legal advice at local level*. London: Ministry of Justice.

Mitchell, G. and Pierce, S., 2009. On the edge of the abyss: legal aid from 2010. *Legal action*, April, 8, 6–9.

Molloy, D., Woodfield, K. and Bacon, J., 2002. *Longitudinal qualitative research approaches in evaluation studies*. Department for Work and Pensions Working Paper Number 7. London: Department for Work and Pensions.

Moorhead, R., Robinson, M. and Matrix Research and Consultancy, 2006. *A trouble shared – legal problem clusters in solicitors and advice agencies*. DCA Research Series 8/06. London: Department for Constitutional Affairs.

Pleasence, P., 2006. *Causes of action: civil law and social justice*. Norwich: Stationery Office.

Pleasence, P. and Balmer, N.J., 2010. The audacity of justice: recession, redundancy, rights and legal aid. *Social policy and society*, 9 (4), 475–488.

Pleasence, P. and Balmer, N.J., 2012. On the rocks: recession-related life problems and relationship stability. *Child and family law quarterly*, 24 (1), 39–59.

Pleasance, P., et al., 2004. *Causes of action: civil law and social justice*. Norwich: Stationery Office.

Pleasance, P., et al., 2008. *Civil justice in England and Wales: report of the 2007 English and Welsh Civil and Social Justice Survey*. London: Legal Services Research Centre.

Ritchie, J. and Spencer, L., 1994. Qualitative data analysis for applied policy research. In: A. Bryman and R.G. Burgess, eds. *Analysing qualitative data*. London: Routledge, 173–194.

Ritchie, J., Spencer, L. and O'Connor, W., 2003. Carrying out qualitative analysis. In: J. Ritchie and J. Lewis, eds. *Qualitative research practice*. London: Sage, 219–262.

Smith, M. and Patel, A., 2008. *Money advice outreach evaluation: cost and effectiveness of the outreach pilots*. London: Legal Services Research Centre.

Smith, M., et al., 2013. Bridging the empirical gap: new insights into the experience of multiple legal problems and advice seeking. *Journal of empirical legal studies*, 10 (1), 146–170.

Spencer, L., et al., 2003. *Quality in qualitative evaluation: a framework for assessing research evidence. A quality framework*. London: Cabinet Office.

Srivastava, A. and Thomson, S.B., 2009. Framework analysis: a qualitative methodology for applied policy research. *Journal of administration and governance*, 74 (2), 72–79.

Walker, J., et al., 2007. *The family advice and information service: a changing role for family lawyers in England and Wales? Final evaluation report*. Newcastle: Centre for Family Studies.

Williams, C., 2004. Access to justice and social inclusion: the policy challenges in Wales. *Journal of social welfare and family law*, 26 (1), 53–68.

Arbitration in financial dispute resolution: the final step to reconstructing the default(s) and exception(s)?

Lucinda Ferguson

University Lecturer in Family Law, University of Oxford; Tutorial Fellow in Law, Oriel College, Oxford, UK

In this article, I argue for caution in embracing family arbitration as a new form of private ordering for resolving parties' financial disputes. I explain that family arbitration may be more successful than other forms of private ordering and final court hearings in enabling certain types of parties to resolve certain types of disputes. I consider why family arbitration may not become numerically significant despite its potential benefits, but may be much more important in normative terms. Lawyer-led negotiations remain the most common form of out-of-court resolution and constitute the de facto default form of bargaining in the shadow of the normative regime framed by ss 23–25 Matrimonial Causes Act 1973. Together with the transformation in approach to nuptial agreements, family arbitration may mark a normative shift towards autonomy and private ordering. I question whether this is a desirable step for family law, at least before we have resolved the underlying policy debate.

Introduction

Speaking in a Court of Appeal case concerning the publication of a judgment in an ancillary relief dispute, Thorpe LJ recognised the value of the full range of alternative dispute resolution mechanisms, and emphasised the strength of the case for renewed attention to family arbitration:

> I see no public policy objection to parties opting for an arbitrator or what is now known as 'private judging'. Resolution have presented a strong case for the introduction of binding arbitration in ancillary relief. The abstraction of cases from the Family Justice System, whether for alternative dispute resolution, collaborative practice or non-binding arbitration is generally to be welcomed. (*Lykiardopulo* v. *Lykiardopulo* [2010] EWCA Civ 1315, [69])

Two recent developments suggest a renewed impetus for divorcing couples to resolve their financial disputes through arbitration. Whilst both government policy and practitioner interest drives the recent mediation initiative,[1] the renewed focus on family arbitration is primarily practitioner-driven, and centres around the new Institute of Family Law Arbitrators (IFLA).[2] In addition to the IFLA scheme, the Arbitration and Mediation Services (Equality) Bill has been progressing through the House of Lords.

I argue that we should be cautious to invest significant energy into arbitration as a panacea for the perceived problems in resolving parties' family disputes, especially given the fate of mediation.[3] It may well be that family arbitration can be more successful than mediation in enabling parties to resolve certain types of disputes. Given that lawyer-led negotiations remain the most common form of out-of-court resolution, however, it may be that family arbitration's impact will not be numerically significant. But family arbitration may be very important in normative terms. For some time, bargaining in the shadow of family law has meant that the default normative financial dispute regime has been one of viewing s 25 of the Matrimonial Causes Act 1973 (c. 18 (MCA 1973)) through the lens of 'fairness', (as outlined in leading cases such as *White* v. *White* [2000] 1 AC 596; *Miller* v. *Miller*; *McFarlane* v. *McFarlane* [2006] UKHL 24) whilst the *de facto* default has been lawyer-led negotiations.[4] Along with the change in attitude to nuptial agreements, the rise of family arbitration has the potential to privatise the very types of cases that shape the normative default and risks disrupting that status quo. I question whether this is a desirable step for family law, at least before we have resolved the larger family policy debate this raises.

Two recent developments in arbitration: The IFLA Scheme; the Arbitration and Mediation Services (Equality) Bill

In February 2012, the IFLA launched a family arbitration scheme, which will be discussed in more detail below. In brief, it sets out guidelines for the exercise of arbitration by specialist trained arbitrators, as well as providing the framework for training those individuals who will act as arbitrators. Concern has been expressed that this might lead to the development of a 'shadow system of family justice' (Gardner 2012). Private ordering of financial disputes has long been characterised as 'bargaining in the shadow of the law' (Mnookin and Kornhauser 1979), so why should we be concerned about emphasising one particular form of private ordering? Does the adjudicatory feature or alleged enforceability of arbitrated 'awards' make family arbitration particularly troubling or promising for the family justice system?

The Arbitration and Mediation Services (Equality) Bill was introduced by Baroness Cox as a Private Member's Bill and arose out of her concern that women were being treated unequally by tribunals operating under Sharia law (HL Deb 19 October 2012, col. 1683), although on its terms, it addresses not just all forms of religious arbitration, but arbitration tout court. Reading the Bill is somewhat confusing. Clause 4 proposes to insert s80A into the Arbitration Act 1996 (c. 23 (AA 1996)) to specify that '[a]ny matter which is within the jurisdiction of the criminal or family courts cannot be the subject of arbitration proceedings'. Clause 7 of the Bill originally envisaged criminalising the claiming of jurisdiction in relation to either of these matters,[5] although Baroness Cox (col. 1716) has since recognised the need to confine that to matters within the jurisdiction of the criminal courts.[6] Yet, in 2008, when he was Lord Chancellor and Justice Secretary, Jack Straw MP stated that '[a]rbitration is not a system of dispute resolution that may be used in family cases' (HC Deb 24 November 2008, col. 866W). Straw was responding to a question focused on Sharia law and the government's policy towards agreements reached by parties using Sharia councils. However, his answer is a broader comment on the status of all forms of family arbitration. If the Justice Secretary considered that there could not be any family arbitration in 2008, had matters really changed by the introduction of the IFLA scheme in 2012?

The IFLA scheme was grounded in the AA 1996 presumably because those involved took the view that family arbitration was as valid a subject-matter for arbitration as commercial disputes. Yet, Straw and the 2012 Bill assume otherwise. Perhaps both of the latter are simply too broadly expressed and were in fact concerned solely with enforceability and the assertion thereof, rather than with the occurrence of arbitration at all. Even then, as discussed in section 5, below, the enforceability of family arbitration is a matter of debate. Alternatively, if Straw and the 2012 Bill are addressing the idea of arbitration in family law disputes more generally, then it is clear that we need to consider the case for family arbitration so that we do not prematurely stifle the fledgling IFLA scheme.

A proposed amendment to Clause 4 suggests that we might try to regulate separately religious and other family arbitration.[7] But such a differentiation would be fraught with difficulty and uncertainty. How would one assess a religious arbitration that explicitly claimed to operate in accordance with the non-religious IFLA scheme or the provisions of the MCA 1973?[8] Arguably, both Straw's remarks and the 2012 Bill turn on an implicit distinction between non-religious and religious family arbitration. If there is a good case to be made for family arbitration generally, the debate over the place of religious family arbitration will need to be settled.

The urgency of this debate is heightened by trends within the family justice system more generally. When it comes into force in April 2013, the Legal Aid, Sentencing, and Punishment of Offenders Act 2012 will introduce a new basis for assessing entitlement to legal aid in the family law sphere. It is debatable to what extent this will result in more litigants in person in court (Miles 2011a, 2011b, Harris 2012), but the downward pressure on the legal aid budget is clear. This sits alongside increased policy emphasis on parties pursuing alternative dispute resolution instead of having their cases settled in a final hearing. The recommendations in the Family Justice Review (Norgrove 2011), for example, '... are intended to enable divorcing couples to dissolve their marriage efficiently and, wherever possible, to reach an agreement on financial arrangements without using the court' (p. 36). Stowe (2011) argues that family arbitration 'would certainly seem to have all the advantages that other ADR methods lack, and therefore appears to be a highly attractive proposition'. Yet, given that it will likely be out of the reach of those individuals who no longer qualify for legal aid, who will benefit from these advantages? Can it effectively move individuals out of litigation or only out of other forms of ADR? Arbitration may work well in the commercial context, but the family justice system and the family court system it seeks to replace in some cases are quite distinctive,[9] with an informal, flexible process and without being shown to increase the level of conflict between the parties.[10]

An outline of the IFLA scheme[11]

The Family Procedure Rules 2010 (SI 2010/2955 (FPR 2010)), which came into force in 2011, require the court to '... consider, at every stage in the proceedings, whether alternative dispute resolution is appropriate' (R.3.2). This has been supplemented by Practice Direction 3A, the Pre-Application Protocol for Mediation Information and Assessment, which requires anyone seeking a financial remedy (Annex B, para. 2) to arrange to attend a Mediation Information and Assessment Meeting (MIAM) (Annex A, para. 2). Whilst the requirement is to contact a family mediator, other forms of ADR, including arbitration, are discussed in the meeting. This insertion of ADR into the process suggests that arbitration has much potential for growth.

There is evidence, however, that the courts are not treating the MIAM as a true pre-condition. Fifty-six per cent of respondents to a Resolution (2012) survey of its members' experiences at over 100 courts reported that court staff did not require evidence that a party had attended a MIAM. Seventy-eight per cent reported that their local courts did not enquire at any stage whether ADR was appropriate. MIAM-referrals also seemed to be heavily practitioner-dependent. Approximately one-third of respondents reported referring 91–100% of clients to MIAM, whereas one-fifth had only referred 0–10%. It surely cannot be that clients are so very, very different in terms of suitability for any form of ADR?

In its pre-legislative scrutiny of the Children and Families Bill 2012, the House of Commons' Justice Committee (2012) recognised the need to ensure consistency in the requirement to attend a MIAM, proposing that inclusion in the FPR 2010 would achieve this. Depending on the precise content of the MIAM and client interest in pursuing arbitration as a result, this might suggest additional scope for growth in use of family arbitration ([112], Recommendation 23). How attractive is the scheme? What follows is a very brief outline. Currently, the scheme applies only to financial matters, such as disputes under Part II of the MCA 1973 and Schedule 1 of the Children Act 1989 (c. 41), which cannot include any children issues (Art. 2 Rules).[12] The inclusion of disputes involving the Trusts of Land and Appointment of Trustees Act 1996 (c.47) has the potential to create some difficulties in practice, given that that statute is governed by the Civil Procedure Rules 1998, rather than the FPR 2010, and some cases are more appropriately heard in the Chancery Division rather than the Family Division.

Arbitrations under the IFLA Rules are to be conducted in accordance with the mandatory and non-mandatory provisions of the AA 1996 (Art. 1.3). The critical provisions to note are the s 1 general principles, which set out the aims for arbitration; the s 33 general duty of the tribunal; and the s 40 general duty of the parties. The s 81 preservation of the common law will be discussed below insofar as it relates to the debate over the enforceability of arbitrated 'awards'. Certain non-mandatory provisions may be excluded, replaced, or modified by either the Rules and/or the parties' agreement. The law of England and Wales governs arbitrations under the scheme (Art. 3). Parties refer a dispute to arbitration under the scheme by submitting an 'ARB1' form, which can include the nomination of a particular arbitrator. There are two possible arbitration procedures under the scheme: the general procedure set out in Art. 10 and the alternative procedure set out in Art. 12, which more closely mirrors that in Part 9 of the FPR 2010. Either the parties can agree or the arbitrator can choose which procedure to follow. At the conclusion of the arbitration, the arbitrator makes an 'award.' Its status is hotly debated and will be discussed in detail below.

Arbitration within the landscape of private ordering

Before evaluating the advantages and disadvantages of family arbitration, it is important to understand the landscape in which it is intended to sit. We need to determine whether we should evaluate family arbitration by contrasting it with a final court hearing, with one or more particular other forms of private ordering, or with all other options by simply considering any benefits that make it the most appropriate method of dispute resolution in particular contexts.

I suggest that there are at least three models of private ordering (including family arbitration) and court involvement: firstly, family arbitration might be seen as one method on a sliding scale that moves from the least to the most state involvement in dispute resolution; secondly, we might decide that it is better to consider the various methods of dispute resolution simply as alternative approaches to be contrasted; thirdly, it might be that the various methods of dispute resolution relate as intersecting circles, most significant where distinctive, i.e. where not overlapping.

Sliding scale

If family arbitration is on a spectrum, we might think of it as occupying a distinct position on a scale that moves from processes that are participant-directed to those that are court-directed. This would fit with some of the practitioner-led narrative, such as Hodson's earlier description of family arbitration as '... a crucial middle ground between court and mediation' (2002, writing at the time of the earlier family arbitration project). One version of this model might be as follows: (1) administrative financial arrangements (whereby the parties themselves simply reach an agreement directly and have it represented in a Consent order); (2) such an agreement reached between the parties, but with some minimal assistance, such as information provided via an automated phone service or online; (3) nuptial agreements; (4) mediation (which might be categorised in a number of ways); (5) collaborative family law, including co-operative family law; (6) early or third party neutral evaluation; (7) private financial dispute resolution (FDR); (8) family arbitration; (9) court involvement, from an initial FDR appointment to a final hearing.

This model presupposes that each form of dispute resolution is sufficiently discrete and internally coherent so that it can occupy only one position on the scale. It also assumes that there is only one key variable here – the degree of state intervention. Whilst there is some support for this sliding scale approach to thinking about dispute resolution, it immediately encounters difficulties. Whilst there is no real debate over how to define family arbitration, there are multiple ways of understanding what we mean by mediation and the most appropriate way to construct mediation in this context. For example, should we distinguish between family counselling and legally-oriented mediation?[13] What if we preferred Boulle's categorisation between 'settlement', 'facilitative', 'evaluative', and 'therapeutic' mediation (cited by Spencer and Brogan 2006, p. 100)? What of the more recent 'transformative' (Fisher 2006, p. 2),[14] and 'narrative' (Winslade and Monk 2000, p. 3) terminology? Should in-court conciliation be seen as mediation for the purpose of this assessment?[15] This uncertainty of scope and categorisation is not a criticism of the use of mediation in financial disputes as its flexibility is central to its success. Yet, it does make it very difficult to suggest that it can occupy a single place on a sliding scale of state intervention in financial dispute resolution.[16]

The place of family arbitration on such a sliding scale is also less straightforward than it initially appears insofar as, whilst there is indeed less state intervention in most forms of mediation and collaborative law, the nature of the intervention is different. In family arbitration, the parties freely choose to enter into the process with no intervention at all; the detail of the process is then governed by a mixture of state-imposed – AA 1996 – and party-chosen provisions. The outcome is then determined by the arbitrator and only indirectly participant-led in the sense that the identity of the arbitrator is selected by the parties. In mediation and collaborative law, however, both the process and outcome are shaped by the participants, but neither is generally freely determined by them. Using such a sliding scale might also create a risk of confusion as parties might move back and forth between different forms of dispute resolution adjudged to be more and less interventionist as part of a larger process. For example, family arbitration or mediation can often occur during the adjournment of ongoing court proceedings.

A single variable approach with 'triage'[17] based on the degree of state intervention is thus unhelpful as it requires us to accept only one version of each type of dispute resolution in order to place it on the scale. This overlooks the qualitatively different nature of state intervention and can only respond to the extent of intervention. It also assumes that the extent of state intervention is indeed the only critical variable.

Might we remedy these concerns by transforming the sliding scale approach into one that contains multiple variables on intersected sliding scales? One scale might consider the degree of state intervention, another the speed of the process, another the costs incurred, and so forth. But the flexibility within individual types of dispute resolution, such as mediation and arbitration, as well as the flexibility needed for particular clients, makes it very difficult, if not impossible, to situate types of dispute resolution at only one point on any of these scales. Much of the success of particular dispute resolution processes depends on how individual clients experience the process as adapted to them. The sliding scales approach appears incapable of capturing this necessary subjectivity. Further, it cannot straightforwardly accommodate those variables which do not exist on a scale and operate in a binary manner, such as concern for confidentiality, in relation to which one might conclude that all forms of private ordering that do not require a court hearing all respect confidentiality to a similar degree.

Category-based comparison of alternative approaches

Instead of attempting to situate the various models of financial dispute resolution on a single sliding scale or multiple intersecting sliding scales, we might instead simply approach them as alternatives to be compared and contrasted. This model presupposes that each method is sufficiently discrete to be isolated for comparison purposes. It also presumes that there are sufficient shared variables to enable such a comparison to illuminate the key elements of each approach. Barlow *et al.*'s ongoing research (2012–15)[18] into three pathways to resolution appears to fit this model. Their project assesses lawyer-led negotiation, mediation, and collaborative law in terms of their scale of adoption, user and practitioner perception, and suitability for particular types of disputes and/or clients (Barlow *et al.* 2012–15).

This category-comparison approach constitutes one of the key narratives of private ordering. Lord Falconer, chair of the IFLA, for example, commented that '[a]t a time when there is a need to find solutions in family disputes outside the courtroom, it is a logical next step to offer arbitration as another means of doing so' (quoted in IFLA 2012a). His remarks identify family arbitration with private ordering, so that the perceived need to avoid court and use private ordering can provide additional justification for the turn to family arbitration. In a similar move, and as Eekelaar (2010, p. 315) explains, the Interim Report of the Family Justice Review and the government's proposals on legal aid identified private ordering with mediation in its contrast with adjudication. In relation to mediation, Genn (2010) notes that '[its] benefits ... are ... expressed in opposition to adjudication, despite the fact that most civil cases are settled out of court, rather than by means of judicial determination' (p. 196). Yet, can we understand the landscape in this way? Can we use arguments in favour of private ordering in general in order to underpin particular types of private ordering? The variation within private ordering, and the prevalence of private ordering compared with resolution through final court hearings, suggests not.

At least part of this narrative strategy may be explained by the difficulty in delineating individual categories of dispute resolution within private ordering. Mediation illustrates this well. Whilst we might be able to identify the hallmarks of mediation, such as the mediator's impartiality and the voluntariness of the process (McCrory cited in Roberts 2008),[19] the variation between practitioners might make this sort of category-based comparison similarly reductionist. Indeed, given the fluidity of the nature of parties' engagement with private ordering, it might yield a clearer understanding if any attempt to create a model of categories for comparison were empirically-led. Instead of starting with pre-determined categories of dispute resolution and then looking to their content and variation therein, it might be more profitable to start by observing disputing couples and their engagement with dispute resolution. We could then examine those activities to consider what categories of resolution process emerge, which might not neatly fit the existing typology of private ordering. This gap in strong empirical research would also further shed light on the possibility for determining critical variables for a more complex sliding scale model.

Intersecting circles

Finally, we might view family arbitration and other forms of financial dispute resolution as intersecting circles, each being most significant where it is distinctive, i.e. where not overlapping with other types of dispute resolution processes. The starting-point for this intersection approach might lie in the early recognition that law and mediation are already blending: mediators operate with a view to agreements being acceptable to court[20] and, in order to lead their clients to settlement, lawyers are necessarily somewhat therapeutic in their approach (e.g. Eekelaar *et al.* 2000). Focusing on the non-overlapping aspects of each category enables us to overcome some of the concern over the fluidity between different forms of private ordering. In the absence of strong empirical research, it also permits us to isolate known key strengths and weaknesses of each approach.

One might argue, for example, that the most important aspect of collaborative law – that marks it out from other forms of private ordering, such as mediation – is the commitment not to litigate, unless with another lawyer, by the signing of a 'participation agreement'. Focusing on this particular feature might enable us to identify particular types of parties or conflicts that are especially well- or ill-suited to a collaborative approach. With family arbitration, one might focus on the additional procedural protections for vulnerable parties, and use that to direct particular types of parties or conflicts towards or away from arbitration.

However this intersecting circles approach may require oversimplification of the content of the various elements that overlap. For them to be perceived as intersecting, our model needs to assume that each dispute resolution process thinks of each element in the same way. This works straightforwardly in relation to respect for confidentiality. Each dispute resolution process can be assessed as either respecting client confidentiality or not; there are no competing accounts of what it means to respect confidentiality. This is not the case for other apparently common elements, such as respect for autonomy. Whilst both mediation and family arbitration can be said to respect client autonomy in a sense, it is not clear that it is in the same sense. One might imagine that the empowerment aspects of mediation differ from the respect for autonomy in the adjudicatory features of arbitration. As a result, whilst mediation and family arbitration appear to intersect in terms of respect for autonomy, they may not in fact do so. An intersecting circles model works only if the common elements they share in fact are the same, not if they merely appear to be the same.

In addition, family arbitration is currently being considered only in relation to financial dispute resolution. If arbitration were expanded into children issues it is not clear whether we would be able to employ the same model of its place within private ordering or whether we then might require two complex diagrams, one for financial disputes and another for children issues. All that is clear at this stage is that private ordering is complex, setting out its interplay with court-led adjudication even more complex, and we should be wary of categorisations and points of comparison constructed without good empirical evidence.

A contextualised evaluation of the proposed benefits of family arbitration

In their Joint Ministerial Foreword to the Government's Response to the Family Justice Review, the Justice and Education Secretaries outlined the problems in private family law as follows:

> Too often, divorcing couples end up arguing over deeply sensitive and emotional issues in the adversarial environment of the courtroom, when they might have resolved their disputes more quickly, simply and consensually outside it. (Ministry of Justice and Department of Education 2012, p. 4)

As has been discussed above, this misrepresents the current landscape. Yet, this attitude also underpins the evaluation of the proposed benefits of family arbitration. Its potential is expounded in contradistinction to final hearings and adjudication more generally, despite the reality of financial dispute resolution. This assumption of comparators within the dispute resolution field will be shown to affect the strength of the proposed benefits of family arbitration.

The proposed benefits

Singer argues that the 'potential benefits ... are piled pretty high in those cases and for those clients for which and for whom arbitration may be appropriate' (2012a, p. 1359). Family arbitration is thus envisaged as the new, preferred approach to financial dispute resolution for some, but not all, cases and clients. Yet, we are left to work out which types of parties and/or disputes that might include. In what follows, I address the benefits proposed by the IFLA (2012c) as well as some additional possible benefits.

Confidentiality

The IFLA suggests that a key benefit of the IFLA scheme is confidentiality. The parties select the venue and there is no possibility of media access, hence no publication of either the occurrence of the arbitration or the 'award' made. This may well be a critical distinctive benefit given that the general approach under the Family Proceedings (Amendment) (No. 2) Rules (SI 2009/857) is to allow accredited members of the press to attend ancillary relief proceedings (Practice Direction: Attendance of Media Representatives at Hearings in Family Proceedings [2009] 2 FLR 157). In *Lykiardopulo*, the Court of Appeal recognised the importance of confidentiality for some parties in financial disputes. Mrs Justice Baron had agreed to publication in anonymised terms out of concern for the impact of the publicity on the husband's health and the family business (Thorpe LJ, [56], [61]). The Court of Appeal decided to publish in redacted, un-anonymised terms because of the lack of evidential basis for the alleged harms that such publication would inflict on the husband's health, the family business, and the children (Thorpe LJ, [65], [68], [70], [73]). In his concurring judgment, Stanley Burton LJ agreed with Thorpe LJ's reasoning ([81]), but also suggested that the husband's non-disclosure and perjury in respect of his business assets prevented him from claiming entitlement to respect for confidentiality in relation to affected documents and information (Stanley Burton LJ, [79]).

In the High Court, Baron J also expressed more general concern for the '*Spencer* Factor,' i.e. that, following publicity surrounding the proceedings, the parties would not continue to a full hearing but, in order to avoid further publicity, would instead settle their dispute privately (Thorpe LJ, [63–64]). Her concern was couched in terms of the possible injustice that might be suffered by one of the parties, though Baron J noted that, with the withdrawal of the parties from the judicial process, such speculation was impossible (Thorpe LJ, [63]).

Confidentiality in family arbitration is better seen as a key benefit for at least one party, but not necessarily for both. Subject to any need to obtain a Consent order or opportunity to appeal, there may not be any judicial oversight over the 'award' made in family arbitration; hence confidentiality may hide potential injustice to one party. Yet, this is no less oversight than in relation to private ordering more generally and the arbitrator and arbitration process may provide greater protection for both parties' interests than in other forms of private ordering.

Cost

The IFLA suggests that in many cases arbitration would be cheaper than court proceedings (2012c). This would represent a potential saving for the parties and definite savings for HM Courts and Tribunal Service. Yet, the parties must pay a fee for the arbitrator, the venue, and so forth. Further, the appropriate comparator may not be the cost of proceeding to a final hearing. Might these couples have resolved their disputes through the usual out-of-court lawyer-led negotiations or mediation? If so, that is the accurate comparison. In the absence of evidence as to the appropriate comparator, it is much more difficult to assess the value of this stated benefit. Singer (2012b, p. 1497) suggests that the speed of the resolution would offset the arbitrator's fee. We might then ask if the argument for reduced costs depends upon quick resolution. More generally, is this argument for reduced costs even relevant beyond wealthy clients? The reported recent rise in self-represented litigants (Pendlebury Cox 2012)[21] in financial disputes hints that those who cannot get access to legal aid are more likely to avail themselves of the court service for free and rely on the ever-more strained court resources than pay for arbitration. Given the formalities of entry into the IFLA process, it is unclear whether self-represented clients would avail themselves of arbitration. The IFLA (2012c) 'strongly recommend[s] that each party takes legal advice before entering into the arbitration agreement'. It further provides (2012c) that as '[a]rbitration has some similarities with court proceedings … being represented by a lawyer may be the most effective way to present a case and legal arguments'. As a result, empirical evidence for reduced costs and for whom is required before it can be stated as a clear benefit.

Speed

The IFLA identifies the speed of the arbitration process as a marked benefit over the court process. However, we have no evidence of this to date. Further, as noted above, it is not clear that the appropriate comparator is the court process rather than other forms of private ordering such as lawyer-led negotiations. To the extent that the parties would have otherwise proceeded to a final hearing, it may be significantly beneficial that they can appoint an arbitrator without delay, in contrast to the usual months-long delay for a court date. To make family arbitration more attractive, Ryder J noted that the Money and Property working group engaged in family justice reform would consider the possibility of an expedited Consent order process where 'awards' needed to be so recognised (Ryder 2012, [62]).[22] The value of this proposed reform depends in large part on the view we take of the enforceability of arbitrated 'awards', as discussed below.

Flexibility

Grounded in the AA 1996, the IFLA scheme is designed to be flexible. The parties can define the terms of reference for arbitration, as well as aspects of the procedure to be followed. Singer notes, for example, that the parties can choose to make written submissions only (2012b, p. 1496). The parties can also choose the time and the place of any hearings. Where an expedited process is desirable, the flexible process enables it. The flexibility of the process also enables a slower process, so that the arbitrator can 'encourage the parties' to address individual issues or the dispute as a whole via other forms of ADR as appropriate (IFLA 2012b, Arts 17.1–2). As a result, the benefit of flexibility may impact on the potential benefit of speed in any particular case. Whilst flexibility will be of benefit to busy clients, empirical evidence would be needed to show that, in the larger context of individuals' experience of family disputes, this flexibility was more than a minor benefit to them.

Interplay with other types of ADR

As noted, the flexible family arbitration process enables the parties to move in and out of other forms of ADR during the arbitration process and vice versa. This interplay with other forms of ADR may also be important of itself as part of the larger aim of enabling the parties to avoid the need for a final hearing wherever possible. Singer provides the example of an imperilled mediation where there are entrenched disagreements on particular issues that can be severed, resolved by arbitration, and then fed back into the larger mediation process (2012b, p. 1497). Further data is required, however, to show that simply avoiding a final hearing through some combination of private ordering is of real benefit to clients.

Choice of arbitrator

This reflects both the flexibility of the process and the participants' ownership of it. The parties are free to choose an arbitrator from the IFLA's directory. Again, the IFLA compares this to the inability to choose which judge will hear their case in court (2012c). Much of the significance of this proposed benefit turns on the particular arbitrator. Speaking extra-judicially, Lord Wilson suggested that such an arbitrator

> ... will need to be as wise as the family judge whose outstanding judicial qualities are intended to have been identified in the course of the appointments system and who in many cases will have developed the art of wise decision-making by experience over the years. (2011)

Even with specialist training in arbitration, might new family arbitrators not be as skilled in making these kinds of decisions as family judges? Singer suggests that arbitrators would come out of the comparison more favourably, arguing that '... there is no guarantee that the judge allotted by the court listing officer will have the same degree of specialist knowledge or experience in resolving financial disputes nor be conversant with the often highly complex financial arrangements that the parties are seeking to unravel' (2012b, p. 1498). Unlike in the case of the judiciary, there is no independent body to whom parties can complain about arbitrators' appointments process or arbitrators' conduct (Geffin 2012, p. 9).

Given that these arbitrations will be confidential, it will be difficult to gather more than anecdotal evidence as to whether there is a notable difference in the quality of the decision-maker. In any event, as noted previously, final hearings in court may not be the appropriate comparator. If correct, we would need to instead compare parties' freedom to choose an arbitrator together with their solicitors, alongside the other party and their lawyers, to their freedom to choose solicitors to negotiate with the other party's solicitor on their behalf. Such a comparison does not appear to suggest a distinct advantage in the family arbitration context.

Respect for autonomy

Whilst not necessarily an independent benefit, this might represent an important consequence of other particular benefits such as the procedural flexibility and choosing the arbitrator. Singer argues that arbitration '... allows the parties the dignity of having as much 'ownership' of the progress of what is after all their process' (2012a, p. 1353). We might extend the idea of ownership to that of enabling parties to be as autonomous as possible. Yet, it is only the process and not the outcome that the parties choose; the parties merely make representations before the arbitrator decides on the appropriate 'award'. Whilst the process is flexible, the AA 1996 and IFLA scheme Rules mean that the parties do not have complete control over the arbitration procedure and that family arbitration envisages the parties being legally represented. As the IFLA scheme is new, it is not yet clear how parties experience this process and whether it empowers them in any way that the usual lawyer-led negotiations do not.

Protection of vulnerable parties

This potential benefit might be seen as an aspect of respect for the parties' autonomy, and includes particular concerns about parties in cases involving domestic violence. Concerns have been expressed about the capacity of mediation to ensure equal treatment of the parties' interests. Davis (2001), for example, concludes that:

> Mediation is essentially a form of assisted negotiation, and as such it cannot be an effective alternative to certain other aspects of the service that is provided to vulnerable people by their lawyers. Specifically, mediation does not offer the same level of support, it is unlikely to be able to contain overwhelming bitterness and anger, and it does not connote authority... (Conclusion)

Similarly, instead of the mediation process enabling the parties to be treated as equal, Baroness Deech suggests that mediation is valuable '... *provided that* the parties meet on equal terms' (emphasis added, HC Deb 19 November 2012, col. 1704). Writing extra-judicially, Lady Hale (2011) expressed concern about the possibility of compulsory mediation in terms of '... the power imbalances between the parties. Unless it is very professionally conducted, there is plenty of scope for the strong to bully the weak into agreeing a solution which is against their best interests.'

Would the more legalistic procedural protections of the AA 1996, the IFLA scheme Rules, and the role of the arbitrator remedy this concern in relation to family arbitration? Baroness Deech suggests not. She argues that '[a]rbitration ... may perpetuate irregularity of status that goes down the generations to the disadvantage of children if it is presented as the legal solution to a situation that needs finality in civil law' (HC Deb 19 November 2012, cols 1704–1705). Although her remarks are made in the context of religious arbitration, the divide between religious and non-religious arbitration is debatable and difficult to sustain.

The IFLA does not raise this as a potential benefit. Yet, if family arbitration is to be an adjudicatory alternative to court proceedings, procedural protection is important. Articles 8.4–8.6 of the Rules set out the arbitrator's powers to respond to failure to comply with obligations such as disclosure, including adverse inferences [Art.8.5] and allowing the other party to apply to court for a similar direction [Art.8.6]. To the extent that this procedural protection turns on judicial proceedings, we might see this as a weak point in the argument for family arbitration. The guiding role for lawyers in family arbitration, however, may of itself bring a measure of protection for weaker parties. But what if lawyer-led negotiations, for example, equally protect and empower the parties? Empirical evidence would be required to evaluate the comparison. Yet, the privatised nature of these various processes might make this difficult to obtain.

Reduced acrimony and impact on children

Hailed as a key feature of both mediation and collaborative law (e.g. Trinder *et al.* 2002, Kelly and Emery 2003), it would be important to assess how the unique place of family arbitration within private ordering affects its potential to reduce conflict between the parties and indirectly thereby benefit any affected children.

Enforceability

Finally, what of enforceability? If arbitrated 'awards' are enforceable, this might be a distinct benefit over other forms of private ordering. This would be advantageous to the extent that finality is beneficial for the parties. Yet, it would also heighten the need for sufficient arbitrator training and procedural safeguards. If arbitrated 'awards' are not enforceable, these concerns are less relevant. But consequentially non-enforceability makes family arbitration less distinctive as a form of private ordering and potentially less desirable to those parties seeking a confidential substitute for a final hearing. This debate will be discussed in more detail below.

The value of a commercial law comparison

The foregoing discussion makes clear that some of the potential benefits of family arbitration, such as confidentiality, are clearly supported by evidence, though they only apply to specific types of parties and disputes. Secondly, some potential benefits have been assumed without empirical support due to the ongoing policy rhetoric of contrasting court hearings with private ordering, including family arbitration. Finally, some of the potential benefits, such as enforceability, have been asserted on the basis of key elements of successful arbitration in the commercial context. Lord Falconer explains that

> [a]rbitration has a long history in certain areas. For example, many commercial and construction contracts provide for dispute resolution in this way. Arbitration in family law will be another tool in the box of methods of alternative dispute resolution. (quoted in IFLA 2012a)

But is this link between commercial and family arbitration more than mere rhetoric? Stowe suggests that we might make sense of how family arbitration might operate by considering how it works in the commercial context. She explains:

> Commercial arbitration is to my knowledge swift, private and in many cases considerably cheaper than incurring two sets of legal costs during a protracted court process. Commercial arbitrators impose their own timetable which can short circuit the issues in dispute. Parties to a commercial dispute can have as much or as little legal representation as they choose and hearings take place in more informal settings than a courtroom and are therefore less emotionally burdensome. A major attraction of any commercial arbitration process is that it does have teeth and a legally binding certainty of outcome. The arbitrators who deal with these disputes are also experts in their own particular field. A specific arbitrator can be appointed by agreement between the parties or nominated by the Chartered Institute of Arbitrators. It is therefore in their own interests to have prepared beforehand, which is at odds with many cases held in the courtroom before judges, who are often too pressured to give each case similar standards of care. (Stowe 2011)

These outlined benefits of commercial arbitration read much like the proposed benefits of the IFLA's scheme. Yet, there is insufficient empirical evidence to support many of these benefits in the family context such as speed, reduced costs, and reduced levels of conflict, especially when we recognise that final hearings may not provide an appropriate comparison. In addition, the debate over the enforceability of arbitration 'awards' in financial dispute resolution may undermine the comparison to the commercial context where, as Born notes, the enforceability of the award is a 'defining characteristic' of arbitration (2012, p. 5). Finally, it may be that the public policy concerns that underpin the default MCA 1973 substantive regime require a distinctive approach to process and outcome, which makes the commercial approach an inappropriate analogy. Marks and Tecks (2012) suggest that:

> ... the award, as the classic arbitral form of resolution that settles the issues it purports to decide once and for all, may need to be adapted to the family law context, where there is a greater requirement for decisions which allow the possibility of review and amendment.

However, family law might not be suitable for arbitration, at least not as an analogue to the commercial form. There are distinct public policy issues at stake in the financial provision context, which mean that it may not be possible to simply adapt the commercial approach. If a good argument can be made for greater state oversight of the parties' settlement, for example, there may be no way to adapt an enforceable arbitration award to accommodate this concern. The IFLA's decision to confine its roll-out to financial disputes and exclude children issues itself recognises the potentially significant difficulties in adapting arbitration to family law.[23] I return to the impact of public policy arguments and the default regime below.

Enforcement and the nature of private ordering

As noted above, the enforceability of an arbitration 'award' is cited by some as a critical distinction from other aspects of private ordering and one of the features that makes it a clear, confidential alternative to proceeding to a final hearing in court. An assessment of the literature to date reveals that some practitioners and potentially also the IFLA scheme Rules have assumed enforceability. However, the terms of the AA 1996, the proposed use of Consent orders, the status of separation agreements, and a careful understanding of the Supreme Court's decision in *Radmacher (formerly Granatino)* v. *Granatino* [2010] UKSC 42 militate against enforceability.

The assumption of enforceability

Writing in 2002 at the time of the earlier attempt to introduce family arbitration, Hodson commented that the '[t]he stumbling block in England is of course the inability to bind the family court by agreement, arbitration or otherwise'. In 2008, as quoted above, then-Justice Secretary Straw concluded that arbitration could not be used in family cases. Yet, shortly before the launch of the IFLA scheme, Scott QC (2011) stated that '[t]he [parties] agree in the form ARB 1 that the arbitrator's decision will be final and binding and that if necessary they will apply for a court order to give effect to it' ([7]).[24] Article 13.3 of the IFLA scheme Rules also describes the 'award' as 'final and binding' (IFLA 2012b) subject to limited grounds of challenge and appeal. This certainly seems to suggest the IFLA intends an 'award' to be enforceable in its own right. Arguably, even the term 'award' itself suggests finality. If that is so, it is hard to understand the intention of Article 13.4, which reads as follows:

> If and so far as the subject matter of the award makes it necessary, the parties will apply to an appropriate court for an order in the same or similar terms as the award or the relevant part of the award... In this context, 'an appropriate court' means a court which has jurisdiction to make a substantive order in the same or similar terms as the award,

whether on primary application or on transfer from another division of the court. (IFLA 2012b)

If an 'award' is 'final and binding,' when would it be 'necessary' to apply for a court order in the same or similar terms? The need for a Consent order implies that the arbitrated 'award' has no greater status than a draft Consent order reached via mediation or collaborative law. Scott QC elsewhere seems to recognise that these 'awards' are not enforceable:

> It is possible that at some point there may be a case which will test the precise juridical status of an award made e.g. under the Matrimonial Causes Act. It may be arguable as a matter of strict legal theory that since the jurisdiction of the court cannot be ousted, the court will not be bound to make an order which mirrors the award. (2012, [32])

He concludes that '[i]t seems extremely unlikely that a Judge would exercise judicial discretion in a way which departed from an award' (Scott QC 2012, [33]). But is it not misleading to present 'awards' as being enforceable when that outcome is contingent upon judicial practice? Given the centrality of enforceability to seeing family arbitration as an alternative to litigation, theoretical coherency is more than a mere technical nicety.

The technical position: non-enforceability

Singer sets out the legal relationship between arbitration 'awards' and the surrounding family law context. He notes that '[i]t is beyond dispute that the jurisdiction of the court may not be ousted' (Singer 2012b, p. 1500) and that, in this context, the court's decision-making is governed by s 25 MCA 1973. Similarly, Howell (2012) explains that

> [o]nly the court has the jurisdiction to make a final financial remedy order dismissing claims. Accordingly, it is only the court that can provide finality which is why on entering into arbitration, the parties must specifically agree to make an application for a consent order in the terms of the award.

The basis for this technical position lies in the AA 1996. Ahmed and Calderwood Norton explain that '... most family law matters cannot be resolved through arbitration ... because the Act preserves certain matters to be governed by the common law. Moreover, the jurisdiction of civil family courts cannot be ousted by contractual agreement' (2012, p. 368). In the absence of clear contrary authority, I would agree.

Section 81(1)(a) reserves to judicial decision-making 'matters which are not capable of settlement by arbitration'. To the extent that the court's s 25 MCA 1973 jurisdiction cannot be ousted, s 81(1)(a) can be understood to mean that matrimonial financial disputes are not capable of being the subject-matter of enforceable arbitration awards under the 1996 Act. Even if arbitrated awards were treated as akin to maintenance agreements (considered below) under s 34(1) MCA 1973, this only means that, if we took a narrow view of the scope of s 81(1)(a), they might withstand s 81(1)(a) scrutiny, not that they would be enforceable in a way that ousted the court's jurisdiction. In any event, arbitrated 'awards' would be likely to remain incapable of being seen as enforceable because of s 81(1)(c). Subsection (1)(c) entitles courts to refuse to recognise and/or enforce an arbitration 'award' on public policy grounds. It is likely that a court would rely on the public policy interest in the s 25 MCA 1973 exercise in order to avoid holding any arbitrated 'award' enforceable. Eekelaar (2011, pp. 1212–1213) suggests a different conclusion might be reached, though this would be where neither party wished to challenge the 'award'. Whilst such an 'award' would not be challenged, it would not in fact be enforceable. I contend that it would devalue the policy choices that underpin s

81 to argue that it is mere technicality that an arbitrated 'award' in relation to financial provision is not enforceable.

As good as enforceable?

In considering an application for a Consent order, Singer '... anticipate[s] that it will only be in rare circumstances that the court will decline to uphold the award, given the parties' agreement at the outset to be bound by it' (2012b, p. 1500). This final point lies at the heart of this debate: if it is only rarely that the court will independently redistribute the parties' income and assets, is the lack of enforceability of arbitrated 'awards' only of interest to academic lawyers? There are at least four arguments to be made to the contrary.

Public perception

There are dangers in perpetuating the perception of enforceability. In the House of Lords' debate over the Arbitration and Mediation Services (Equality) Bill, discussed above, discussants likely intended to refer to religious arbitration only but spoke of arbitration generally, thus inadvertently extending their comments to non-religious arbitration such as the IFLA scheme. In this context, suggesting that arbitration 'awards' are enforceable, when in fact they are not, might be conversely misunderstood as extending to religious arbitrations. The House of Lords' debate reveals the significance of the public's awareness of the law. There is good evidence, discussed above (e.g. Malik 2012, Douglas *et al.* 2012), that religiously-based tribunals understand the limits of their jurisdiction. Most recently, in *AI* v. *MT* [2013] EWHC 100 (Fam), a case concerning Jewish religious arbitration in relation to both financial and children matters, Ryder J adjourned proceedings to allow for religious arbitration and specifically recognised the non-binding nature of such arbitration ([31]). However, he also cited with approval Singer's suggestion (2012b, p. 1503) that an arbitrated 'award' should be treated as a 'lodestone (more than just a yardstick' by any court ([31]). Can we expect the parties before the court or the public in general to understand the difference between something of magnetic importance and something that is binding and enforceable? Spreading the incorrect view of arbitration 'awards' as being in a sense enforceable might unnecessarily risk public misunderstanding of the nature of religious tribunals' work. If these 'awards' definitely are not enforceable in law, why risk such misunderstanding?

Consent orders and public policy

Singer characterises judges who revisit the issues in exercise of their s 25 jurisdiction as '... employing what some might in the ordinary case regard as over-intrusive technicality or zeal ...' (2012b, p. 1500). His remarks needs to be viewed in light of research findings that demonstrate the lack of scrutiny of parties' applications for Consent orders, regardless of process followed that result in the draft orders (e.g. Davis *et al.* 2000, Wright 2007). Given that we have specifically reserved to judges oversight of Consent orders where necessary to protect the parties' interests, judges would be no more zealous in revisiting matters under s 25 than if the parties had produced the draft simply as a result of the usual lawyer-led negotiations. If we do not consider it a mere technicality that the output of such negotiations is not enforceable before being represented in a Consent order, why are we entitled to take a different view of arbitrated 'awards'? Any disagreement relates to the Consent order model as a whole, rather than the particular treatment of family arbitration. Has this public policy changed?

Nuptial agreements and public policy

Parties are free to negotiate their own division of finances at the end of their marriage, which they may choose to have recognised by means of a s 33A MCA 1973 Consent order. If they do not do so, the agreement is governed by the terms of ss 34–36 MCA 1973. Section 34(1)(a) provides that any provision in a separation agreement that purports to oust the court's jurisdiction is treated as void. This provision is grounded in public policy. As Lord Hailsham LC reasoned in *Hyman* v. *Hyman* [1929] AC 601:

> ... the power of the court to make provision for a wife on the dissolution of her marriage is a necessary incident of the power to decree such a dissolution, conferred not merely in the interests of the wife, *but of the public*, and that the wife cannot by her own covenant preclude herself from invoking the jurisdiction of the court or preclude the court from the exercise of that jurisdiction. (emphasis added, p. 614)

I suggested above that this framework for private ordering and the s 25 MCA 1973 exercise also gives content to s 81 AA 1996 as it applies to determine the status of any family arbitration 'awards' in relation to financial provision. I contend that there are no strong policy arguments that suggest that arbitrated 'awards' should be of greater effect than separation agreements, particularly because, in theoretical terms, family arbitration might best be thought of as the process by which such separation agreements are reached.

The IFLA scheme and its 'strong[.] recommendation' (2012c) for legal advice enables one to assume that arbitrated 'awards' have likely been reached by a process involving at least minimal legal protection for both sides. The same assumption cannot be made for separation agreements reached by other processes. However, the arbitrated 'award' might yet be substantively 'not ... fair', as set out in the Supreme Court's decision in *Radmacher* (majority, [75–76]), which transformed the approach to all nuptial agreements, whether made before or after marriage. Courts will now 'give effect to a nuptial agreement that is freely entered into by each party with a full appreciation of its implications unless in the circumstances prevailing it would not be fair to hold the parties to their agreement' (majority, [75]). Marks and Tecks (2012) suggest that this new approach to nuptial agreements means that

> ... the courts will look favourably on awards made under the scheme. An award will be the outcome of an impartial adjudication following a recognised process – supported by the Act – whose object is to achieve a fair result. There is arguably less scope for inappropriate influence, unevenness of representation or some of the other factors which might adversely affect a negotiated settlement.[25]

This reference to 'fairness' implies decision-making in accordance with the principles governing the s 25 MCA 1973 exercise. Yet, there is nothing in the scheme Rules that requires this approach. Indeed, Article 1 of the Rules makes clear that the scheme is grounded in the AA 1996, so that the only room for the MCA 1973 regime is that reserved via s 81 AA 1996. As a result, it is not clear that a court should be entitled to assume the outcome of the IFLA scheme process is 'fair', only that the process is likely fair. Empirical evidence on the interactions between the parties, their solicitors, and the arbitrator is needed before we can confirm whether Marks and Tecks are right that the family arbitration process might be fairer than the usual lawyer-led negotiations.

Even if it were more likely to be fairer, that does not counter the substantive policy concerns. Without parliamentary intervention, the family arbitration process should be seen as insufficient to satisfy the public interest in protecting vulnerable parties. Whilst the content of the parties' arbitrated 'award' may most often be reflected in any order made by the court exercising s 25 MCA 1973, characterising any departure therefrom as merely technical overlooks the significance of the public interest. Overplaying the likely lack of judicial departure from arbitrated 'awards' also risks distorting any attempt to develop a coherent picture of the relationship between private ordering generally and the s 25 MCA 1973 exercise. Section 25 expresses public policy in this area. If it were possible to entirely exclude the application of s 25 or to treat it as if it might as well be so excluded, the section would lose its normative value.

Desirability of enforceability

Might the issue of enforcement be one of desirability, rather than technicalities, with the desirability of enforceability turning on the precise form that family arbitration takes in practice? Writing about the Arbitration and Mediation Services (Equality) Bill, Eekelaar notes that '... it could be claimed that a family arbitration procedure is privatised justice on the cheap, with no quality control, and carries special risks for children and the vulnerable' (2011, p. 1213). If that became the reality of family arbitration, we would not want arbitrated 'awards' to be enforceable. Whereas, we would likely be content with arbitrated 'awards' being enforceable if family arbitration were freely available to all, with procedural safeguards shown to protect the parties' independent interests, and backed by good empirical evidence showing that it reduced conflict between the parties and negative impacts on any children. Such data would also enable us to revisit the public policy message that should be sent by the s 25 MCA 1973 default regime. As matters currently stand, we should be cautious before assuming the value of treating the factual default of private ordering as if it could straightforwardly replace the normative default of the s 25 MCA 1973 exercise.

Nuptial agreements, autonomy, and the default regime

De facto and normative defaults: autonomy and fairness

In the absence of parliamentary intervention, might we argue that judicial consideration of the place of nuptial agreements evidences a shift in the underlying nature of the default regime? As noted above, and as Maclean explains, private ordering has long been the *de facto* default:

> It is extraordinary that, in a jurisdiction where there is so little adjudication, the debate has become framed in terms of ADR versus court-imposed rulings. This false dichotomy ignores the main mode of dispute management in family (and other civil matters), which is lawyer-led negotiation, usually concluded in a settlement culture without a court appearance except to check and record a consent order for the purpose of fairness and enforceability. (2010, p. 106)

Is private ordering now also on the brink of becoming the normative default? The majority in *Radmacher* reasoned that '[t]he fact of the agreement is capable of altering what is fair' ([75]). Taken with this approach to nuptial agreements, might the IFLA scheme's introduction of family arbitration come to signify the moment at which the *de facto* default also took on deeper, normative significance?

Family arbitration in practice

Will family arbitration become sufficiently widespread to bring about such a normative shift? Would a rise in nuptial agreements make family arbitration more or less likely, or might it have no impact? Geffin (2012) notes that:

> With divorce, the only opportunity to agree to an arbitral resolution in advance is through a prenuptial agreement. At this stage it is far from being a given that many couples will be

prepared to agree in advance to contract into arbitration. This is unlikely to happen until it has become firmly embedded in the culture of family law.

There is not yet any clear evidence either way. One might imagine that the types of clients who would wish to settle their financial arrangements privately via arbitration would also consider entering into nuptial agreements. Yet, the correlation may not be very strong because the former concerns procedure and the latter concerns substantive provisions.

In addition to considering the broader relationship between the two forms of private ordering and autonomy, one might focus on those parties who have chosen to enter into a nuptial agreement. Are they likely to include an arbitration clause or, should a disagreement over interpretation of the agreement arise, to take it to arbitration? On one view, the types of individuals who enter into nuptial agreements may intend to fix the financial outcomes at that stage, thus might include an arbitration clause only to the extent it governs disagreements over interpretation. On another view, at least some parties might be less content with a fixed determination at the stage of a nuptial agreement but, whether for reasons of confidentiality or otherwise, be content to agree to arbitrate should the relationship break down. But could such an agreement even be enforced within the terms of the AA 1996? In the commercial context, arbitration clauses are common at the time of contract formation because the parties often envisage the need for ongoing business relationships after any individual disputes have been settled. This is much less obvious in the family context – whilst some parties might view their relationship that way, particularly if they already have children together before entering into a nuptial agreement, it is unclear how many would.

The Law Commission contrasts the decision to enter into nuptial agreements in England and Wales to the decision to do so in European jurisdictions with matrimonial property regimes. These decisions cannot be treated as equivalent, it argues, because in English law the parties are 'opting out of a discretionary regime and into certainty' (Law Commission 2011, [5.38]; cited with approval: *B* v. *S (Financial Remedy: Marital Property Regime)* [2012] EWHC 265 (Fam), Mostyn J, [7]) whereas, in those other European jurisdictions, 'they are opting for a different set of rules' (Law Commission 2011). The decision to enter into a nuptial agreement may be a complex one, and the relationship between decisions made in respect of nuptial agreements and family arbitration may also be similarly complex and similarly depend at least in part on the governing default regime. The interrelationship can only be fully tested over time as evidence emerges from practice.

Normative consequences

In their Matrimonial Survey 2012, Grant Thornton asked 139 family lawyers whether or not they believed that family arbitration would become a significant form of private ordering in the next five years. Forty-eight per cent thought that it would whereas 52% thought that it would not (p. 5). Speed and confidentiality for wealthy and celebrity clients were cited as reasons by those who thought it would grow (p. 5). Those who thought it would not grow significantly believed that it would have little attraction 'in the provinces' and for the 'average client' (p. 5). If these views are predictive, it may be that nuptial agreements are more important than family arbitration for any normative shift to autonomy.

The expansion of arbitration and nuptial agreements may represent a move toward two-tier family justice, at least in relation to financial matters. As discussed above, legal aid is now for the few, and is accompanied with a requirement for assessment for mediation. Carefully drafted nuptial agreements and family arbitration might thus appear as privatised, luxury dispute resolution whilst the majority must either make do with a less expensive form of private ordering, sometimes lacking in such expert guidance or, more rarely, become self-represented litigants in court proceedings. The approach to the s 25 MCA 1973 exercise has been significantly shaped by courts' reasoning in 'big money' cases. Without the wealthier clients, whose disputes have conventionally shaped the larger normative principles in landmark higher court decisions such as *White* and *Miller; McFarlane*, how will the law in the shadow of which the majority will continue to need to bargain be developed?

One might reply that the problem lies in the nature of the s 25 MCA 1973 exercise and in media access to court proceedings. Whilst both of these points are well taken, that does not assist the average future client who will not benefit from the ongoing judicial refinement of the discretionary regime in response to societal change.

In her judgment in *Lykiardopulo*, Baron J notes that one can never know if a party was denied justice through resorting to these private processes (quoted by Thorpe LJ, [63]). So, one might well argue that if we really want to avoid two tier family law, we would need to reverse our approach to openness and publication regarding divorce and ancillary relief proceedings. Given that this is impossible, perhaps the growth of family arbitration is inevitable. Mr Justice Ryder suggests in *AI* v. *MT* that, with the IFLA scheme, 'the Rubicon has been crossed' ([31]).

If family arbitration is to become part of the new default, how can we ensure family law's end users remain at the heart of its normative impact? The very idea of confidential family arbitration makes supervision and development in accordance with public policy concerns difficult. At the least, we will need legislation to both recognise the new normative default and to settle the debate over its enforceability. In his written evidence to the Justice Committee, David Hodson (2010) calls for primary legislation to secure enforceable family arbitration. If autonomy is set to become the normative default, this has much to commend it. However, I would caution against such legislation before we have resolved the difficult matter of the relationship between non-religious and religious arbitration. As long as non-religious family arbitration remains non-enforceable, we can avoid resolving this complex issue, though the debate over the Arbitration and Mediation Services (Equality) Bill has added a sense of urgency.

The normative shift to autonomy marked by the rise of nuptial agreements and family arbitration may itself not be a straightforward issue. In *Radmacher*, the majority reasons:

> The circumstances surrounding the conclusion of a contract will either result in the contract being of full effect, or of no effect at all. The courts have always adopted a more nuanced approach to ante- and post-nuptial agreements. We cannot see why it mattered whether or not the agreement in *MacLeod* was a contract.
>
> In summary, we consider that the Board in *MacLeod* was wrong to hold that post-nuptial agreements were contracts but that ante-nuptial agreements were not. That question did not arise for decision in that case any more than in this and does not matter anyway. It is a red herring. Regardless of whether one or both are contracts, the ancillary relief court should apply the same principles when considering ante-nuptial agreements as it applies to post-nuptial agreements. ([62–63])

This hints at a more sophisticated, family law-specific understanding of autonomy. Just as 'fairness' has come to mean something quite particular, so respect for the parties' 'autonomy' may be much more nuanced than the importation of commercial conceptions. In relation to family arbitration, Singer argues that '[i]t would be illogical if 'respect for autonomy' were to prove to be a divisible concept, applying only to substantive resolution by way of pre- or post-nuptial agreement but not also to the parties' choice for procedural resolution' (2012b, p. 1503). Yet, the complexity of family law and policy, may mean that it develops quite different consequences in relation to procedural and substantive aspects of private ordering in financial disputes.

Conclusion

Geffin (2012) suggests that '... the most significant issue [for family arbitration] is whether there will be much of an uptake for arbitration as an alternative to litigation'. Indeed, we will have to wait to find out whether we are at a crucial moment for financial dispute resolution and private ordering. For the reasons outlined above, we need to be cautious in embracing family arbitration as a new panacea to address perceived problems in family financial dispute resolution. Without sufficient supporting evidence, claims have been made that family arbitration has the potential to be more successful than other forms of private ordering and final court hearings in enabling certain types of parties to resolve certain types of disputes. However, family arbitration is confidential, the process is flexible, and the arbitrators themselves are experts within the field. But even the standard claims of increased speed and reduced cost (e.g. *AI* v. *MT*, Ryder J, [32]) require additional empirical evidence.

The potential for family arbitration and nuptial agreements to transform the normative default in relation to financial provision highlights the need to develop a clearer sense of the interrelation of different aspects of private ordering and litigation. Significant empirical research is required. I have suggested three starting-points for thinking about the landscape here – sliding scale, category-based comparators, and intersecting circles. As private ordering becomes even more central to the family justice system, a clearer picture of the map of dispute resolution would help identify which approaches are best suited to which types of parties and disputes. This would also work to clarify the validity of comparing particular approaches, such as family arbitration and mediation, or family arbitration and litigation, as a means of evaluation.

Considering the potential for family arbitration alongside mediation and collaborative law, Stowe (2011) comments that she 'know[s] of no family lawyer who regards alternative dispute resolution methods as widely successful or even vaguely popular among divorcing couples'. Yet, as Mostyn J notes in *B* v. *S*, 'the functioning of the family justice system depends on a high rate of settlement of these cases' ([79]). If private ordering and respect for autonomy are set to become the new normative default, family justice reform needs to (re)inspire the public.

Acknowledgements

Thanks to both Mavis Maclean and John Eekelaar for constructive advice and discussion. Any errors that remain are mine alone.

Notes

1. Dingwall (2010) provides an excellent overview of the earlier and more recent attempts to embed mediation in family law dispute resolution.
2. The stakeholders in the new not-for-profit Institute for Family Law Arbitrators (IFLA) are Resolution, the Family Law Bar Association, and the Chartered Institute of Arbitrators. The IFLA is also working together with the Centre for Child and Family Law Reform, London Metropolitan University.

3. Stowe (2011), a leading practitioner in this area, reasons as follows: '... I think the fascination with [mediation and collaborative law] now mostly rests with the professionals who conduct it. ADR has singularly failed to capture the imagination of the public, because there are so many perceived disadvantages which simply cannot be surmounted, no matter how hard one may try or attempt to gloss them over ...' In this regard, it is also interesting to note that the 2012 scheme is the second attempt at launching family arbitration. Burton (2012, p. 117) explains that '... several years ago, [the Chartered Institute of Arbitrators] and Resolution experimented in Family arbitration, which was them not taken forward'.
4. Resolution (n.d.) reports that over 90% of cases handled by its lawyers are resolved without the need for a final hearing in court. See also Roberts (2008, p. 14).
5. But Malik (2012) found that there was very little empirical evidence of empirical councils asserting jurisdiction in this way. See also Douglas *et al.* (2012, p. 156); Eekelaar (2011, p. 1209).
6. Lord Bishop (HL Deb 19 October 2012, col. 1693) explicitly expresses concern about the impact of this provision on the IFLA scheme.
7. Clause 4 is proposed to be amended as follows: '(2) Any agreement using religious laws concerning matters in this section shall have no effect.'
8. Currently, parties who present an agreement to court to be recognised in a Consent order do not have to declare the basis upon which the agreement was reached, i.e. who officiated the arbitration. Without a precondition that the parties declare the basis, the court could not know whether reasonable agreements were either religious or non-religious. Ahmed and Calderwood Norton (2012, p. 370) note that the government has considered introducing this requirement.
9. In his judgment in *Lykiardopulo*, Thorpe LJ ([36]) provides a good list of the ways in which family court proceedings are special.
10. Dingwall (2010) provides an insightful analysis of the relationship between the assumption made about the family court system and the policy drive for expanding the use of mediation.
11. Sir Peter Singer (2012a, 2012b) provides an excellent outline of the IFLA scheme, particularly in terms of the detailed rules of procedure envisaged to apply and connect the IFLA scheme to the AA 1996, the FPR 2010 and the Civil Procedure Rules 1998 (CPR 1998).
12. By comparison, the new Scottish arbitration scheme envisages certain children issues. The Family Law Arbitration Group (Scotland), FLAG(S), was established shortly after the general Arbitration (Scotland) Act 2010 (asp 1) was enacted. It is interesting to note that there is no procedural requirement similar to Practice Direction 3A in Scotland. Crandles and Loudon (2012) outline the current role of arbitration in the family law context. See also Note 23 below.
13. Taxonomic uncertainty might be one interpretation of Dingwall and Greatbatch's suggestion of the increasing multiplicity of mediators' objectives (2000, p. 251).
14. Fisher (2006) notes that Boulle now substitutes 'transformative' for 'therapeutic.' Fisher (2006, p. 2) also suggests that the term 'transformative' may not have an agreed meaning, noting that Bush and Folger, for example, define it as a process that qualitatively changes the nature of conflict.
15. Roberts (2008, p. 7) notes that '[t]he terms 'mediation' and 'conciliation' were often used interchangeably in Britain in the context of family disputes'. Herring (2011, p. 138) refers to this as 'in-court mediation' and discusses the debate over its status.
16. Similarly with nuptial agreements, the detail of the agreement may greatly affect where on such a sliding scale it would belong. One might compare an agreement reached between the parties that is simply formally drafted by a solicitor, an agreement that is the result of protracted negotiations between two parties and their solicitors, and a more flexible agreement that specifically includes an arbitration clause to authorise post-separation arbitration to finalise financial matters.
17. Dingwall (2010, p. 113) discusses 'case triage' by court staff in the mediation context, but we might consider extending the idea to referrals to a range of ADR options.
18. Barlow *et al.*'s (2012–15) ongoing ESRC-funded evaluates three overlapping methods: solicitor-led negotiation, collaborative law, and mediation.
19. The other two core characteristics Roberts (2008) proposes are confidentiality and procedural flexibility.
20. Dingwall and Greatbatch (2001), for example, argue that mediation has changed from focusing on parties' relationships and empowerment to focusing on managing settlements.

21. Pendlebury Cox (2012) explains that '[i]ncreasing costs and cuts in public funding are just two of the factors leading to an escalation of the numbers of Litigants in Persons or Self Represented Litigants . . . '. The Ministry of Justice's literature review (Williams 2011) notes that the precise numbers involved are uncertain.
22. Such an expedited process would be similar to that adopted by Coleridge J in relation to draft consent orders that result from a collaborative law process: *S* v. *P (Settlement by Collaborative Law Process)* (Fam Div) [2008] 2 FLR 2040 '. . . to provide as much encouragement as possible to people to resolve their difficulties in this civilised and sensible way' ([5]).
23. Interestingly, whilst the Scottish approach is also currently confined to financial disputes, subsequent roll-out to children cases is also envisaged. Wise (quoted in Nicholson 2010) reasons: 'Why not? Just as people can resolve disputes about children without involving the courts at all, in principle there is no reason why you couldn't arbitrate. But the focus of our group is on financial provision cases.'
24. In the Scottish context (governed by the Arbitration (Scotland) Act 2010), Jones (2012) assumes that arbitration is binding, and implies that is one of the key benefits, reasoning that '[i]n family matters, arbitration is the only alternative to litigation that allows for a final, legally binding determination to be made by an impartial decision maker'.
25. Their comments closely reflect those of the IFLA in its scheme FAQs, which also state that the object of the scheme '. . . is to achieve a fair result' (IFLA 2012c).

References

Ahmed, F. and Calderwood Norton, J., 2012. Religious tribunals, religious freedom, and consent for vulnerable women. *Child and family law quarterly*, 24, 363–388.

Arbitration and Mediation Services (Equality) Bill. London: TSO (Bills 2012–13, (7)).

Arbitration and Mediation Services (Equality) Bill: Amendment to be moved in committee. London: TSO (Bills 2012–13, (7)) (13 November. Available at: http://www.publications.parliament.uk/pa/bills/lbill/2012-2013/0007/amend/am007-a.htm [Accessed 10 January 2013].

Barlow, A., et al., 2012–15. Mapping paths to family justice. News release. Available at: http://socialsciences.exeter.ac.uk/law/news/title_147249_en.html [Accessed 6 January 2013].

Born, G., 2012. *International arbitration: law and practice*. Alphen aan den Rijn, Netherlands: Kluwer Law International.

Burton, F., 2012. *Family law*. London: Routledge.

Crandles, G. and Loudon, A., 2012. Arbitration will keep family law cases out of court. *New Scotsman*, 5 March. Available at: http://www.scotsman.com/the-scotsman/scotland/gillian_crandles_and_alasdair_loudon_arbitration_will_keep_family_law_cases_out_of_court_1_2153328 [Accessed 10 January 2013].

Davis, G., 2001. Reflections in the aftermath of the family mediation pilot. *Child and family law quarterly*, 13, 371–382.

Davis, G., et al., 2000. Ancillary relief outcomes. *Child and family law quarterly*, 12, 43–65.

Dingwall, R., 2010. Divorce mediation: should we change our mind? *Journal of social welfare and family law*, 32, 107–117.

Dingwall, R. and Greatbatch, D., 2000. The mediation process. In: G. Davis, et al. eds. *Monitoring publicly funded family mediation: report to the Legal Services Commission*. London: Legal Services Commission.

Dingwall, R. and Greatbatch, D., 2001. Family mediators: what are they doing? *Family law*, 31, 378–382.

Douglas, G., et al., 2012. The role of religious tribunals in regulating marriage and divorce. *Child and family law quarterly*, 24, 139–157.

Eekelaar, J., 2010. 'Not of the highest importance': family justice under threat. *Journal of social welfare and family law*, 33, 311–317.

Eekelaar, J., 2011. The Arbitration and Mediation Services (Equality) Bill 2011. *Family law*, 41, 1209–1215.

Eekelaar, J., et al., 2000. *Family lawyers: the divorce work of solicitors*. Oxford: Hart.

Fisher, T., 2006. Transformative mediation: differentiating principles from illusions: p[art 1. *ADR bulletin*, 9 (3), Article 2.

Gardner, C., 2012. What's legal about family arbitration? *The Guardian*, 23 February. Available at: http://www.guardian.co.uk/law/2012/feb/23/is-family-arbitration-legal [Accessed 10 January 2013].

Geffin, M., 2012. New family arbitration scheme is no alternative to litigation. *Solicitors journal*, 156/9, 9.

Genn, H., 2010. Civil mediation: a measured approach?. *Journal of social welfare and family law*, 32, 195–205.

Grant Thornton, *Matrimonial Survey 2012*, Available at: http://www.grant-thornton.co.uk/Global/Publication_pdf/Matrimonial-Survey-2012.pdf [Accessed 10 January 2013].

Hale, Lady, 2011. Sir Henry Hodge memorial lecture: Equal access to justice in the big society. Law Society, London June. *Family law*, September Newsline Extra.

Harris, P., 2012. Legal aid cuts? What legal aid cuts? *Family law*, 42, 1267–1268.

HC Deb, vol. 483 written answers col. 866W (24 November 2008). Available at: http://www.publications.parliament.uk/pa/cm200708/cmhansrd/cm081124/text/81124w0012.htm [Accessed 15 December 2012].

Herring, J., 2011. *Family law*. 5th ed. Harlow: Pearson.

HL Deb, vol. 739 col. 1682–1716 (19 October 2012) Available from: http://www.publications.parliament.uk/pa/ld201213/ldhansrd/text/121019-0001.htm#12101923000438 [Accessed 13 March 2013].

Hodson, D., 2002. Family law arbitration. *Family law*, 32, 694–698.

Hodson, D., 2010. FC 16: written evidence submitted to the Justice Committee – *6th report of session 2010–12: operation of the family courts*. Available at: http://www.publications.parliament.uk/pa/cm201012/cmselect/cmjust/518/518vw15.htm [Accessed 10 January 2013].

Howell, G., 2012. Financial remedy cases: piecing together the jigsaw. *Family law week*, 20 April. Available at: http://www.familylawweek.co.uk/site.aspx?i=ed97230 [Accessed 10 January 2013].

Institute of Family Law Arbitrators, 2012a. Family arbitration scheme launched by the newly formed Institute of Family Law Arbitrators (IFLA). News release, 22 February. Available at: http://ifla.org.uk/news/family-arbitration-scheme-launched/ [Accessed 10 January 2013].

Institute of Family Law Arbitrators, 2012b. *Family law arbitration scheme: arbitration rules*, 2nd ed., 20 March. Available at: http://ifla.org.uk/cms/wp-content/uploads/2012/03/Rules-Final-2012-2nd-edition-200312.pdf [Accessed 10 January 2013].

Institute of Family Law Arbitrators, 2012c. FAQs: what are the benefits of arbitration? Available at: http://ifla.org.uk/what-is-arbitration/faqs/ [Accessed 10 January 2013].

Jones, S., 2012. Keeping it in the family. *The journal of the law society of Scotland*, 19 March. [Available at: http://www.journalonline.co.uk/Magazine/57-3/1010906.aspx [Accessed 10 January 2013].

Kelly, J. and Emery, R., 2003. Children's adjustment following divorce: risk and resilience perspectives. *Family relations*, 52, 352–362.

Law Commission, 2011. *Marital property agreements: a consultation paper*, Consultation Paper No. 198. HMSO. Available at: http://lawcommission.justice.gov.uk/docs/cp198_Marital_Property_Agreements_Consultation.pdf [Accessed 10 January 2013].

Maclean, M., 2010. Editorial: family mediation: alternative or additional dispute resolution? *Journal of social welfare and family law*, 32, 105–106.

Malik, M., 2012. *Minority legal orders in the UK: minorities, pluralism and the law*. London: British Academy.

Marks, T. and Tecks, J., 2012. A new arrival. *New law journal*, 162 (7500), 201–2.02.

Miles, J., 2011a. Legal aid, Article 6 and 'exceptional funding' under the Legal Aid etc. Bill 2011. *Family law*, 41, 1003–1009.

Miles, J., 2011b. Legal aid and 'exceptional' funding: a postscript. *Family law*, 41, 1268–1270.

Ministry of Justice and Department of Education, 2012. *The government response to the family justice review: a system with children and families at its heart*, Cmnd 8273. Available at: https://www.education.gov.uk/publications/eOrderingDownload/CM-8273.pdf [Accessed 10 January 2013].

Mnookin, R.H. and Kornhauser, L., 1979. Bargaining in the shadow of the law: the case of divorce. *Yale law journal*, 88, 950–997.

Nicholson, P., 2010. Agreeing to disagree. *The journal of the law society of Scotland*, 13 December. Available at: http://www.journalonline.co.uk/Magazine/55-12/1009018.aspx [Accessed 10 January 2013].

Norgrove, D. (Chair), 2011. *Family Justice Review – final report*. Available at: http://www.justice.gov.uk/downloads/publications/moj/2011/family-justice-review-final-report.pdf [Accessed 14 December 2012].

Pendlebury Cox, L., 2012. Litigants in person cases: it doesn't have to be like this. *Family law week*, 13 April. Available at: http://www.familylawweek.co.uk/site.aspx?i=ed97034 [Accessed 10 January 2013].

Pre-Legislative Scrutiny of the Children and Families, Bill 2012: fourth report of sessions 2012–13 (14 December 2012). Available at: http://www.publications.parliament.uk/pa/cm201213/cmselect/cmjust/739/73902.htm [Accessed 20 December 2012].

Resolution, n.d. What makes Resolution lawyers special? Available at: http://www.resolution.org.uk/moreaboutus/ [Accessed 10 January 2013].

Resolution, 2012. First anniversary of mediation assessment meetings marked, as survey reveals they are not working as they should. *News release*, 4 April. Available: http://www.resolution.org.uk/news-list.asp?page_id=228&n_id=177 [Accessed 10 January 2013].

Roberts, M., 2008. *Mediation in family disputes: principles of practice*. 3rd ed. Aldershot: Ashgate.

Ryder, Mr Justice, 2012. *Judicial proposals for the modernisation of family justice*. Judiciary of England and Wales. July. Available at: http://www.judiciary.gov.uk/Resources/JCO/Documents/Reports/ryderj_recommendations_final.pdf [Accessed 10 January 2013].

Scott QC, T., 2011. Family arbitration: an introduction. *Family law week*, 5 December. Available at: http://www.familylawweek.co.uk/site.aspx?i=ed90447 [Accessed 10 January 2013].

Singer, P., 2012a. Arbitration in family financial proceedings: the IFLA scheme: part I. *Family law*, 42, 1353–1560.

Singer, P., 2012b. Arbitration in family financial proceedings: the IFLA scheme: part 2. *Family law*, 42, 1496–1504.

Spencer, D. and Brogan, M., 2006. *Mediation law and practice*. Melbourne: Cambridge University Press.

Stowe, M., 2011. *Family law arbitration: a new dawn for ADR?* Available at: http://www..marilynstowe.co.uk/2011/11/30/family-law-arbitration-a-new-dawn-for-alternative-dispute-resolution/ [Accessed 10 January 2013].

Trinder, L., et al., 2002. *Making contact: how parents and children negotiate and experience contact after divorce*. York: Joseph Rowntree Foundation.

Williams, K., Litigants in person: A literature review. *Ministry of Justice research summary 2/11*. Available at: http://www.justice.gov.uk/downloads/publications/research-and-analysis/moj-research/litigants-in-person-literature-review.pdf [Accessed 10 January 2013].

Wilson, Lord, 2011. Keynote address. *Collaborative family law reception*, Reform Club, 29 November. Available at: http://www.supremecourt.gov.uk/docs/speech_111129.pdf [Accessed 10 January 2013].

Winslade, J. and Monk, G., 2000. *Narrative mediation: a new approach to conflict resolution*. San Francisco, CA: Jossey Bass.

Wright, K., 2007. The role of solicitors in divorce: a note of caution. *Child and family law quarterly*, 19, 481–495.

When legal rights are not a reality: do individuals know their rights and how can we tell?

Catrina Denvir, Nigel J. Balmer and Pascoe Pleasence

Faculty of Laws, University College London

Public knowledge of rights has been the subject of a number of empirical enquiries over the last decade. In England and Wales, knowledge of rights and its relationship with an individual's capacity to 'self-help' and 'self-represent' when faced with a civil justice problem has become the subject of renewed attention following changes to legal aid which, from March 2013, will see the availability of legal advice and representation dramatically reduced. Previous studies focusing on public knowledge of rights in this (and other) jurisdictions have illustrated a lack of knowledge amongst the general population and more specifically, a widespread tendency of individuals to assume that the law aligns with their own moral, ethical or social attitudes. However, many of these studies have also suffered from methodological shortcomings. In attempting to address some of these shortcomings this study uses an open-ended format to ask individuals with one or one or more civil or social justice problems to describe their rights/legal position. We find that whilst an open-ended question approach to exploring knowledge of rights yields insight not acquired by other formats, its utility is constrained by difficulty reconciling articulation and actual knowledge of rights. We discuss the implications of these findings as they relate to the development of future research in the field of family and social welfare law, Public Legal Education (PLE) and access to justice post-March 2013.

Introduction

In 2010 the British Government proposed wide-ranging reforms to the legal aid system in England and Wales (Ministry of Justice 2011). They noted that although 'successive changes (had) managed to contain the growth in overall spending on legal aid, such changes (had) not addressed the underlying problems facing the scheme' (Ministry of Justice 2010b, p. 3). In the long term, the Government agreed that simplification of the justice system to make its navigation easier for lay individuals was necessary; in the meantime, the availability of publicly funded specialist advice and representation across a range of matter types would be substantially curtailed (Ministry of Justice 2010a, 2010b, 2011). Deciding which areas of law would and would not qualify for publicly funded legal advice and assistance under the new legal aid scheme was justified in part, by reference to whether the public could utilise (self-help and) self-representation for their particular problem (Ministry of Justice 2010a, 2010b, 2011).[1] Consequently, the reforms heralded by the Legal Aid, Sentencing and Punishment of Offenders Act (LASPO) 2012, detailed (explicitly and implicitly) that self-help/self-representation would from April 2013 onwards, become a key route to resolving civil justice problems.[2]

Public legal capability, education and knowledge of rights

The idea that individuals are capable of handling civil justice problems without professional advice, anticipates a level of existing competence from the population – particularly those individuals who are neither eligible for legal aid, nor able to secure alternative legal services. How public legal capability is assessed and improved, or for that matter, the characteristics necessary to produce individual legal 'capability' remains an issue of some debate. One factor generally considered relevant, is the extent to which individuals know their legal rights (see, e.g., PLEAS Taskforce 2007, Gramatikov and Porter 2010, Buck *et al.*, 2008, Balmer *et al.*, 2010, Bowal 1999). It is argued that without such knowledge, individuals will more often fail to vindicate their rights (Bowal 1999); fail to take steps to protect themselves against the likelihood of a particular eventuality (Kim 1999, Meager *et al.*, 2002); fail to uphold their civic responsibilities (Bowal 1999); and experience diminished success when self-representing in court (Moorhead and Sefton 2005). A lack of knowledge has also been said to potentially generate unrealistic expectations of lawyers and judges (Bowal 1999) and the risk of experiencing a civil justice problem (Williams 2009) and is further linked with the adoption of poor problem handling techniques and lower levels of satisfaction with outcome when an individual seeks to handle their problem alone (Buck *et al.*, 2008, Balmer *et al.*, 2010, Denvir *et al.*, 2012).

In the Public Bill Committee debates regarding the passage of the LASPO Bill, it was said that changes to legal aid demanded greater public knowledge of rights if individuals were to be expected to self-help and self-represent more often (Public Bill Committee 2011). It follows, then, that as part of an on-going effort to safeguard access to justice, whether the general public have knowledge of their rights or not will remain one of the key issues facing public policy makers in the years to come. Studies which have previously sought to measure knowledge of rights have found that citizens in a number of jurisdictions frequently admit to lacking knowledge (see, e.g., Cortese 1966, Williams and Hall 1972, Saunders 1975, Baker and Emery 1993, Parle/IARS 2009, Casebourne *et al.* 2006; Genn *et al.*, 2006, Tennant *et al.* 2006, Albrecht and Green 1977) with this lack of knowledge more prominent among certain subsections of the population, namely young people, the mentally ill, and those without educational qualifications (see, e.g., Williams and Hall 1972, Ruck *et al.*, 1998, Youth Access 2002, Parle/IARS, 2009, Casebourne *et al.* 2006, Buck *et al.*, 2008, Denvir *et al.*, 2012). These concerns have been the basis for a range of policy initiatives aimed at improving public knowledge of rights, referred to as 'Public Legal Education' (PLE) (PLEAS Taskforce, 2007).[3] Such interventions seek to rectify an absence of knowledge, and thus require an understanding of the existing level of knowledge amongst the general population. Yet measuring public knowledge of rights or for that matter the benefits that may flow from increased knowledge is no easy feat, as existing research in the field has illustrated.

Measuring knowledge of rights

Self-reporting knowledge

Existing studies have generally taken one of two approaches in measuring public knowledge of rights. The first approach, as used by both Denvir *et al.*, (2012) and Buck *et al.*, (2008) has involved asking respondents to self-report the extent to which they know their rights, with results highlighting low levels of knowledge amongst the general population and certain groups. However, as recognised in the methodological literature (see, e.g., Baldwin 2009) whilst self-reporting is a convenient approach, it is not without issues. These include the fact that long reference periods in any type of survey may impact upon memory recall (Deming 1950, Bradburn *et al.*, 1987), that respondents to face-to-face surveys may be inclined to answer in certain ways (for a variety of reasons, see, e.g., Groves *et al.*, 2009, Calahan 1968), and that the acquisition of knowledge after the event may lead people to incorporate post-event information in their memory of the experience (Groves *et al.*, 2009). This last issue has particular relevance given that an individual's propensity to incorporate post-event information has ramifications for any attempt to link the presence of knowledge with the problem-resolution strategies individuals adopt. More problematic however, is the assumption that those who report knowing their 'legal rights' actually do. In the absence of an understanding of what respondents actually believe their rights to be, Buck *et al.*, (2008) and Denvir *et al.*, (2012) may simply indicate an individual's level of confidence in their knowledge, especially given that existing research also highlights individuals answer more confidently when asked fixed choice questions (see, e.g., Schuman and Presser 1981, Schwarz and Hippler 1991).

Fact-based questions with/without a contextual hypothetical scenario or 'vignette'

Studies which have attempted to verify the self-reporting of knowledge such as Meager *et al.*'s (2000) employment rights research, have adopted a second approach. Using self-assessment questions alongside a number of other question types, including (prompted and unprompted) awareness of various employment related legislation, and questions which ask whether a hypothetical situation represents a breach of the law alongside requiring participants to name the law breached. Via these methods, Meager *et al.*, (2002) were able to demonstrate that although two-thirds of respondents to their study claimed to be well informed or very well informed about their rights, substantive knowledge varied by individual problem-type, with individuals often able to identify a breach of the law in a hypothetical situation, but unable to substantiate this breach by naming the relevant legislation.[4] The authors concluded that individuals often identified breaches of the law based on perceptions of fairness or natural justice, rather than knowledge of the relevant legislation (Meager *et al.*, 2002) suggesting that self-reporting remained a crude proxy for actual knowledge.

Yet, whilst utilising a range of approaches, the authors failed to comment on the fact that the ability to name legislation was not necessarily a good measure of knowledge of rights or of the content of the legislation itself. By focusing more on whether respondents were able to link what they perceived to be unfair behaviour with the corresponding legislation, rather than exploring whether respondents actually understood their rights, the results provided only limited insight into 'knowledge of rights'. Similar such limitations were evident in Kim's earlier (1999) work exploring US employees' knowledge of rights regarding at-will-dismissal. Respondents were required to indicate whether they felt the dismissal was lawful or unlawful in respect of a number of circumstances. But whilst incorrect responses were said to indicate a confusion of legal norms and ethical or social norms, correct responses were deemed to indicate 'knowledge' of rights, rather, than as may well have been the case, a situation in which ethical/social norms and the law happened to align (Kim 1999) or 'educated' or 'wild' guesses happened to be correct (Nadaeu and Niemi 1995).[5,6]

A different approach to exploring public knowledge of rights (whilst retaining a fact-based questioning approach) was utilised a few years later by Barlow *et al.* in 2005. With the intent of exploring existing levels of knowledge among the general population as to the rights of a cohabitant vis à vis the rights of a spouse,[7] the authors developed a series of fact-based questions relating to the legal rights of a protagonist in a hypothetical scenario (or 'vignette') which were then added to the 2004 British Social Attitudes Survey (BSAS). Finding that individuals held erroneous beliefs in respect of time-dependent accrual of benefits[8] and a belief in the equivalence of paternal rights and responsibilities between married and unmarried couples, Barlow *et al.* (2005, p. 45) concluded that people's beliefs about cohabitation law, whether accurate or not, were based less on acquired knowledge, and more upon 'notions of social logic, fairness and morality'.

Whilst findings corroborated those of other related studies (e.g. Meager *et al.*, 2002, Kim 1999) as Pleasence and Balmer (2012) observed, the BSAS questions relied on a presumption that people had good knowledge of the spousal rights against which cohabitants' rights were being compared, resulting in conflation between knowledge of spousal rights and knowledge of cohabiting rights. Thus, in their 2012 study on the same topic using respondents to the English and Welsh Civil and Social Justice Panel Survey (CSJPS), Pleasence and Balmer (2012) also developed a series of fact-based questions in relation to a hypothetical scenario but randomly varied the duration of the relationship (one month to 20 years – allowing formal modelling of time dependency in beliefs about accrual of rights) and its status (cohabiting or married). Whilst employing a different methodology, like Barlow *et al.*, (2005), Pleasence and Balmer (2012) found evidence of ongoing public misconception of cohabitation law, leading the authors to propose that in the absence of an actual understanding of the law, the public tended to believe the law aligned with the rights they thought it ought to protect.

Although Pleasence and Balmer (2012) were able to address some of the issues evident in the 'vignette' approach taken by Barlow *et al.*, (2005) this does not leave the approach limitation-free. Other signs point to the fact that responses to hypothetical questions may, like self-reporting, provide only a rough measure of knowledge for a number of reasons. Nadaeu and Niemi (1995) note that some individuals, even when unsure of an answer, will be compelled to respond in a manner other than 'don't know' with some people inclined to answer knowledge-based questions even in the face of considerable uncertainty (Chong 1993). For some, these uncertain answers are 'educated guesses', for others they may be 'wild guesses' (Nadaeu and Niemi 1995). In addition, it has been said that most people 'construct' attitudes when asked a question (Tourangeau and Rasinski 1988), meaning that a respondent without actual knowledge may answer a fact-based question in manner no different to how they would answer an attitudinal question; perhaps explaining why previous research has found that individuals respond with answers indicative of what they think the law *should* be, rather than what it actually is. The question that these issues highlight, is whether there might be an alternative approach to exploring public knowledge of rights, and if so, what form it would take?

Alternative approaches to exploring public knowledge of rights

In the exploration of public knowledge of rights, open-ended questions appear to have remained if not unused, then seemingly unreported. This is somewhat surprising since as Hruschka *et al.*, (2004) and Geer (1988) note, the use of open-ended questions offers a number of benefits, including capturing data of (potentially) greater accuracy or relevance to the individual, alongside capturing unanticipated responses. What may offset these benefits (and account for the lack of use to date) is as both Griffith *et al.* (1999) and Johnson *et al.*, (1974) note (although contested by Burchall and Marsh 1992) these benefits may come at the expense of higher response rates, possibly because some individuals (more often those without educational qualifications according to Geer 1988) struggle to articulate their responses.

However, neither of these suggested limitations would appear to outweigh the potential insight open-ended questions might provide when used to explore how the public defines and describes their rights. This is particularly so in respect of knowledge of the law, since self-help and self-representation rely (to varying degrees) on an individual's ability to identify and articulate an infringement of their rights. In the context of wide-ranging changes to public legal aid in England and Wales and a presumed increase in self-help and self-representation (Public Bill Committee 2011), open-ended questions present a fresh approach to the measurement of public knowledge of rights across a range of civil and social justice issues.

Accordingly, in this study we explore how individuals with one or more civil or social justice problems respond when asked to briefly describe their rights/legal position in the context of a quantitative survey. Our findings contribute to the existing methodological and PLE literature by: (a) examining the merits of using open-ended questions to explore public knowledge of rights; and (b) exploring how the public articulate their rights when asked to do so and what may be inferred about their level of knowledge. With the changes contained in the Legal Aid, Sentencing and Punishment of Offenders Act 2012 (LASPO) imminent, this study is particularly timely.

Aims and hypothesis

In this study, we draw on data from the 2010 English and Welsh Civil and Social Justice Panel Survey (CSJPS) to build upon earlier studies exploring public knowledge of rights. Utilising self-assessment and open-ended (verbatim) responses from the CSJPS, this study sets out to determine: whether an open-ended question format can provide useful insight into an individual's knowledge of their rights and/or the validity of their self-assessment and the extent to which findings might provide useful lessons for research and policy development.

Referring to self-assessed knowledge of rights and on the basis of the issues raised in the extant literature (including the findings of Williams and Hall 1972, Caseborne *et al.* 2006, Genn *et al.*, 2006, Tennant *et al.* 2006, Buck *et al.*, 2008 and Denvir *et al.*, 2012) we hypothesise that the majority of those experiencing one or more civil or social justice problems do not report having knowledge of their rights and that the majority report a failure to acquire knowledge of their rights, but as found by Kim (1999) and Meager *et al.*, (2002) these rates will vary by problem-type. Based on Deming's (1950) concerns regarding issues of memory recall in relation to self-assessed questions, we also hypothesise that those who self-report report knowing their rights in Wave 1 of the CSJPS in respect of a particular problem, frequently answer inconsistently when they are asked whether they knew their rights in Wave 2 (in relation to the same problem). We further hypothesise that many of the people who profess to have knowledge of rights are unable to articulate these rights in response to the open-ended format, however unlike Geer (1988) we propose that the failure to articulate knowledge of rights will not be associated with education level.

Methods

Data

Data used for this study came from the 2010 CSJPS,[9] a nationally representative survey of 3806 individuals aged 16 or over, living in 2318 households across 194 sample points in England and Wales. The survey explored respondents' experience of, and response to a broad range of problems involving legal rights. The survey was conducted face-to-face in respondents' homes, with all members of households interviewed separately. The survey averaged 37 minutes, with a household response rate of 88% and a cumulative eligible adult response rate of 54%. For further technical details of the CSJPS, see Pleasence *et al.*, (2011). Table 1 shows incidence of each of the broad problem types in the survey

In addressing some of the limitations of earlier research, the 2010 CSJPS included a series of open-ended questions, including questions designed to ascertain if individuals knew their rights/legal position. It did so by asking individuals who reported one or more civil or social justice problem the following: 'Thinking about the time the problem first started, to what extent did [you/your partner] understand [your/their] legal position - for example, what [your/their] legal rights were?' Which had a scale of answers as follows: (1) completely; (2) mostly; (3) partly; (4) not at all; (5) don't know. Those who answered with (3), (4) or (5) were then asked 'To what extent do [you/they] now understand what [your/their] legal position was?' This differed from the wording of the continuous Civil and Social Justice Survey (upon which Buck *et al.*, 2008 and Denvir *et al.*, 2012 relied) which asked 'At the time of the [problem descriptor], did you know what your legal rights were relating to this problem?' with the intent of negating some of the memory recall problems (Deming 1950, Groves 2009) mentioned above by distinguishing between those who knew their rights from the offset and those who acquired knowledge. Those who stated that they knew their rights at the start of the problem 'completely' or 'mostly' and those who indicated that they now knew their rights 'completely' or 'mostly' were additionally asked whether they '[could] describe, briefly, what [your/your partner's] legal position was?'

In Wave 2 of the CSJPS, all follow-up respondents were asked again 'To what extent do [you/they] now understand what [your/their] legal position was?' in respect of the same problem, with the same range of responses available ('completely', 'mostly', 'partly', 'not at all', 'don't know'). This enabled the tracking of the self-assessment respondents gave, across CSJPS waves. However, owing to timing restrictions, follow-up respondents in Wave 2 were not asked to briefly describe their rights, so where an individual responded

Table 1. Prevalence of civil justice problems of different types.

Problem type	N	%
Neighbours	359	9.3
Consumer	338	8.9
Employment	211	5.5
Money	202	5.3
Debt	185	4.9
Benefits	166	4.4
Personal Injury	155	4.1
Rented housing	144	3.8
Relationship breakdown	80	2.1
Education	71	1.9
Owned housing	59	1.6
Clinical negligence	53	1.4
Divorce	41	1.1
Domestic violence	39	1.0
Care proceedings	9	0.2

that they knew their rights 'partly', 'not at all' or 'don't know' in Wave 1, but in Wave 2 indicated that they now knew their rights, the verbatim responses of these individuals were not captured.

Analysis

Firstly we set out the extent to which respondents to the 2010 CSJPS (Wave 1) self-report knowledge of rights and how this varies with problem-type so as to provide an overview of the cohort and a basis for comparison with existing studies. We describe the rate at which individuals knew their rights at the start of their problem and the rate at which individuals acquired knowledge of their rights, distinguished by problem-type.

Exploring how self-reported knowledge changes over the course of the reference period, using descriptive statistics, we compare individuals' self-reported knowledge in Wave 1, against their self-reported knowledge in Wave 2, looking also at the extent to which knowledge varies by problem-type across Wave 1 and Wave 2 of the CSJPS.

Finally, we look at how individuals answered the open-ended question asking them to describe their rights. We code these verbatim responses into one of seven categories as outlined below. Whilst responses were not 'marked' as correct or incorrect, we anticipated that those inferring the intended meaning from the question and capable of articulating their legal position/rights, would provide an answer that gave insight into their position of (legal) power relative to the other party. For example, someone who purchased a faulty coat and reported a consumer problem could (in an ideal scenario) answer the question as follows: (a) 'under the Sale of Goods Act I was allowed to claim a refund or exchange on my faulty coat'. Those without knowledge of or reference to the legislation might have offered a similar explanation such as: (b) 'the store had to provide me with a refund or exchange'. In consideration of the fact that in the context of a long quantitative survey some participants might have (reasonably) opted to explain their legal position with greater brevity (see further Herzog and Bachman 1981), we could also have expected answers such as (c) 'I could get a refund' which although shorter, remained illustrative of an individual's knowledge of their rights/legal position.

Whilst the range of expected answers was rather broad, individuals actually answered in a far more varied manner than this. Analysis of all verbatim responses identified seven different responses types that individuals tended towards in answering the question. These categories included:

(1) Those who described their situation or the outcome they experienced (e.g. 'My zipper was broken on my coat' or 'The shop offered a refund');
(2) Those who referred to legislation, used legal terminology, spoke of 'positive' rights, or provided a common sense interpretation of their rights (e.g. see (a), (b) and (c) above);
(3) Those who referred to legislation, used legal terminology, or spoke of 'positive' rights but whose response indicated that they may have misinterpreted their legal position, or over/underestimated their rights (e.g. an example of an overestimate of rights might have included: 'Under the Sale of Goods Act my rights were to get a new coat and the shop had to replace it with a better quality brand than previously and compensate me for inconvenience caused'. Whereas an underestimation of rights might have been: 'I was entitled to a refund or return but it was the manufacturer I needed to contact not the store');
(4) Those who made a value judgement about the fairness of the legal system, the individuals involved, or their position in it (e.g. 'I was right, the coat was faulty' or

'No point in complaining, the Government is acting to take away the rights of consumers');

(5) Those who referred to broad rights that did not suggest any knowledge of their rights in relation to their problem, but were indicative of a more general understanding of the legal system or with moral or ethical interpretations of the concept 'right' (e.g. 'Human Rights', 'The right to voice my opinion', 'I could appeal', 'I had the right to be listened to');

(6) Those who claimed to have no legal position/rights or to be 'in the wrong ' (e.g. 'No rights', 'I should have noticed the zip was broken before I took the coat home, it was my fault I didn't check');

(7) Those who claimed not to know, or who failed to articulate anything.

Whilst the answers provided were for the most part discrete, where an individual provided a response that could have fallen into two categories, they were assigned to a category based on the length of their answer.[10] This was not the case where an individual provided a response that may have fallen into category (2) and another category, they were coded only as (2) since the central issue was whether they could explain their legal/position rights, and not the information they provided surplus to this.

In exploring open-ended responses, we compare verbatim response-type against problem type, looking also at how individuals verbalised their rights, before turning to explore whether response and articulation type varied by level of educational attainment.

Results

Perceived knowledge and the acquisition of perceived knowledge of rights

Out of 1760 problems, respondents said they knew their rights at the outset of the problem, 'completely' for 396 problems (22.5%), 'mostly' for 319 problems (18.1%), 'partly' for 356 problems (20.2%), 'not at all' for 612 problems (34.8%). For a further 68 problems (3.9%)[11] respondents suggested that they did not know whether or not they knew their rights. For those 1036 problems where the respondent answered 'partly', 'not at all' or 'don't know', they were additionally asked whether they later came to understand their rights. For 140 problems (13.6%) respondents claimed to have acquired knowledge of their rights 'completely' in relation to the problem, for 205 problems respondents acquired knowledge of their rights 'mostly' (19.9%), 'partially' for 345 problems (33.5%), for 289 problems (28.1%) respondents claimed still to have obtained no knowledge and for 51 problems respondents claimed not to know (5%).

In total, discounting those who provided no response, for 715 problems (41%) respondents claimed to know their rights completely or mostly at the start of the problem. For a further 345 problems (20%) respondents came to acquire knowledge of their rights, and for 685 problems (39%), respondents did not come to acquire knowledge of their rights. Table 2 identifies these individuals on the basis of problem type.

As is shown in Table 2, those with consumer problems more often knew their rights from the outset at 58.4% but were relatively less likely to acquire knowledge of their rights, followed by owned housing at 49.1% where the acquisition of knowledge was higher than non-acquisition. In domestic violence cases the acquisition of knowledge was higher than its rate at the outset, but those with domestic violence problems were more likely still, to not acquire knowledge at all, at a rate of 37.8%. A failure to acquire knowledge was particularly prevalent for care proceedings, clinical negligence, education and neighbours cases.[12]

Table 2. Problem types and knowledge of rights.

	Knew rights at outset		Acquired knowledge		Did not acquire knowledge	
Problem type	*N*	*Row %*	*N*	*Row %*	*N*	*Row %*
Consumer	174	58.4	38	12.8	86	28.9
Employment	69	35.0	47	23.9	81	41.1
Neighbours	103	40.9	33	13.1	116	46.0
Owned housing	26	49.1	15	28.3	12	22.6
Rented housing	41	34.5	24	20.2	54	45.4
Debt	61	36.1	39	23.1	69	40.8
Money	72	39.3	38	20.8	73	39.9
Benefits	43	33.0	28	21.7	58	45.0
Education	22	33.8	11	16.9	32	49.2
Personal injury	29	42.6	17	25.0	22	32.4
Clinical negligence	19	39.6	5	10.4	24	50.0
Divorce/relationship breakdown	44	37.0	35	29.4	40	33.6
Domestic violence	10	27.0	13	35.1	14	37.8
Care proceedings	2	25.0	2	25.0	4	50.0

Self-reported knowledge across CSJPS waves

Owing to the panel format of the CSJPS, individuals at Wave 1 were asked whether they knew their rights at the start of the problem or whether they later came to acquire knowledge. In Wave 2, follow-up respondents (i.e. the same respondents as Wave 1) were again asked whether they 'now knew' their rights in relation to the same problem, allowing an exploration of whether respondents changed their self-assessment over time. Results found that 92 respondents (24.6%) claimed to have lost knowledge – that is to say they reported knowing their rights to a higher degree in Wave 1, than they did in Wave 2. 135 respondents (36.1%) claimed the same level of knowledge, and 147 respondents (39.3%) claimed to have gained knowledge. Table 3 displays the rate at which knowledge was lost, gained or remained the same by problem type.

As is shown in Table 3, those with neighbours (51.3%), personal injury (50%), employment (45.7%), clinical negligence (45.5%), and education (45.5%) problems were more likely to report gains in knowledge than those with other problem types. Those with owned housing (71.4%) and consumer (58.8%) were most likely to report the same level of knowledge across waves, with those with rented housing and personal injury problems reporting a loss in knowledge more frequently than other problems types. However, at a rate of 34.6% for rented housing and 33.3% for personal injury, approximately two-thirds of individuals with these sorts of problems reported the same, or a gain in knowledge. For all problem types, more individuals reported either gaining or retaining the same level of knowledge than reported losing knowledge.

Open-ended articulation of rights

For the 1056 problems where individuals claimed to know their legal position/rights 'completely' or 'mostly' at either the outset of the problem or later during the course of the problem, individuals were asked to briefly explain their legal position/legal rights. Analysis of the responses revealed some common themes categorised as described previously.

Table 3. Whether respondents lost, gained or retained the same level of knowledge of their rights by problem-type.*

	Lost		Same		Gained	
	N	*Row %*	*N*	*Row %*	*N*	*Row %*
Consumer	6	17.6	20	58.8	8	23.5
Employment	10	21.7	15	32.6	21	45.7
Neighbours	20	25.6	18	23.1	40	51.3
Owned housing	1	7.1	10	71.4	3	21.4
Rented housing	9	34.6	10	38.5	7	26.9
Debt	9	21.4	17	40.5	16	38.1
Money	11	30.6	13	36.1	12	33.3
Benefits	5	23.8	8	38.1	8	38.1
Education	3	27.3	3	27.3	5	45.5
Personal injury	4	33.3	2	16.7	6	50.0
Clinical negligence	2	18.2	4	36.4	5	45.5
Divorce/relationship breakdown	10	31.3	10	31.3	12	37.5
Domestic violence	2	20	4	40	4	40.0

*With only one respondent the category 'care' was removed from the table, this respondent reported that their knowledge had stayed the same.

Table 4 examines the categorisation of verbatim responses in relation to problem-type. As can be seen, 25.9% of verbatim responses were categorised as instances where the respondent described the situation or outcome of the dispute. Forty-two per cent of respondents detailed their legal position/rights referring to the legislation, legal terminology or presenting a lay interpretation and fewer (8%) individuals provided a more general/vague interpretation of their rights. Less frequently, individuals gave responses which suggested they may have under or overestimated their rights or the strength of their legal position at a rate of 2.6%, with 4.5% claiming that they had no rights in respect of their problem or that their 'legal' position was that they were to blame or at fault. 6.1% made a value judgement about the legal system in response to the question, with a further 11.1% claiming that they did not know or could not verbalise their rights/legal position when asked.

Setting aside the categorisation of verbatim responses related to care proceedings given the small numbers contained within that group (four in total) results further highlight how individuals with certain problems tended to reply in certain ways. This was not so evident in respect of those who responded to the open-ended question in a manner that described their situation or outcome. Here, relatively high rates of responding in this manner were seen across most problem types and differences were relatively small with the exception of those with education problems (at 12.1%). Where respondents did describe their situation or outcome, their answers provided relatively little if any insight in to what they believed their rights to be, making it difficult to deduce whether they had any clear understanding of their rights as they believed they did. Examples of those who claimed they knew their legal position/rights included: 'Took out a joint mortgage with a friend who had unknown to me a poor credit rating' and 'The agency gave me a poor score I had not done anything wrong they would not let me see my score in details'. Individuals with debt problems frequently spoke of the nature of their problem, rather than articulating what their legal entitlements were. Examples included one who simply stated that they

Table 4. Categorisation of verbatim responses against problem-type.

	(1) Situation/ Outcome		(2) Rights/ Legal Position		(3) Potential Error		(4) Value Judgement		(5) Vague Rights		(6) No Legal Position/ Rights		(7) Don't Know	
	N	*Row %*	*N*	*Row %*	*N*	*Row %*	*N*	*Row %*	*N*	*Row %*	*N*	*Row %*	*N*	*Row %*
Consumer	46	21.7	111	52.4	12	5.7	5	2.4	14	6.6	7	3.3	17	8.0
Employment	32	27.6	36	31.0	7	6.0	9	7.8	11	9.5	11	9.5	10	8.6
Neighbours	33	24.3	41	30.1	2	1.5	17	12.5	20	14.7	8	5.9	15	11.0
Owned housing	12	29.3	13	31.7	0	0.0	3	7.3	6	14.6	1	2.4	6	14.6
Rented housing	17	26.2	32	49.2	3	4.6	1	1.5	4	6.2	0	0.0	8	12.3
Debt	29	29.0	46	46.0	0	0.0	2	2.0	2	2.0	3	3.0	18	18.0
Money	39	35.5	43	39.1	0	0.0	6	5.5	8	7.3	5	4.5	9	.2
Benefits	14	19.7	34	47.9	0	0.0	6	8.5	0	0.0	4	5.6	13	18.3
Education	4	12.1	15	45.5	2	6.1	2	6.1	1	3.0	3	9.1	6	18.2
Personal injury	12	26	17	37.0	0	0.0	9	19.6	4	8.7	1	2.2	3	.5
Clinical negligence	7	29.2	6	25.0	0	0.0	1	4.2	6	25.0	1	4.2	3	12.5
Divorce/relationship breakdown	23	29.5	36	46.2	1	1.3	3	3.8	3	3.8	3	3.8	9	11.5
Domestic violence	4	20.0	13	65.0	0	0.0	0	0.0	3	15.0	0	0.0	0	.0
Care	2	50.0	0	0.0	0	0.0	0	0.0	2	50.0	0	0.0	0	.0
Total	274	25.9	443	42.0	27	2.6	64	6.1	84	8.0	47	4.5	117	11.1

'went over their overdraft' and another who explained that 'I gave girlfriend money to look after she spent it all.'

In respect of those who did answer the question in the manner expected by describing their rights/legal position, these types of responses were most common among those experiencing domestic violence problems at a rate of 65%. Responses such as 'I could get him nicked' or 'I had the right to press charges' were typical of domestic violence cases. Those with consumer, rented housing, benefits, divorce/relationship breakdown, debt and education problems also had high rates of providing answers that indicated that they had an understanding of their legal position/rights at a rate of between 52–45%. However, whilst responses were indicative of some level of knowledge, the extent to which respondents were familiar with the legislation varied from individual to individual. For example, some respondents provided relatively simplistic and short responses, such as 'had to pay the money'. Whilst this response presents an efficient explanation in the context of a long quantitative survey it is distinguished from those who demonstrated willingness to provide a more detailed response, by stating their obligations, along with their entitlements, e.g. 'had to repay the money in affordable instalments' or 'I had to pay the money back at a payment that was affordable to me and not what they were asking'. Some individuals gave specific reference to the relevant legislation in their answers with this more common in the case of those reporting clinical negligence or consumer problems. For example, whilst some responses were again simplistic, e.g. 'could get a refund', others were more sophisticated, e.g. 'goods not sold as described so they did not meet Sale of Goods Act', with another detailing that they had a 'right to receive goods fit for purpose'. Although, individuals did not always recall the name of the legislation correctly, for example, one respondent claimed to be 'entitled to a replacement under the (non-existent) faulty goods act' this error did not compromise their understanding of their rights - namely that they were entitled to a replacement.

Yet, although frequently reporting their rights/legal position as expected, those with consumer problems along with those experiencing employment, rented housing and education problems were also more frequently categorised as responding to the open-ended question in a manner that indicated they may have erred in their understanding of their rights, along with either potentially over or underestimating their entitlements (5.7%, 6%, 4.6%, 6.1% respectively). Generally, this overestimation appeared to derive from a misunderstanding of the relevant legislation or its application. Some errors had the potential to impact upon the resolution of the problem and an individual's satisfaction with this resolution. For example, one respondent claimed to have 'had the right to (have his vehicle repaired) to (his) satisfaction' when in fact the relevant legislation (Sale of Goods Act 1979) imposes an objective test of satisfactory quality (under s14 (2) and s48B as it relates to repair) suggesting the individual may have been waiting for an outcome which holds the other party to a higher standard than the legislation does. There also appeared to be confusion surrounding tenancy rights, including one individual who erroneously believed it was within their rights to 'withdraw rent until (their) property (was) sorted', a position which is not only legally incorrect, but places the individual at risk of eviction. Conversely, individuals also appeared to occasionally underestimate their rights, including one individual who claimed that 'if you order something and pay on the Internet and tick the terms and conditions you have no rights' a position at odds with the entitlements enshrined in the Consumer Protection (Distance Selling Regulations) 2000 and potentially also the Unfair Terms in Consumer Contracts Regulations 1999.[13] There was indication of potential underestimation of rights in respect of employment, with a number of individuals claiming that they had to put up with changes to the terms and conditions of their employment or get another job. Whilst understanding that they did not have to agree to such changes, they did not appear to have an appreciation of the fact that (legally speaking) getting another job was not their only alternative.

Value judgements were most common amongst those with neighbours (12.5%) and those with personal injury (19.6%) problems. Typically these were the types of problems where individuals provided very matter-of-fact and short responses to the question asked by detailing that they were 'in the right', 'wholly innocent' or 'had done nothing wrong'. Whilst these were legitimate responses to the question asked, particularly since the question asked individuals to detail their 'legal position', they did not elicit the desired information, namely greater insight into what people thought their rights were. It was also somewhat surprising to find responses discussing issues such as guilt/innocence in relation to a civil, rather than a criminal justice problem. However, this is perhaps less surprising given that personal injury problems tend to focus on the attribution of blame and responsibility, whilst neighbours problems can often straddle both the civil and criminal law.

In a similar vein, those with employment and education problems more frequently gave answers indicative of them having 'no rights' with one individual claiming that they had no rights because they '(could not) argue against council or government decision'. At a rate of 5.9% and 5.6% those with neighbours and benefits problems also expressed their belief that they had 'no rights' when asked. However, whilst some appeared to be more of a political statement than an expression of legal understanding, for example one individual in respect of a benefit problem who claimed that the 'government acting (was) to remove rights', other responses appeared illustrative, not of knowledge (or a lack thereof) but whether a right could reasonably be upheld by the individual. For example, one respondent with a neighbour problem claimed that 'essentially we had little rights, collecting evidence would be difficult and time consuming and we have to prove damage to property and then start civil action'. Similar such statements were evident in relation to employment problems where individuals often claimed that they had 'no rights', not because none existed, but more often because they believed exercising such rights would put their job at risk.

Common sense interpretations of rights were most often given in respect of clinical negligence, domestic violence, neighbours and owned housing. Examples included those who identified a 'right to take an individual to court', 'the right to an appeal', 'human rights', or the 'right to be heard' or 'voice an opinion'. Whilst these responses were again, not incorrect, they were indicative of a more general understanding of an individual's position based on common sense or principles of fairness, one not reliant on knowledge of the law in relation to a particular problem. Of course many people may also have had knowledge of the law in respect of the question asked – indeed one individual did make a distinction between what she saw as legal and moral rights in stating in respect of her employment problem that she 'Did not have legal right to move but had moral rights not to be moved further away from home'. However, because the rights these individuals professed to have were so generic, it made it difficult to determine the extent to which these individuals had any clear understanding of the specific rights relative to their legal problem, or whether they were simply relying on a broad understanding of concepts of 'natural justice' or legal common sense.

Importantly, verbatim responses highlighted a disjuncture between an individual's belief that they knew their rights/legal position and their ability to articulate this. This was more so the case for those reporting debt, benefits, education and owned housing problems than those reporting other problem types. For 117 problems (11.1%) individuals responded that they '(didn't) know' when asked to articulate their rights, suggesting that they were confident enough to believe that their problem engaged a right but they could not explain this in legal terms. Indeed, one respondent said as much, claiming that they '(couldn't) really describe it'.

Education level and responses to the verbatim question

Table 5 shows the categorisation of verbatim responses in relation to the level of educational attainment of the respondents. Whilst there are some minor differences apparent in Table 5 as shown below, there was no significant relationship emerging between type of verbatim response and level of education qualification. [14]

Discussion

Our results indicate that most individuals felt unsure of their rights at the outset of their problem. For 41% of problems, respondents claimed to know their rights completely or mostly at the start of the problem, for a further 20% of problems respondents acquired knowledge, and for 39% of problems respondents did not come to acquire knowledge.

Knowledge varied by problem type (see Table 2), with those with consumer problems more often reporting knowledge of their rights from the outset at 58.4% but relatively less likely to acquire knowledge of their rights, followed by owned housing at 49.1% where the acquisition of knowledge was higher than non-acquisition. In domestic violence cases the acquisition of knowledge was higher than its rate at the outset, but those with domestic violence problems were more likely still, to not acquire knowledge at all, at a rate of 37.8%. A failure to acquire knowledge was particularly prevalent for clinical negligence, education and neighbour problems.

Utilising data from both Waves of the CSJPS highlighted that 24.6% of respondents claimed to lose knowledge with 39.3% claiming a gain in knowledge. As is shown in Table 3, those with neighbours (45.7%), personal injury (50%), employment (45.7%), clinical negligence (45.5%), and education (45.5%) problems were more likely to report gains in knowledge than those with other problem types. Those with owned housing (71.4%) and consumer (58.8%) problems were most likely to report the same level of knowledge across waves. Those with rented housing (34.6%) and personal injury (33.3%) problems reported a loss in knowledge more frequently than those with other problem types.

Analysis of verbatim responses demonstrated a number of response types, most common of these were responses in which individuals were able to give a brief overview of their rights/legal position. However, response types varied from those who supported their answer with reference to the relevant legislation to those who simply stated their rights. In respect of this latter group, although their answer appeared correct in relation to their dispute, it was not possible to deduce the basis of their knowledge, i.e. whether it stemmed from an understanding of the legislation, or whether it was based on a common sense position as found by Kim (1999), Meager *et al.*, (2002), Barlow *et al.* (2004) and Pleasence and Balmer (2012). Individuals also frequently reported their situation or the outcome of the dispute rather than their legal/rights and tended to also provide very vague responses which did not appear to have specific relevance to their particular dispute. In addition, whilst claiming to know their rights, 11.1% went on to claim they 'didn't know' in relation to the question. Less frequently, 2.6% of respondents gave verbatim responses which implied an over/under assessment of their rights. Results did not suggest any connection between interpretation of or response to the verbatim question and level of educational attainment.

Table 5. Categorisation of verbatim responses in relation to level of education attainment of respondent.

	(1) Situation/ Outcome		(2) Rights/ Legal Position		(3) Potential Error		(4) Value Judgement		(5) Vague Rights		(6) No Legal Position/ Rights		(7) Don't Know	
	N	*Row %*	*N*	*Row %*	*N*	*Row %*	*N*	*Row %*	*N*	*Row %*	*N*	*Row %*	*N*	*Row %*
None	41	24.1	66	38.8	3	1.8	10	5.9	19	11.2	6	3.5	25	14.7
Higher degrees	21	24.7	34	40.0	3	3.5	5	5.9	4	4.7	6	7.1	12	14.1
First degrees or equiv.	63	29.4	97	45.3	5	2.3	7	3.3	13	6.1	6	2.8	23	10.7
Diplomas in HE or equiv.	35	27.3	48	37.5	5	3.9	11	8.6	10	7.8	6	4.7	13	10.2
A/AS levels or equiv.	40	27.4	55	37.7	6	4.1	9	6.2	15	10.3	9	6.2	12	8.2
GCSE A-C or equiv.	15	23.4	35	54.7	1	1.6	3	4.7	2	3.1	2	3.1	6	9.4
GCSE D-G or equiv.	13	24.1	21	38.9	1	1.9	5	9.3	6	11.1	2	3.7	6	11.1
Trade apprentice	44	23.7	85	45.7	3	1.6	13	7.0	13	7.0	10	5.4	18	9.7
Other	2	22.2	2	22.2	0	0.0	1	11.1	2	22.2	0	0.0	2	22.2

Who knows what and when?

In keeping with our first hypothesis, most individuals did not have knowledge of their rights to begin with. These findings are not surprising and are in line with the findings of previous studies, notably that of Buck *et al.*, (2008), Denvir *et al.*, (2012), Parle/IARS (2009) and Casebourne *et al.* (2006). As also hypothesised, the majority (60.7%) of respondents who reported a lack of knowledge at the outset of the problem did not go on to acquire knowledge of their rights to the standard of 'completely' or 'mostly'.

As found by Kim (1999) and Meager *et al.*, (2002) and in keeping with our second hypothesis, we found that the rate of existing knowledge and acquisition of knowledge varied by problem type. Interestingly, many of the problem types for which knowledge was poor at the outset, were related to social exclusion and vulnerability, including rented housing, money, debt, benefits, education and domestic violence as has been noted by both Buck *et al.* (2005, 2008), Balmer *et al.*, (2010) and Denvir *et al.*, (2012). This may be related to the complexity of the problem, or potentially the low rate at which individuals with these problem types seek professional advice (see further Pleasence *et al.*, 2011, p. 43). This would also explain why individuals with divorce and owned housing problems were more likely to acquire knowledge of their rights since these are problem types for which the obtaining of professional advice is far more common (Pleasence *et al.*'s 2011, p. 43).

In keeping with our third hypothesis, based on Deming's (1950) and Groves *et al.*'s (2009) concerns regarding issues of memory recall in relation to self-assessed questions, we found that those who self-reported knowing their rights in Wave 1 of the CSJPS in respect of a particular problem, frequently answered inconsistently when asked whether they knew their rights in Wave 2 (in relation to the same problem). However, more often people professed to having the same if not greater levels of knowledge in relation to their problem in Wave 2. That reductions in levels of knowledge happened more frequently for rented housing, money and personal injury problems may be a reflection of the complexity of dealing with such issues or the fact that individuals tended to overestimate their knowledge of rights in relation to these problem-types more frequently, only realising later down the line. This was certainly the case for those with rented housing problems where 4.6% of verbatim responses were categorised as '(3) Potential Error', the third highest of any other problem group. Interestingly, those with money problems tended towards answering the verbatim question by explaining their '(1) situation/outcome' than those with other problem types and those with personal injury problems tended to report their rights as '(4) Value judgements' than other problem types. The fact that they did not answer the verbatim question in the expected manner and the fact that they answered in it a way that suggested they lacked knowledge of their rights, may account for why by Wave 2 they had lowered their self-reported levels of knowledge. Whilst these results highlight how self-assessed knowledge changes over time, neither comparison between waves nor alteration of our question (to ask participants about both their existing and acquired knowledge) can wholly negate the continued issue of memory-recall noted by Deming (1950) and Groves *et al.*, (2009).

Consistent with our fourth hypothesis that many of the people who profess to have knowledge of rights will be unable to articulate these rights in response to the open-ended format, we found that 11.1% of respondents were not able to articulate their rights/legal position when asked to do so. However, a number of other verbatim response types suggested that individuals had a lack of understanding of their rights. We would contend that this was the case in respect of those 58% of respondents who when asked to explain their rights/legal position instead gave a summary of their problem or its outcome, tended to over- or under-estimate their rights, gave a value judgement, mentioned non-specific rights or claimed to have no rights. Yet, although it suggests as much, we cannot conclusively state (contrary to their self-reporting) that these individuals did not know their specific rights in relation to the problem. Whilst on the face of it such responses imply if not a lack of knowledge of rights/legal position, a lack of understanding of what is meant by the term 'rights'/'legal position', these responses may simply be indicative of participants interpreting the question differently than anticipated although we would not expect this to be the case for the entire 58% of respondents who did not answer the open-ended question as anticipated. What we did not find was any evidence to support Geer's (1988) assertion that response types would vary by education level. Although verbatim responses did vary, it did not appear that education was associated with any clear pattern of response or non-response as Geer (1988) suggests.

What do open-ended questions tell us?

Our results support the proposition that an open-ended question approach to exploring knowledge of rights yields insight into knowledge not acquired by other formats. Unlike hypothetical questions, asking individuals to describe their rights/legal position in their own words gives insight into the knowledge driving their resolution of the problem. The fact that individuals who answered the fixed-choice self-assessment question often then failed to answer the open-ended question (by claiming they 'don't know') highlights, as proposed by Schuman and Presser (1981) and Schwarz and Hippler (1991), the tendency of individuals to answer self-assessed/fixed-choice questions with greater confidence/-frequency than open-ended questions. However, the findings detailed above also suggest that the utility of an open-ended question format in the context of a large-scale quantitative survey will remain constrained by difficulty reconciling articulation and interpretation with actual knowledge. Whilst this problem could be avoided through the use of vignettes it would be difficult to do so with real problems. Although the open-ended question enabled individuals to answer freely, as has been previously noted (Geer 1988) it also enabled them to freely interpret the question. There was also some evidence, as Tourangeau and Rasinski (1988) note in relation to fact-based questions, of individuals providing attitudinal responses rather than directly answering the question, as evidenced by those who provided a value judgment/claimed 'no rights' in response to the open-ended question. While nearly half of respondents were able to articulate their rights/legal position and interpreted the question as anticipated, there was a limit to the extent to which responses provided clear insight. For example, whilst some individuals referenced the relevant legislation, most did not. Respondents may have been relying on 'common sense' when reporting what they believed to be their rights rather than an actual understanding of the law as found by Meager *et al.*, (2002), Barlow *et al.* (2004) and Kim (1999). Conversely, others may have provided an explanation of the situation, even though they did have a clear understanding of their rights. Thus, as found in respect of self-assessed, fact based, and hypothetical questions, an open-ended question is not in itself capable of providing conclusive insight into public knowledge of rights.

Policy implications

Studies seeking to acquire an understanding of the extent to which the public know their rights, will tend to produce an inflated rate of knowledge where they rely on the public's self-assessment alone. As our results highlight, asking individuals whether they knew or acquired knowledge of their rights yields a greater number of individuals saying yes than those capable of articulating these rights. Similarly, approaches relying on tests of knowledge may just reflect the extent to which respondents guess correctly, rather than reflecting any real knowledge. Including an open-ended question provides some degree of verification, however, in order to determine whether the open-ended responses given derive from knowledge of the law, a further question must be asked, designed to determine how the individual knew their rights. Based on both of the aforementioned considerations, a more nuanced question or series of questions would need to deduce not only what individuals thought their rights to be, but also how they arrived at this conclusion. This may involve a number of prompted open-ended questions that do not fit as readily within a quantitative survey format and may be more appropriate within the context of a qualitative study.

Whilst we would caution against concluding that most people were unable to articulate their rights simply because the answer they provided was not what was anticipated (particularly where this answer fell into the '(1) situation/outcome' category) nonetheless our results suggest some priorities for the development of public legal education. In particular, we note that individuals most often appeared unable to articulate their rights in respect of debt, benefits and education problems. Whilst this may be indicative of the complexity of the problem itself or the capacity of the individual, if we are to assume that knowledge and articulation of knowledge of rights plays a key role in problem resolution, then public legal education may have a role to play in improving knowledge in these areas. In addition, individuals more frequently claimed to have 'no rights' in respect of employment and education problems than in respect of other problem types. Rather than a misinterpretation of the question, such responses appear to be indicative of feelings of disempowerment that may stem, not from a lack of knowledge of rights but rather a sense of powerlessness arising from the inequality of the parties. The perceived 'impotence' of these rights suggests the need to consider legislative rather than educational intervention/s. In contrast, those reporting 'vague rights' (neighbours, owned housing, clinical negligence and domestic violence) may benefit from a more specific understanding of the problem as it relates to their rights. The same is also true of consumer, employment, education and rented housing disputes, where over/underestimation of rights occurred most frequently.

When considering family issues (divorce/relationship breakdown and domestic violence) in comparison to the remaining civil justice issues, individuals did tend to provide verbatim responses which were indicative of the fact that they knew and could articulate their rights. If this (and the more frequent acquisition of knowledge for family law problems) is related to their obtaining of professional advice as noted above, any reduction in the availability of advice is likely to have an impact on the extent to which those with family law problems report knowing their rights in the future. Given that family law is one area where legal aid is set to be substantially curtailed, it suggests an ongoing and long-term role for PLE in buffering the impact of legal aid reform.

Yet in spite of what appears to be continued need for PLE and whilst simultaneously promoting self-help for the range of problems soon to be out of the scope of legal aid, the Government has imposed upon itself no duty to promote knowledge of rights, develop just-in-time legal information, share the third sector's burden of equipping citizens to better handle their problems alone or for that matter, inform itself as to the need for public legal education interventions (see further Legal Aid, Sentencing and Punishment of Offenders Act 2012, s 1(3)[15]). Whilst an expectation that the public takes greater responsibility for their legal problems should be complimented with the tools to enable them to do so, thus far it remains to be seen who will take responsibility for both the research underpinning and the development of PLE.

Future research

In this study we have used the articulation of rights as a proxy for actual knowledge. Although we recognise that during the course of a dispute some individuals will never have to put into 'legal terms' the rights they feel have been infringed, our results provide new insight into how the public articulate their rights and whether open-ended questions might produce more reliable data. Nonetheless, further research utilising different methodologies is needed in order to more reliably determine how well individuals know their rights and, crucially, the role knowledge plays in the resolution of civil and social justice problems. Our assumption remains that knowledge of rights leads to 'better' problem-resolution, but there is little reliable evidence to support this assumption and continued difficulty in measuring outcomes. If we are to assume that individuals will in future be required to handle more of their civil and social justice problems alone, it is clear that PLE will continue to have a role to play in access to justice. But whether this role should be to improve knowledge, build confidence, promote early action or a combination of these objectives, cannot be fully understood without further enquiry.

Notes

1. Other key rationales in determining what would and would not remain in scope, included:
   i. The importance of the issue (including personal choices)
   ii. The litigant's ability to present their own case (including the venue before which the case is heard, the likely vulnerability of the litigant and the complexity of the law)
   iii. The availability of alternative sources of funding
   iv. The availability of alternative routes to resolving the issue
   v. The need to fulfil our domestic and international legal obligations (including those under the European Convention on Human Rights).
2. Civil Justice problems can also be referred to as 'justiciable', 'legal-related' or 'rights' problems, or 'problems with a legal dimension'. They are everyday and common-place problems that may or may not be resolved through the civil justice system. Examples of such problems are listed in Table 1.
3. PLE has been used to refer to both 'legal rights-based education' intended to promote general public awareness of the law and legal system and 'self-help/just-in-time' initiatives aimed at guiding people through the resolution of a particular problem and the legal rights it engages (Giddings and Robertson 2003; Lawler *et al*, 2009). Rights-based education has included the introduction of compulsory citizenship classes within the school curriculum since 2005 and Ministry of Justice (MOJ) support of Public Legal Education (PLE) initiatives through the part funding of the Public Legal Education Network (PLEnet) (PLEAS Taskforce 2007). Efforts to provide self-help/just-in-time resources have not been centrally coordinated, but have included the publication of a number of information leaflets available online and in person from a range of agencies including public and third sector organisations (e.g. Shelter, Citizens Advice, Money Advice Trust and government affiliated websites, including the Office of Fair Trading and the now defunct Community Legal Advice, DirectGov and National Debtline to name but a few).
4. This was particularly so in respect of discrimination-like actions which at the time did not fall under discrimination legislation, but which would have fallen under unfair dismissal, including dismissal on the grounds of sexual orientation and age.
5. For policy makers, this is perhaps not a pressing concern where ethical/social norms continue to align, but does suggest that where the law changes, those people deemed to 'have knowledge' may not necessarily hold contemporaneous views any more.
6. In addition, one wonders whether the questions asked of Kim's (1999) respondents were those which individuals could reasonably have been expected to know. An example included a

question which asked whether it was lawful to fire an employee as retaliation for refusing to participate in an illegal billing practice. Whilst the practice was lawful in New York (as opposed to the other two states where the study took place), for New York respondents to have known this would have required a detailed understanding of appeal court case law (Kim 1999, p. 469). Knowing the law in respect of rather obscure (and less likely) dismissal-at-will circumstances is arguably less of an imperative than providing a correct gauge of public knowledge relating to more likely dismissal-at-will events.

7. These situations included a woman's request for financial support post-relationship breakdown, a woman's entitlement to inheritance upon the death of her partner and an unmarried father's right to make decisions regarding medical treatment of his biological child vies-a-vie his rights as a married man.
8. The idea that couples accrued greater rights as time went on.
9. The CSJPS is a substantially developed form of Genn's (1999) Landmark 'Paths to Justice' Survey.
10. So, where an individual provided a response that could have been coded as (1) or (4) for example in relation to an employment problem they said 'I was in the right, I had been a good employee for over four years and I was then fired' they were coded as (1) because their explanation of the outcome of the case was longer than their (4) value judgement.
11. For nine problems respondents refused to give an answer (0.5%).
12. We also fitted two binary logistic regression models in order to predict the likelihood of respondents reporting knowledge of their rights from the outset (Model 1) or later gaining knowledge of their rights (Model 2) by problem-type whilst controlling for a range of socio-demographic characteristics (age, academic qualifications, gender, tenure, family type, illness/disability, mental health, ethnicity and income). Results yielded similar findings to those detailed in Table 2. Readers wishing to know more about these models should contact the authors.
13. For purchases made in England and Wales, with purchases from sellers within the EU protected by the European Union Distance Selling Directive 97/7/EC.
14. Even when splitting education level into a binary 'education qualification' and 'no educational qualifications' category, no significant pattern emerged to suggest that education level had any role to play in type of verbatim response given.
15. Note in particular, the wording used in Section 1(3) of the Legal Aid, Sentencing and Punishment of Offenders Act 2012, where it says 'The Lord Chancellor **may** secure the provision of— *(a) general information about the law and the legal system, and (b) information about the availability of advice about, and assistance in connection with, the law and the legal system.*

    This is a departure from the legal services envisaged under the Access to Justice Act 1999 which by virtue of s4 (1) stated that '*(a) the provision of general information about the law and legal system and the availability of legal services*' was responsibility of the Legal Services Commission and the Community Legal Service.

References

Access to Justice Act 1999 (c. 22).

Albrecht, S.L. and Green, M., 1977. Attitudes toward the police and the larger attitude complex: implications for police-community relationships. *Criminology*, 15 (1), 67–86.

Baker, L.A. and Emery, R.E., 1993. When every relationship is above average – perceptions and expectations of divorce at the time of marriage. *Law and human behavior*, 17 (4), 439–450.

Baldwin, W., 2009. Information nobody else knows. In: A.A. Stone, J.S Turkkan, C.A. Bachrach, J.B. Jobe, H.s. Kurtzma and V.S. Cain, eds. *The science of self-report: implications for research and practice*. Mahwah, NJ: Lawrence Earlbauch Associates, 3–8.

Balmer, N.J., et al., 2010. *Knowledge, capability and the experience of rights problems*. London: PLEnet.

Barlow, A., et al., 2005. *Cohabitation, marriage and the law. Social change and legal reform in the 21st century*. Portland, OR: Hart.

Bowal, P., 1999. A study of lay knowledge of law in Canada. *Indiana international and comparative law review*, 9 (1), 121–141.

Bradburn, N.M., Rips, L.J. and Shevell, S.K., 1987. Answering autobiographical questions: the impact of memory and inference on surveys. *Science*, 236 (4798), 157–161.
Buck, A., Pleasence, P. and Balmer, N.J., 2008. Do citizens know how to deal with legal issues? *Journal of social policy*, 37 (4), 661–681.
Buck, A., Pleasence, P. and Balmer, N.J., 2005. Social exclusion and civil law: experience of civil justice problems among vulnerable groups. *Social policy and administration*, 39 (3), 302–322.
Burchall, B. and Marsh, C., 1992. The effect of questionnaire length on survey response. *Quality and quantity*, 26 (3), 233–244.
Calahan, D., 1968. Correlates of respondent accuracy in the Denver validity survey. *Public opinion quarterly*, 32 (4), 607–621.
Casebourne, J., *et al.*, (Institute of Employment Studies), 2006. *Employment rights at work- survey of employees 2005*. Employment Relations Research Series, No. 51. London: Department of Trade and Industry.
Chong, D., 1993. how people think, reason, and feel about rights and liberties. *American journal of political science*, 37 (3), 867–899.
Consumer Protection (Distance Selling Regulations) 2000 (SI 2000/2334).
Cortese, C.F., 1996. A study in knowledge and attitudes towards the law. *Rocky Mountain social science journal*, 1996 (3), 192–203.
Denvir, C., Balmer, N.J. and Buck, A., 2012. Informed citizens? Knowledge of rights and the resolution of civil justice problems. *Journal of social policy*, 41 (3), 591–614.
Deming, W.E., 1950. *Some theory of sampling*. New York, NY: Dover.
European Union Distance Selling Directive 97/7/EC.
Geer, J.G., 1988. What do open ended questions measure? *The public opinion quarterly*, 52 (3), 365–371.
Genn, H., 1999. *Paths to justice: what people do and think about going to law*. Oxford: Hart.
Genn, H., et al., 2006. *Tribunals for diverse users*. Department for Constitutional Affairs Research Series 1/06. London: Department for Constitutional Affairs.
Giddings, J. and Robertson, M., 2003. Large-scale map, or the A–Z? The place of self-help services in legal aid. *Journal of law and society*, 30 (1), 102–119.
Gramatikov, M. and Porter, R.B., 2010. *Yes, I can: subjective legal empowerment*, Tilburg University Legal Studies Working Paper Series No. 023/2010.
Griffith, L.E., et al., 1999. Comparison of open and closed questionnaire formats in obtaining demographic information from Canadian general internists. *Journal of clinical epidemiology*, 52 (10), 997–1005.
Groves, R.M., et al., 2009. *Survey methodology*. Hoboken, NJ: John Wiley.
Herzog, A.R. and Bachman, J.G., 1981. Effects of questionnaire length on response quality. *Public opinion quarterly*, 45 (4), 549–559.
Hruschka, D.J., et al., 2004. Fixed choice and open-ended response formats: a comparison from HIV prevention research in Zimbabwe. *Field methods*, 16 (2), 184–202.
Hughes, R., 1998. Considering the vignette technique and its application to a study of drug injecting and HIV risk and safer behaviour. *Sociology of health and illness*, 20 (3), 381–400.
Johnson, W.R., Sieveking, N.A. and Clanton, E.S., 1974. Effects of alternative positioning of open-ended questions in multiple-choice questionnaires. *Journal of applied psychology*, 59 (6), 776–778.
Kim, P.T., 1999. Norms, learning, and law: exploring the influences on workers' legal knowledge. *University of Illinois law review*, 1999 (2), 447–515.
Lawler, M., Giddings, J. and Robertson, M., 2009. 'Maybe a solicitor needs to know that sort of thing but I don't' –user perspectives on the utility of legal self-help resources. In: A. Buck, P. Pleasence and N.J. Balmer, eds. *Reaching further: innovation, access and quality in legal services*. London: TSO, 26–46.
Legal Aid, Sentencing and Punishment of Offenders Act (LASPO) 2012 (c. 10).
Meager, N., et al., 2002. *Awareness, knowledge and exercise of individual employment rights*. London: Department of Trade and Industry.
Ministry of Justice, 2010a. *Legal aid reform scope changes: impact assessment*. London: Ministry of Justice.
Ministry of Justice, 2010b. *Proposals for the reform of legal aid in England and Wales*. London: Ministry of Justice.

Ministry of Justice, 2011. *Reform of legal aid in England and Wales: the government response*. London: Ministry of Justice.

Moorhead, R. and Sefton, M., 2005. *litigants in person: unrepresented litigants in first instance proceedings*. London: Department of Constitutional Affairs.

Nadeau, R. and Niemi, R.G., 1995. Educated guesses: the process of answering factual knowledge questions in surveys. *The public opinion quarterly*, 59 (3), 323–346.

Parle, L.J/Independent Academic Research Studies (IARS), 2009. *Measuring young people's legal capability*. London: IARS & PLEnet.

PLEAS Task Force, 2007. *Developing capable citizens: the role of public legal education*. London: Public Legal Education Task Force.

Pleasence, P. and Balmer, N.J., 2012. Ignorance in bliss: modelling knowledge of rights in marriage and cohabitation. *Law and society review*, 46 (2), 297–333.

Pleasence, P., et al., 2011. *Civil justice in England and Wales: report of wave 1 of the English and Welsh Civil and Social Justice Panel Survey*. London: Legal Services Commission.

Public Bill Committee, 2011. *Public Bill Committee transcript of discussions on the Legal Aid and Sentencing of Offenders Act*, Available from: http://www.publications.parliament.uk/pa/cm/cmtoday/cmstand/output/pbc205/pb110906a-01.htm [Accessed 28 March 2012].

Ruck, M., et al., 1998. Adolescents' and children's knowledge about rights: some evidence for how young people view rights in their own lives. *Journal of adolescence*, 21 (3), 275–289.

Sale of Goods Act 1979 (c. 54).

Saunders, L.E., 1975. Collective ignorance: public knowledge of family law. *The family coordinator*, 24 (1), 69–74.

Schuman, H. and Presser, S., 1981. *Questions and answers in attitude surveys*. New York, NY: Academic Press.

Schwarz, N. and Hippler, H.J., 1991. Response alternatives: the impact of their choice and presentation order. In: P.P. Biemer, R.M. Groves, L.E. Lyberg, N.A. Mathiowetz and S. Sudman, eds. *Measurement errors in surveys*. New York, NY: John Wiley, 41–56.

Tennant, R., Taylor, J. and Lewis, J. (National Centre for Social Research), 2006. *Separating from cohabitation: making arrangements for finances and parenting*. London: Department for Constitutional Affairs.

Tourangeau, R. and Rasinski, K., 1988. Cognitive processes underlying context effects in attitude measurement. *Psychological bulletin*, 103 (3), 299–314.

Unfair Terms in Consumer Contracts Regulations 1999 (SI 1999/2083).

Williams, S.H., 2009. Sticky Expectations: responses to persistent over-optimism in marriage, employment contracts, and credit card use. *Notre Dame Law Review*, 84 (2), 733–791.

Williams, M. and Hall, J., 1972. Knowledge of the law in Texas: socioeconomic and ethnic differences. *Law and society review*, 7 (1), 99–118.

Youth Access, 2002. *Rights to access – meeting young people's need for advice*. London: Youth Access.

Index

For Product Safety Concerns and Information please contact our EU representative GPSR@taylorandfrancis.com Taylor & Francis Verlag GmbH, Kaufingerstraße 24, 80331 München, Germany

Batch number: 10732736

Printed by Printforce, the Netherlands